"What a scintillatingly-fresh study of a very traditional theological locus—the doctrine of the atonement—this book is. Using Dante (who would have ever dreamed that he was a clear witness to the biblical truth of this doctrine), Caesarius of Arles, and Haimo of Auxerre (I thought I knew church history well, but I had never heard of this individual before reading Wheaton's book), Dr. Wheaton draws great riches for the explication of this vital truth from the medieval era. Again, one might ask: can any good thing come from the Middle Ages? Well, it turns out that there is a lot of good stuff, if only we have grit and gumption to mine for it. Such mining Wheaton has done for us, and as this book shows, we are the better for it."

—MICHAEL A. G. HAYKIN,
chair and professor of church history, The Southern Baptist Theological Seminary

"Benjamin Wheaton serves as a lively guide on a theological pilgrimage with a ninth-century Benedictine monk, the Florentine poet of the Divine Comedy, and a stately bishop. The destination? A more nuanced understanding of medieval views of the atonement. Written with engaging clarity, *Suffering, Not Power* expands the repertoire of medieval interpretations to include Christ's death as propitiatory and expiatory sacrifice."

—GWENFAIR WALTERS ADAMS,
professor of church history, Gordon-Conwell Theological Seminary

"No scholar of the atonement can fail to grapple with Benjamin Wheaton's careful historical study of its concepts in the Middle Ages. Wheaton illustrates what it means to listen with great care, and in context, avoiding anachronisms and accounting for genres, to the 'great mass of literature' on the atonement. He thereby challenges old mistaken and misleading narratives about the prevalence of certain models in certain periods, and notices nuanced discussions in the tradition of the themes of sacrifice, satisfaction, substitution, expiation, and propitiation that are not merely or even predominantly demonocentric, but theocentric. Here theologians are challenged to be even more rigorously historical in their approach. I highly recommend this work."

—ROSS HASTINGS,
Sangwoo Youtong Chee Professor of Theology, Regent College;
author of *Total Atonement: Trinitarian Participation in the Reconciliation of Humanity and Creation*

SUFFERING, NOT POWER

ATONEMENT

in the

MIDDLE AGES

SUFFERING, NOT POWER

ATONEMENT

in the

MIDDLE AGES

BENJAMIN WHEATON

LEXHAM
ACADEMIC

Suffering, Not Power: Atonement in the Middle Ages

Copyright 2022 Benjamin Wheaton

Lexham Academic, an imprint of Lexham Press
1313 Commercial St., Bellingham, WA, 98225

Print ISBN 9781683595991
Digital ISBN 9781683596004
Library of Congress Control Number 2021948312

Lexham Editorial: Todd Hains, Andrew Sheffield, Jessi Strong, Danielle Thevenaz,
        Mandi Newell
Cover Design: Joshua Hunt, Brittany Schrock
Typesetting: Mandi Newell

For my sister,

Dr. Laura Wheaton

CONTENTS

CONTENTS

ABBREVIATIONS

BLE	*Bulletin de littérature ecclésiastique*
CCSL	Corpus Christianorum Series Latina
PL	*Patrologia Latina*
RevScRel	*Revue des sciences religieuses*
RHR	*Revue de l'histoire des religions*

ABBREVIATIONS

Amour fist Diex du ciel descendre,
Amour li fist char et sanc prendre,
Amour le fist par deniers vendre,
Amour le fist en la crois pendre,
Amour le fist son sanc espandre,
Amour li fist le costé fendre,
Amour li fist l'esperit rendre,
Amour le fist gésir en cendre.
A ceste amour devons entendre.

Love made God come down from heaven,
Love made him take flesh and blood,
Love made him be sold for silver,
Love made him hang on the cross,
Love made him pour out his own blood,
Love made him slit his own side,
Love made him give up his spirit,
Love made him lie down in ash.
We must incline unto this love.

—Anonymous thirteenth-century French poem

CHAPTER I

INTRODUCTION

This book is an experiment, an attempt to grapple with history in all its immensity. Because of history's vast size and scope, it can be very mercurial. Just when we think we have established an accurate narrative about some event or idea, something comes along to upend it and make us doubt ourselves. Then—sometimes—when we have entertained these doubts and allowed them to persuade us to create a new narrative, the facts in all their vast multitude come back to slap us in the face and drive us to realize the old narrative was more right than wrong. At other times, of course, the old narrative has no such renaissance and rightfully slinks away into a corner to die. At still other times, both old and new narratives exist together and clash in brutal trench warfare.

All this is reflected in the study of the history of Christian doctrine. In addition to the normal back and forth of historical discussion, however, the study of church history is fraught with the tensions of confessional difference. It is thus more important than usual for our narratives about this history to be continually subjected to scrutiny from the original sources. And we need not just a few important and famous authors and their books, but the great mass of literature written for all audiences and in all genres to provide a full view of the truth. Yet often this is lacking, especially when it comes to more distant eras, when the immensity of history is especially intimidating.

Although all branches of the Christian faith must wrestle with this tendency, for evangelical Protestants in particular, this is a blind spot, for the focus on the last five hundred years is a matter of confessional identity as much as it is a result of the general human instinct to presentism. As a result, when the first fifteen hundred years of the church are studied, the dominance of preferred narratives over a careful assessment of a broad range of texts is accentuated. This is especially the case for the Middle Ages, the era spanning the years 500–1500 and in terms of location (mostly) referring to the cultures then present in Europe: a diverse, confusing, complicated, yet fascinating time and place. And nowhere is a dominant narrative so firmly lodged, despite all the evidence to the contrary, as in the medieval history of the doctrine of the atonement.

THE CONVENTIONAL NARRATIVE OF
THE HISTORY OF THE ATONEMENT:
PROBLEMS AND SOLUTIONS

There are two problems that need to be addressed regarding this narrative: first, it is mistaken and misleading; and second, attempts to challenge the narrative have all too often been lacking in rigor. The first problem is the most basic—namely, that the conventional narrative is simply wrong. The conventional narrative goes something like this:

> The early church held that Christ's death on the cross was primarily a victory over death and the devil, achieved by means of a ransom (Christ's blood) paid to these enemies and also by tricking these enemies into performing a deed (Christ's murder) that nullified their claim over captive humanity. God could not save mankind from the devil's grip by any other means since after Adam's fall, Satan held rightful title over the whole human race. Christ's death was therefore a triumph over death and the devil, upon which is based the reconciliation of God and mankind. This "demonocentric" view of the atonement, while at times intruded upon by a more "theocentric" conception of Christ's death as a sacrifice for sin, dominated until the time of Anselm and his treatise *Cur Deus homo*, written around 1094, which successfully challenged it. Anselm, drawing on contemporary societal notions of feudal honor, advocated instead for a view that saw Christ's death as an offering made to God that satisfied

his wrath due to his wounded honor. Christ's death was an act of obedience that outweighed the wickedness of human sin, and thus, God's wrath was turned aside, and his honor, restored. At the time of the Reformation, this view was modified, and the new idea of penal substitutionary atonement—that Christ died in our place and suffered our punishment at the hands of the Father, thus freeing us from sin and its consequences—was widely adopted by Protestants.

This is admittedly something of a caricature of the conventional narrative, and its scholarly advocates have laid it out with more sophistication.[1] Still, in terms of popular conceptions of the history of the atonement, it is, I think, fairly accurate; and its gist at least also applies to the more scholarly treatments.

There are two basic mistakes this narrative makes: first, it mistakes the image for the substance; and second, it reverses the priority of the economy of redemption. The imagery of the overthrow of death and the devil was certainly popular, but careful theologians, as we will see, never mistook it for the core of the economy of redemption. So too, the reconciliation of God and mankind was not dependent upon the defeat of the

---

1. The most influential scholarly proponent of this narrative has been Gustav Aulén, *Christus Victor: An Historical Study of the Three Main Types of the Atonement* (New York: MacMillan, 1931); some examples from evangelical authors include Leon Morris, "Atonement," in *New Dictionary of Theology*, ed. S. Ferguson, D. Wright, and J. I. Packer (Downers Grove, IL: InterVarsity, 1988), 54–57; Michael Vlach, "Penal Substitution in Church History," *The Master's Seminary Journal* 20, no. 2 (2009): 199–214; Derek Flood, "Substitutionary Atonement and the Church Fathers: A Reply to the Authors of *Pierced for Our Transgressions*," *Evangelical Quarterly* 82, no. 2 (2010), 142–59; and Joshua McNall, *The Mosaic of Atonement: An Integrated Approach to Christ's Work* (Grand Rapids: Zondervan, 2019), especially 195–202. McNall is far more careful than Aulén and acknowledges the significant presence of sacrificial themes, even of penal substitution itself, in the patristic writings; see, for example, his careful account of penal substitution in the fathers in *The Mosaic of Atonement*, 99–126.

enemy powers; rather the reverse—as we will also see. These two errors are based on a larger deficiency: a refusal to deal with the full range of texts and their contexts that deal with the atonement. Gustav Aulén is the paradigmatic example of this, making sweeping judgments from a very slender base. A careful and comprehensive analysis of patristic and medieval sources shows a very different picture; but this analysis is an intimidating project, and so, most prefer to be carried along by Aulén's and his successors' compelling rhetoric. This is a mistake.

The second problem is that all too often, efforts to refute this narrative have, at least in evangelical circles, been equally poorly based. They have also tended to overread their sources, forcing everything that has even a whiff of sacrifice or substitution onto the procrustean bed of penal substitution. The first issue is a result of both a focus on a few major early church fathers and a tendency to find what one is looking for, without regard for context.[2] Going on hunting expeditions is a perennial temptation of historians, but one that leads all too often to disaster. And narrowing these hunting expeditions to the corpus of a few prominent authors, and extrapolating their views to their successors, all but guarantees this disaster.

The tendency to overread sources is an error so common as to be banal, a fault that everyone who studies history has

---

2. E.g., Michael Vlach, "Penal Substitution in Church History," 199–214; Steve Jeffery, Michael Ovey, and Andrew Sach, *Pierced for Our Transgressions: Rediscovering the Glory of Penal Substitution* (Wheaton, IL: Crossway, 2007), 161–85; and Garry Williams, "Penal Substitutionary Atonement in the Church Fathers," *Evangelical Quarterly* 83, no. 3 (2011), 195–216. Williams's article is based on his PhD thesis on Hugo Grotius, "A Critical Exposition of Hugo Grotius' Doctrine of the Atonement in *De Satisfactione Christi*" (PhD diss., University of Oxford, 1999). Williams is by far the most careful but, again, focuses on snippets—however well contextualized!—from the church fathers. He also maintains a semblance of the conventional narrative: "Let Aulén have his prize," he concludes (Williams, "Penal Substitutionary Atonement in the Church Fathers," p. 215). With respect, no.

indulged in at some time or another. It therefore needs to be guarded against more strictly. In the case of the doctrine of the atonement, this means being careful not to read later concepts into earlier ones. Penal substitution in particular has been read by the opponents of the *Christus Victor* totalizers into generic statements affirming Christ's sacrifice for our sins.[3] Yet sacrifice is broader than penal substitution, while naturally frequently including it as a necessary part. As Joshua McNall wisely notes, "The presence of sacrificial themes (including propitiation) in an author do not necessarily reflect belief in penal substitution, and interpreters should avoid the folly of finding penal substitution in *every* reference to priests and sacrifices."[4]

What then is needed to redress these deficiencies on both sides of the discussion? Two things: we need to grapple properly with the immensity of history and to listen humbly to the voices of our Christian predecessors. Grappling with history's immensity will involve both looking at texts beyond the standard corpus of church fathers or other major theologians like Anselm and Aquinas and looking at the broader historical context of these texts: who were they intended for? How were they received, by both contemporaries and later generations? What controversy did they stir up in their own time? How does that controversy or reception history illumine the conception of the atonement held in society at large? In other words, we need to look at the history of the atonement with the eye of an historian, not a theologian.

---

3. As in Vlach, "Penal Substitution in Church History," 212, where his citations of Severus of Antioch and Oecumenius are overwrought.

4. Joshua McNall, *The Mosaic of Atonement* (Grand Rapids: Zondervan, 2019), 113.

To do this properly requires listening humbly to the voices of the past in their time and place and to the echoes surrounding them. What N. T. Wright said of the apostle Paul applies also to later authors: "We must go slowly, standing where he stood, taking the route he would have taken, listening for other footfalls, echoing in the memory, for hints half guessed and gifts half understood."[5] To listen humbly means to go into the reading of an old author having put aside (for the moment) one's preconceptions and to let oneself be guided along a route not of one's own choosing, encountering strange ideas and passions. Then, the insights gained from this process can be integrated into a more objective whole. But to do this will require further aid from more modern historians. One in particular is due special attention: Jean Rivière.

CRACKING A NUT WITH A SLEDGEHAMMER: JEAN RIVIÈRE VS. JOSEPH TURMEL

If any work on the history of the atonement deserves the title "magisterial," it is that of Jean Rivière. Born in 1878 and educated for the Roman Catholic priesthood at Albi, Rivière completed his doctorate at Toulouse, writing his dissertation on the history of the doctrine of the atonement. This work, published in 1905 as the book *Le dogme de la Rédemption: Essai d'étude historique*, was received with great acclaim and translated into English soon after its publication. Aged only 27, Rivière had taken on an ambitious project whose immediate success showed to all his tremendous intellectual ability. When the University of Strasbourg was founded in 1918, he joined its

---

5. N. T. Wright, *Paul and the Faithfulness of God, Parts I & II* (Minneapolis: Fortress, 2013), 75.

faculty of theology, on which he was to serve as professor for the remainder of his career until his death in 1946. During this time, he wrote an extraordinarily large number of articles and books on various aspects of Catholic theology, always staunchly opposing the modernist theology coming into vogue at that time. At the center of these efforts was his continuing work on the history of the atonement. Rivière continually sought out new documents from the patristic and medieval eras, honing his conclusions and opposing errors promulgated by other scholars. The pinnacle of this long work was three books on the doctrine of the atonement, written between 1928 and 1934, aimed to refute the errors of one modernist in particular: Joseph Turmel.

It is ironic that at the same time Gustav Aulén was giving his lectures on *Christus Victor*, Rivière, a far more insightful and learned historian, produced a comprehensive treatment of the atonement in western Christianity written in response to a man who was crafting a narrative about the history of the doctrine of the atonement very similar to that of Aulén. Aulén gave his lectures on the atonement at the University of Uppsala in 1930, published his book *Christus Victor* in the same year, and had it translated into English in 1931; and between 1922 and 1936, both in the pages of academic journals (e.g., *Revue d'histoire et de littérature religieuse*, *Revue de l'histoire des religions*) and as part of his six-volume work *Histoire des dogmes*, Joseph Turmel put forward his understanding of the history of the doctrine of the atonement. The overlap between the respective narratives of Turmel and Aulén, while not total, was nonetheless significant.

Turmel's work met with fierce opposition from Rivière, whose series of articles between 1927 and 1933 in the *Revue des sciences religieuses* (the house organ of the faculty of theology at the University of Strasbourg) refuting Turmel's narrative was turned into three volumes: *Le dogme de la Rédemption chez saint Augustin* (1928), *Le dogme de la Rédemption après saint Augustin* (1930), and *Le dogme de la Rédemption au début du Moyen Age* (1934). These three works form the great summit of Rivière's scholarship on the atonement, and it is convenient for our purposes that they were written to refute a narrative that insisted *Christus Victor* was dominant in the medieval and patristic church. But who was Turmel, and why did he meet with Rivière's ire?

Born in 1859 in Rennes, Joseph Turmel studied to be a priest there before going to the University of Angers to study theology. He then returned to Rennes to teach theology in 1882. Between the start of his tenure there and 1886, however, he slowly lost his faith, having come under the influence of several German modernist biblical scholars. His doubts were revealed in 1892, and he was deposed from his position and sent to be the chaplain of a hospice of the Little Sisters of the Poor; in 1903, at his request, he was assigned to a Carmelite convent, where he said mass once a week for the nuns. There he remained for many years. From 1895 onward, he devoted his spare time (of which he had a great deal) to his historical scholarship, challenging the received doctrines of the church and exploring the history of Christianity as a product of natural development rather than divine revelation. In 1901, his writings so alarmed his ecclesiastical superiors that they forbade him from publishing anything without first obtaining the imprimatur of his bishop.

To get around this requirement and yet still remain in the Catholic Church, he proceeded to publish his articles under a variety of pseudonyms. Turmel was therefore also, among

other names, Goulvain Lézurec, Denys Lenain, Guillaume
Herzog, and Hippolyte Gallerand. Under the last of these, he
wrote the articles on the history of the atonement to which
Rivière responded.[6] It was these articles that eventually led to
his downfall, when in 1929 the Abbé Louis Saltet confirmed
that the signature of "Hippolyte Gallerand," affixed to a letter
sent to the righteously angry Rivière, matched the handwriting
of Turmel. Saltet had been aware for some years of Turmel's
pseudonymous habit but had hesitated to get involved in this
"tragie-comédie." However, at the urging of Rivière, he published
in 1929 a note in the *Bulletin de littérature ecclésiastique*, the journal of the University of Toulouse, confirming Turmel's pseudonyms. "There is no 'school' here, but a single author," Saltet
drily noted.[7] In 1930, Turmel was summoned before an ecclesiastical tribunal, which in due course defrocked and excommunicated him for heresy. Now freed from any requirement
to dissemble, he continued to publish works on the history of
Christian doctrine, wrote and published an autobiography, and
affiliated with an adoring group of freethinkers in Rennes. He
died in 1943.

It is his three articles on the history of the atonement that
interest us, however, since in them is laid out his view of what
he called the "traditional teaching" or "archaic conception" of the
atonement, which, he argued, prevailed in the western church
from the time of Augustine until Anselm and even after. What

---

6. There were three: H. Gallerand, "La rédemption dans saint Augustin," *Revue d'histoire et de littérature religieuses* 8 (1922), 38–77; H. Gallerand, "La rédemption dans l'Église
latine d'Augustin à Anselme," *RHR* 91 (1925), 35–76; H. Gallerand, "La rédemption dans
les écrits d'Anselme et d'Abélard," *RHR* 91 (1925), 212–41.

7. Louis Saltet, "L'oeuvre pseudonyme et le silence de M. J. Turmel," *BLE* 30 (1929),
213–23. Quoted text is on p. 219: *Il n'y a pas là une école, mais un seul auteur.*

is this "traditional teaching?" In short, *Christus Victor*. Turmel writes of Augustine:

> The flesh of Christ was a ransom that ransomed the human race from the devil; it was also a mousetrap, a trap for the same person. In sum, a ransom of the human race from the devil by means of a ransom which is the human nature of Christ, but a ransom from which results the destruction of the devil's power—such is the redemption for Augustine.[8]

The successors of Augustine thought no differently, their conception of sacrifice thoroughly subordinate to the defeat of the devil:

> When the teachers of the early Middle Ages mention reconciliation, propitiation, the forgiveness of sins achieved by the death of Christ, their goal is to make us aware of the final result of the victory won by Christ over the devil; they wish to complete the scene of this victory, not to correct it. And the conclusion that emerges from our inquiry is that, from Augustine to Anselm, the theory of the redemption by means of destroying the power of the devil ruled without rival in the Latin church.[9]

---

8. Gallerand, "La rédemption dans saint Augustin," 75. *La chair du Christ a été une rançon qui a racheté le genre humaine au diable; elle a été aussi une souricière, un piège pour le même personnage. En somme, rachat du genre humain au diable au moyen d'une rançon qui est la nature humaien du Christ, mais rachat d'où résult la destruction de l'empire du diable, telle est la rédemption pour Augustin.*

9. Gallerand, "La rédemption dans l'Église latine d'Augustin à Anselme," 74. *Quand les docteurs du haut moyen-âge mentionnent la réconciliation, la propitiation, la rémission des péchés opérées par la mort du Christ, leur but est de nous faire connaître le résultat ultime de la victoire remportée par le Christ sur le diable; ils veulent compléter le tableau de cette victoire, non le corriger. Et la conclusion que se dégage de notre enquête est que, d'Augustin à Anselme, la théorie de la rédemption par le destruction de l'empire du diable a régné sans rivale dans l'Eglise latine.*

This description of the traditional teaching of the atonement, in which Christ's death on the cross and the redemption as a whole is seen through the lens of the defeat of the devil's power over humanity, is almost identical to the conventional narrative laid out by Aulén and many scholars to this day.[10]

Jean Rivière responded to these claims by writing three voluminous works on the atonement, in which he meticulously and acidly dismantled Turmel's arguments. While his reaction might seem akin to taking a sledgehammer to crack a nut—against articles totaling around 109 pages he wrote ones totaling over 437—it is difficult to deny his effectiveness in thoroughly burying Turmel's credibility. More importantly, these three works enabled him to present his mature view of the history of the doctrine of the atonement. They are not merely refutations, in other words; they are a whole new history of the doctrine's development. And his conclusion was that through all periods of Christian history, the atonement was at its root seen as a sacrifice of expiation and propitiation made by God to God, thereby reconciling mankind to God and God to mankind.

Against Turmel's sneers at the apologists who naïvely thought that history backed them, Rivière thunders:

An assault in great strength is launched in the name of history against the doctrine of the redemption; it will not

---

10. Compare the statement of Aulén in *Christus Victor:* "God is pictured as in Christ carrying through a victorious conflict against powers of evil which are hostile to His will. This constitutes Atonement, because the drama is a cosmic drama, and the victory over the hostile powers brings to pass a new relation, a relation of reconciliation, between God and the world." Gustav Aulén, *Christus Victor: An Historical Study of the Three Main Types of the Idea of the Atonement,* tr. A. G. Herbert (New York: MacMillan, 1931), 21. To be fair, Aulén does not go quite so far as Turmel and, unlike the French historian, denies that the devil was portrayed as having a legal right over humanity.

be said that the assailant found nothing in front of him but a deserted rampart. And no doubt, whether now or later, there will be some judges competent enough to say on which side, between the "apologists" of the Church and its supposedly "critical" adversaries, lay on this matter the respect for texts, a sense of history and of its laws.[11]

Fighting words, indeed, and a challenge. On whose side lay the balance of history? Rivière invites us to make that decision. He has no doubt as to the result.

Jean Rivière and the History of the Doctrine of the Redemption

Rivière takes up two tasks: first, acknowledging the ubiquity of *Christus Victor* language in the primary sources, he carefully explains what it is actually referring to and what its priority is in the atonement as a whole; and second, he gives more examples of texts that Turmel did not explore that give a more accurate view of the state of things. I will draw on the conclusions from his work dealing with Late Antiquity rather than his work on Augustine or the early Middle Ages since he approaches each period and author in a similar way. In all three works, he systematically investigates four questions: (1) Did the devil have rights over humanity that God was obliged to respect? (2) Does the justice of God as revealed in the cross refer to his respect for the devil's rights? (3) How is this justice applied in the salvation of

---

11. Jean Rivière, "Le dogme de la Rédemption après saint Augustin," *RevScRel* 9, no. 1 (1929): 16. *Un assaut de grand style est mené au nom de l'histoire contre le dogme de la Rédemption: il ne sera pas dit que l'assaillant n'ait trouvé devant lui qu'un rempart désert. Et sans doute, aujourd'hui ou plus tard, se trouvera-t-il des arbitres assez compétents pour dire de quel côté, entre les «apologistes» de l'Église et ses adversaires prétendus critiques, fut sur ce point le respect des textes, le sens de l'histoire et de ses lois.*

the human race? (4) What is the role of the devil in the whole of the divine plan?

In answer to the first, he makes the case that the devil was the agent of God's wrath, and our slavery to him a result of the divine decree. So, when discussing the sermons of Pope Leo I (400–461), he writes: "It is nonetheless clear that our spiritual slavery and the death that is its main effect results from a divine decree. ... In this sense, the devil can be nothing but an agent of execution."[12] The devil is an *exactor* of God's wrath, no more; our predicament is a result of God's just judgment on our sin. The language of the devil's rights is just an image:

> This "right" is, at the end of it all, nothing but another manner of expressing the providential order of secondary causes. In any case, everything excludes the idea of a "right" in a strict sense that would be prior to the will of God.[13]

This is his conclusion about the bulk of the other fathers and medieval thinkers as well. While, as we will see later, the expression of this image could get out of hand, Rivière insists that careful theologians never gave it undue weight.[14]

---

12. Rivière, "Rédemption après saint Augustin," 20–21. *Il est clair cependant que notre esclavage spirituel et la mort qui en est la principale suite résultent d'un décret divin ... À cet égard, le démon ne saurait être qu'un agent d'exécution.*

13. Rivière, "Rédemption après saint Augustin," 31. *Ce «droit» ne serait, en définitive, qu'une autre manière d'énoncer l'ordre providentiel des causes secondes. En tout cas, tout exclut l'idée d'un droit proprement dit, qui serait antérieur aux vouloirs de Dieu.*

14. Aulén is in essential (though not total) agreement with Rivière here in his description of the patristic teaching: "God in Christ overcomes the hostile powers which hold man in bondage. At the same time these hostile powers are also the executants of God's will. The patristic theology is dualistic, but it is not an absolute Dualism. The deliverance of man from the power of death and the devil is at the same time his deliverance from God's judgment." Aulén, *Christus Victor*, 75.

What does Rivière think the justice of God refers to? Does it mean that God was obliged to respect the devil's rights over humanity and so order the economy of redemption around satisfying those "rights?" By no means. As he writes in his treatment of Gregory the Great (540–604):

> Saint Gregory and his contemporaries, as in their predecessors Saint Augustine and Saint Leo, like without a doubt to bring into the goals of the divine wisdom, for the sake of "fittingness," the demonstration of "justice" with regard to the devil, whose "rights" they have with greater or lesser confidence recognized. But neither of them knows anything of a firm law that might limit for God the growth of his power or paralyze the passionate rush of his generosity.[15]

The key word here is "fittingness," that is, *convenance*; it is this that represents the fathers' use of the word "justice" with regard to the redemption. It is suitable to God's character to act in a certain way to redeem humanity, but this does not represent an external bond upon his actions. As Rivière writes of Leo's teaching on the atonement, "Concerning the 'justice' that he discovers therein, the devil, if we may speak of it in this way, is nothing but the subject and the circumstance: it is in God himself and in God alone that it has its beginning and its law."[16]

---

15. Rivière, "Le dogme de la Rédemption après saint Augustin," *RevScRel* 9, no. 3 (1929), 328–29. *Saint Grégoire et ses contemporains, comme auparavant saint Augustin et saint Léon, aiment sans nul doute faire entrer dans les fins de la sagesse divine, à titre de convenance, la manifestation de la «justice» à l'égard du démon don't ils ont avec plus ou moins de fermeté reconnu les «droits». Mais ni les uns ni les autres ne savent rien d'une loi stricte qui limiterait en Dieu l'expansion de sa puissance ou paralyserait les élans de sa bonté.*

16. Rivière, "Rédemption après saint Augustin," *RevScRel* 9, no. 1 (1929), 41. *De la «justice» qu'il y découvre le démon n'est, si l'on peut ainsi dire, que la matière et l'occasion: c'est en Dieu même et en Dieu seul qu'elle a son principe et sa règle.*

And how is this justice applied in the course of the redemption? Is it a ransom paid to the devil, or is he tricked into forfeiting his rights? Rivière maintains that these are images pertaining to the "fittingness" of the economy of redemption mentioned above. He writes of Leo:

> There is no need to say again that God was able to dispense with this "justice" and that all these speculations do not go beyond the order of "fittingness." What remains characteristic of Saint Leo is the insistence with which he delights in seeing that justice entered into the designs of God and to show in this fact a suitable goal for his eternal wisdom of one more dazzling demonstration of his attributes toward the devil.[17]

The attributes of God are always front and center for the fathers and their successors when speaking of the atonement. There is much more to be said on this, and he says it in his answers to the last question.

What is the role of the devil in the whole of the divine plan, and what is, in fact, the core of the economy of redemption? First, Rivière insists that human sin is constantly linked to our state of captivity to death and the devil, which are metaphors of the effects of our guilt. In his discussion of Leo's take on Christ destroying death in his crucifixion, he writes:

---

17. Rivière, "Rédemption après saint Augustin," *RevScRel* 9, no. 2 (1929), 164. *Il n'est pas besoin de redire que de cette «justice» Dieu pouvait se dispenser et que toutes ces spéculations ne dépassent pas l'ordre de la convenance. Ce qui reste caractéristique de saint Léon, c'est l'insistance avec laquelle il se plaît à faire voir qu'elle est entrée dans les desseins de Dieu et à montrer dans ce fait une fin digne de son éternelle sagesse pour une plus éclatante manifestation de ses attributs en regard du démon.*

This terminology is elastic enough to designate as well eternal death and, consequently, in a manner more or less implicit, the state of guilt that is its cause. It is not rare, moreover, that sin is expressly associated with either the devil's work or death itself. All this suggests that these are similar realities, if not identical, and allows us to clarify the still rather unclear images that surround the latter [i.e., human sin] by the more tangible ones of the former [i.e., death].[18]

He states slightly later on: "[For Leo,] sin concerns our moral relations toward God. It is not only a blemish to remove, but an 'offense' that demands expiation."[19] The problem, then, for the main Latin fathers after Augustine was humanity's sin, which was justly punished. The devil's rule over captive humanity was but a metaphor for the wrath of God against us due to sin.

What then did the cross do? What was the defeat of the devil? Was it primarily the devil's overstepping his rights by attacking the bait of Christ on the cross? Or was it achieved through a ransom to the devil or to death that resulted in our liberation? No: on the contrary, although these images are prominent in the rhetoric of preachers and moralists, they are always put alongside and even subordinate to the notion of a sacrifice made to God for the forgiveness of our sin. Rivière

---

18. Rivière, "Rédemption après saint Augustin," *RevScRel* 9, no. 2 (1929): 166–67. *D'autant que ce terme est assez élastique pour désigner aussi la mort éternelle et, par conséquent, d'une manière plus our moins implicite, l'état de culpabilité qui en est la cause. Il n'est pas rare, au surplus, que le péché soit expressément associé, soit à l'oeuvre du démon, soit à la mort. Ce qui suggère qu'il s'agit là de réalités voisines, sinon identiques, et permet d'éclairer les images encore un peu vagues don't s'enveloppent celles-ci par le contenu déjà plus concret de celle-là.*

19. Rivière, "Rédemption après saint Augustin," *RevScRel* 9, no. 2 (1929): 169. *Le péché intéresse nos relations morales envers Dieu. Il n'est pas seulement une tache à effacer, mais une «offense» qui demande expiation.*

writes of a passage from Leo's *Sermon 68*, which states that Christ was an offering made to God for the forgiveness of sins:

> Without a doubt this text is preceded, at a short distance, by a rapid line where it is said that Christ came *to destroy death and the author of death by his own passion.* This is enough for H. Gallerand to judge it without more commentary [as referring to *Christus Victor*]. But it is quite evident that an assertion that is so general does not fit any precise theory and cannot prevail over the explicitly theocentric meaning of the following argument. It is the sacrifice of Christ, so neatly proclaimed, which, by a good method, clarifies the destruction of death and of its author to such an extent that the latter must depend on the former to the point of full absorption.[20]

And as for the destruction of the devil's power? "It is nothing but a partial element of it [the atonement], an exuberant one perhaps, but in the end secondary, in the whole of a mystery ordered to restore us to the grace of God."[21]

For Gregory the Great, the sacrifice for sin and the defeat of the devil are two separate elements of the atonement that nonetheless do not conflict:

---

20. Rivière, "Rédemption après saint Augustin," *RevScRel* 9, no. 2 (1929): 175. *Sans doute ce texte est-il précédé, à petite distance, d'une ligne rapide où il est dit que le Christ est venu* mortem et mortis auctorem sua passione destruere. *Ce qui suffit à H. Gallerand pour se l'adjuger sans autre commentaire. Mais il est bien évident qu'une assertion aussi générale ne comporte aucune théorie précise et ne saurait prévaloir sur le sens explicitement théocentrique du développement qui suit. C'est le sacrifice du Christ, si nettement énoncé, qui, en bonne méthode, éclaire la destruction de la mort et de son auteur, bien loin que celle-ci doive réagir sur celui-là au point de l'absorber.*

21. Rivière, "Rédemption après saint Augustin," *RevScRel* 9, no. 2 (1929): 187. *Il ne s'agit là que d'un élément partiel, exubérant peut-être mais secondaire en définitive, dans l'ensemble d'un mystère ordonné en vue de nous rendre la grâce de Dieu.*

When it comes down to it, nothing prevents one and the same reality being able to have many aspects. This is why, taken in the moral sense of sanctity, the innocence of Christ is very much able to have, in the eyes of saint Gregory, power before God to make from his death a fitting sacrifice to purify us from our faults; yet also that, taken in the judicial sense of inviolability, it rests at the root of this abuse of power which has to bring about the punishment of our conqueror according to the rules of justice.[22]

Turmel had asserted that the "traditional redemption" was *Christus Victor*; but as Rivière insists:

> It is time, in fact, to recognize the existence of a tradition on this point, but one that, with a few extraneous elements regarding the devil, nonetheless directed the faith of believers and the reflection of the teachers towards the effectiveness and, in a certain sense, the necessity before God of the sacrifice of Christ for the forgiveness of our sins.[23]

---

22. Rivière, "Rédemption après saint Augustin," *RevScRel* 9, no. 4 (1929): 492. *Rien n'empêche, au demeurant, qu'une seule et même réalité puisse avoir divers aspects. C'est pourquoi, prise au sens moral de sainteté, l'innocence du Christ peut fort bien, aux yeux de saint Grégoire, valoir devant Dieu pour faire de sa mort un sacrifice propre à nous purifier de nos fautes, cependant que, prise au sens juridique d'inviolabilité, elle fonde cet abus de pouvoir qui doit amener le châtiment de notre vainqueur selon les règles de la justice.*

23. Rivière, "Rédemption après saint Augustin," *RevScRel* 9, no. 4 (1929): 511. *Il y a lieu, en effet, de reconnaître l'existence d'une tradition sur ce point, mais qui, avec quelques surcharges relatives au démon, n'en dirigeait pas moins la foi des croyants et la réflexion des docteurs vers l'efficacité et, dans un certain sens, la nécessité devant Dieu de l'immolation du Christ pour la rémission de nos fautes.*

Rivière's point is this: the core of the atonement in the Latin fathers and their successors is not the traditional redemption but sacrifice.[24]

The reason why Rivière's arguments are outlined here is to provide an introduction to his work, which will be of considerable importance to our study. Moreover, Rivière's method of systematically exploring primary texts in depth is precisely the method we will adopt. While his extensive citations of primary sources have not been included in this introduction for the sake of brevity, we will encounter some of his interactions with the primary texts in the following chapters. The principal weakness in Rivière's work is simply that of outdatedness: we have many more edited texts available to us, and historical research has progressed to a remarkable degree since his death. So I will occasionally find reason to disagree with his conclusions. Still, on the whole, my approach and conclusions are correlated with his own. In any case, I believe we would do well to recover his contribution, virtually ignored until now.

---

24. Aulén on this point is, apart from the concept of the devil's rights, with Turmel, not Rivière: "The Sacrifice is the means whereby the tyrants are overcome; yet there is a close connection between the tyrants and God's own judgment on sin. The idea that God receives the sacrifice is not based on a theoretical calculation of what God must demand from man's side for the satisfaction of His justice before atonement can be effected. Rather the idea is that sacrifice stands in the Divine Economy as the means whereby the Divine will-to-reconciliation realises itself, and which also shows how much it costs God to effect the Atonement." Aulén, *Christus Victor*, 74. And later: "The Atonement is set forth as the Divine victory over the powers that hold men in bondage. Yet at the same time these very powers are in a measure executants of His own judgment on sin. This opposition reaches its climax in the tension between the Divine Love and the Divine Wrath. But here the solution is not found in any sort of rational settlement; it is rather that the Divine Love prevails over the Wrath, the Blessing overcomes the Curse, by the way of Divine self-oblation and sacrifice. The redeeming work of Christ shows how much the Atonement 'costs' God." Aulén, *Christus Victor*, 171.

THE MEDIEVAL ATONEMENT:
A SACRIFICE BY GOD TO GOD

This book has two purposes: first, to shine a bright light on three sets of overlooked yet important texts and their authors, illuminating them from multiple angles to let readers come to their own conclusions about their take on the atonement; and second, to suggest that they show the core of the medieval atonement as being a sacrifice of propitiation and expiation made by God to God for the sake of reconciling God to mankind and mankind to God. But what do we mean by a sacrifice of expiation and propitiation?

Propitiation refers to a sacrifice that changes the attitude of a deity toward the offeror from hostility to benignity. In the opening of the *Iliad*, the god Apollo is angered at the Achaeans on account of the insult done to his priest Chryses, leading to him launching a plague against them. Kalchas the seer tells the assembled lords that the wrath of Apollo must be appeased:

> Therefore the archer sent griefs against us and will send
> them
> Still, nor sooner thrust back the shameful plague from
> the Danaans
> Until we give the glancing-eyed girl to her father
> Without price, without ransom, and lead also a blessed
> hecatomb
> To Chryse; thus we might propitiate and persuade him.[25]

Thus, the Achaeans, after returning his daughter to Chryses, offer a sacrifice, a burnt offering (the ἑκατόμβη) and a grain

---

25. *Iliad* 1.96–100, tr. R. Lattimore.

offering, to Apollo followed by a feast and singing, all of which
serves to propitiate the god and end the plague (*Iliad* 1.446–
474). This conception of a sacrifice of propitiation is a commonplace throughout the ancient world.

The Old Testament includes this idea as well, although
modified. For example, when Noah offers a burnt offering to
God after the flood, we are told, "The Lord smelled the pleasing aroma and said in his heart: 'Never again will I curse the
ground because of man, even though every inclination of his
heart is evil from childhood. And never again will I destroy
all living creatures, as I have done'" (Gen 8:21). Here we have
a key phrase denoting a sacrifice of propitiation in the Old
Testament: "The Lord smelled the pleasing aroma." It is important to see that there is not necessarily a penal element to this;
it is Noah's gift, his act of obedience, that pleases God and
reverses his attitude toward his creation. On the other hand,
other iterations of sacrifices of propitiation do have a penal element. The first chapter of Leviticus states, "He [i.e., the offeror]
is to lay his hand on the head of the burnt offering, and it will
be accepted on his behalf to make atonement for him ... It is a
burnt offering, an offering made by fire, an aroma pleasing to
the Lord" (Lev 1:4, 9). So, propitiation is essentially a sacrifice
that makes God propitious towards someone. How exactly
this happens is somewhat mysterious, although both the obedience of the offeror and the penalty symbolically exacted by
the offering are often clear elements.[26]

---

26. For more on this subject, see John Stott, *The Cross of Christ* (Leicester: Inter-
Varsity Press, 1986), 197–204. Stott notes the crucial difference between pagan and biblical
understandings of propitiation: "The sacrifices were recognized not as human works but
as divine gifts. They did not make God gracious; they were provided by a gracious God in

Expiation refers to a sacrifice that purges sin. As opposed to propitiation, which is directed upward toward a deity, expiation is directed downward toward the offeror. It makes a person or a people holy from a state of unholiness, innocent from a state of guilt. Thus, in the play *Eumenides* by the ancient Greek playwright Aeschylus, Orestes, guilty of slaying his mother, is hunted by the Furies to avenge her blood. Orestes pleads his case to Athena:

> It is the law that the man of the bloody hand must speak
> No word until, by action of one who can cleanse,
> Blood from a young victim has washed his blood away.
> Long since, at the homes of others, I have been absolved
> Thus, both by running waters and by victims slain.[27]

Orestes avers that he has been cleansed from the guilt of murder by sacrifices of expiation made by priests at the temples of gods other than Athena. This, too, was a common conception of expiation in the ancient world.

A sacrifice of expiation was also an integral part of God's law in the Old Testament. In Leviticus, the regulations for expiating sin offerings are laid out, as in this example:

> When a leader sins unintentionally and does what is forbidden in any of the commands of the Lord his God, he is guilty. When he is made aware of the sin he committed, he must bring as his offering a male goat without defect. He is to lay his hand on the goat's head and slaughter it

---

order that he might act graciously towards his sinful people." Stott, *The Cross of Christ*, 203. See also Gordon Wenham, *The Book of Leviticus* (Grand Rapids: Eerdmans, 1979), 55–63.

27. Aeschylus, *Eumenides*, tr. R. Lattimore, 448–52.

at the place where the burnt offering is slaughtered before the Lord. It is a sin offering. Then the priest shall take some of the blood of the sin offering with his finger and pour out the rest of the blood at the base of the altar. He shall burn all the fat on the altar as he burned the fat of the fellowship offering. In this way the priest will make atonement for the man's sin, and he will be forgiven (4:22–26).

In the case of sacrifices of expiation, the penal aspect is much clearer—the shedding of the sacrificial victim's blood is in place of the blood of the sinner: "He is to lay his hand on the goat's head and slaughter it."[28] However, the penal aspect does not exhaust the meaning of expiation.

The Old Testament sacrifices are ultimately fulfilled in the sacrifice of Christ on the cross. It is a sacrifice made by God to God, a sacrifice of both propitiation and expiation, that results in the averting of his wrath from sinners as well as their cleansing from sin. It is to this dual concept of sacrifice that we should look to find the foundation of the medieval doctrine of the atonement. Going on hunting expeditions to find what may or may not be penal substitution, or *Christus Victor*, or vicarious satisfaction, or some other image or structure, is the wrong way to go about discovering what medieval Christians thought.

---

28. For more on the sin offerings as expiation, see the discussion of Thomas Schreiner, *The King in His Beauty* (Grand Rapids: Baker Academic, 2013), 52–56; also, Bruce Waltke, *An Old Testament Theology* (Grand Rapids: Zondervan, 2007), 465; and Wenham, *The Book of Leviticus*, 88–89.

THREE VIGNETTES OF THE
MEDIEVAL ATONEMENT

What is, then, the right way to discover what medieval Christians thought? As stated above, we must listen humbly to their voices. This means, first, learning about who they were (What were their lives like? How were they educated? What motivated them?), then carefully reading the texts that deal with atonement, and finally, seeing them in their proper context (Who were their audiences? Why were they written?) and considering how they were received both by contemporaries and by those who lived later in the medieval period. This book does not pretend to be a comprehensive treatment of the subject; as Rivière's career shows, such a project would take a lifetime. But what I hope to achieve in the following pages is to sketch out what such an approach would look like, then to engage in a limited experiment using this approach with three sets of texts, and finally to give a brief glimpse in these texts of the centrality of sacrifice and the nuance with which it was integrated into medieval Christian thought.

I have chosen to examine three figures whose writings and historical contexts are both widely varied and little known to most modern chroniclers of the doctrine of the atonement. They are Dante Alighieri, Caesarius of Arles, and Haimo of Auxerre. The Middle Ages spanned a millennium and was far from homogeneous. Thus, I have chosen to use figures from its end, beginning, and middle to represent a variety of time periods and cultures. I have also selected a wide variety of literary genres: political treatise, epic poem, sermon, and commentary. Dante, Caesarius, and Haimo are also three very different people: respectively, layman and poet, statesman and bishop, teacher and monk. The sources they drew on and the audiences to which they spoke are also quite diverse. At the same time, they are not typical choices for those seeking to describe the doctrine of the atonement in the Middle Ages.

Dante is famous for his *Divina Commedia* but less so for his other works, such as the *Monarchia*. And his take on the atonement is at best a footnote in histories of the doctrine. Both the *Divina Commedia* and the *Monarchia* feature in the two chapters devoted to him. Caesarius of Arles is reasonably well known to historians of Late Antiquity and the early Middle Ages, but his sermon "Why the Lord Jesus Christ freed the world through harsh suffering, not power," which forms the center of his two chapters, has remained virtually unstudied. Haimo of Auxerre is the least known of the three, familiar only to specialists. His commentaries on Romans and Hebrews, sections of which are the focus of the two chapters dealing with him, are also known only to specialists. All three of these figures exemplify fascinating approaches to the atonement and deserve more attention in historical theology.

Each figure is investigated in the following manner. First, an account of the life and times of each is given: namely, his political context, education, and career. Second, the key texts on the atonement are introduced, with an introduction to their genres and contexts. Third, the relevant parts of each text are presented and explained. Fourth, key contemporary authors and texts that shed light on the conception of the atonement in the main texts are similarly introduced and examined. Fifth, the understanding of the atonement displayed in each central work and author is outlined. Sixth, what the modern scholarly voice of Jean Rivière (and, in the case of Dante, Bruno Nardi) says on the text and author in question is presented to provide another perspective on its role in the history of the doctrine of the atonement. Seventh and last, I suggest a conclusion about the medieval view of the atonement that challenges the received narrative.

NOTE ON THE TEXT

I have included extensive quotations from the primary texts we engage with to provide readers as wide as possible a base for coming to their own conclusions about the medieval atonement. I give in the footnotes the original language of each excerpt; my own rendering in English (unless noted otherwise) is in the body of the text.

Dante Alighieri: I have used previous translations for Dante's own work, given the high quality of existing scholarship on him and my own lack of expertise in medieval Italian. The translation of the *Monarchia* by Prue Shaw is more accessible (in the series Cambridge Texts in the History of Political Thought), but that by Richard Kay is of superior quality. I have used Charles Singleton's prose translation of Dante's *Commedia*. For most of the supplementary texts examined in this chapter, English translations do not exist, however, so this option cannot be exercised. The text of the commentators on Dante may be found in the excellent resource of the *Dartmouth Dante Project* (dante.dartmouth.edu). There is a translation of Guido Vernani's attack on Dante in Anthony Cassell's monograph on the subject, but I found his translation unsatisfactory. I have therefore translated from the text of N. Masseini's critical edition of Vernani.

Caesarius of Arles: Good critical editions of the sermons of both Caesarius of Arles and the Eusebius Gallicanus collection may be found in the Corpus Christianorum series. The sermons of Caesarius have also been translated for the Fathers of the Church series by Mary M. Mueller; I have, however, used my own translation for this book. The quote from Augustine's De Trinitate has been taken from the Patrologia Latina rather than from the modern critical edition contained in volume 50 of the Corpus Christianorum series due to lack of availability.

Haimo of Auxerre: For this section, the original texts are in an unsatisfactory state. The only available printed edition of Haimo's commentary, from the early sixteenth century, was incorporated into Migne's Patrologia Latina in the middle of the nineteenth century. It is sometimes unreliable, therefore, and I have on one or two occasions had to correct the Migne text by consulting the original manuscripts. When this occurs, I mention it in the relevant footnote. The same goes for the Pauline commentaries of Hrabanus Maurus. The commentary on Paul by Claudius of Turin has never been printed, so I have used a ninth-century manuscript to provide the necessary original text. All manuscripts used are available for free online on the website of the Bibliothèque nationale de France (bnf.fr).

Most of the other works cited have been taken from the Patrologia Latina. The same strictures concerning textual quality mentioned above occur in these as well, but this is easily the most accessible resource for the writings of the patristic period and the early Middle Ages. All volumes are available for free on Google Books. While I would have preferred to cite whenever possible the modern critical edition, that has sometimes not been possible. All citations from the Bible that are not drawn from the Latin are from the NIV 1984 translation.

The articles of Jean Rivière and his contemporaries are all available for free online at either the website of the *Bibliothèque nationale de France* (bnf.fr) or persee.fr, the open-source scholarly website maintained by the University of Lyon in tandem with the French Ministry of Higher Education, Research, and Innovation. I have had many occasions over the past year or so during the COVID-19 pandemic to be grateful for the generosity of the French public as shown in these superb resources, and I urge readers to make use of them as well.

DANTE ALIGHIERI, PART I

Penal Substitution
in the *De monarchia*

The first vignette belongs to the period of the late Middle Ages, to the region of Northern Italy, and to two genres: political tract and epic poem. Written by the poet Dante Alighieri, the political pamphlet *De monarchia* and the epic poem *Paradiso* both contain expositions of the meaning of Christ's atonement. How did Dante, educated in the intricate theology of the scholastic theologians, portray Christ's work on the cross in these two works? Furthermore, what does this portrayal say about how his contemporaries viewed the atonement? This chapter and the next will deal with these questions.

This book begins with the latest, most developed understanding of Christ's work on the cross since it is closest to that
of the Reformers in both time and conception, and yet is thoroughly medieval. Dante is an interesting representative of this
era and place because he not only was the foremost (and most
deeply orthodox) poetic expositor of its Christianity but also
had a number of unusual quirks that help shed light on his contemporaries. He also had the gift of being able to address many
different audiences; the *Monarchia* is addressed to a learned
audience, the *Paradiso* to an unlearned one. This diversity will
also be of use to us.

Naturally, a full account of Dante's theology of redemption
would have to encompass his entire oeuvre. Still, these two works,
the *Monarchia* and the *Paradiso*, are central to any understanding
of Dante's view of the atonement. They therefore make a useful
vignette for the present book. What this vignette reveals is an
atonement doctrine that holds out Christ's death on the cross
as a sacrifice of propitiation and expiation performed by God
and offered to God. However, what is unique about it among
our three vignettes is that it adheres to a precise understanding
of the atonement as an act of penal substitution, integrated into
a broader framework of vicarious satisfaction.

This chapter will explore the *Monarchia* and its reception.
First, there will be an introduction to Dante himself, including
his life, education, and writings. Second, the chapter will place
the *Monarchia* in its historical context, laying out its message
and intent. Third, it will look at the *Monarchia's* use of the
atonement in its political argument. Fourth, it will examine
the reaction of Dante's contemporary Guido Vernani to its
argument and doctrine.

The Life and Writings of Dante

Dante was born in 1265 to the Florentine citizen Alighiero Alighieri, a landowner and financier. He was given a good, though rather narrow, education in the local grammar schools of Florence in preparation for a career as a notary. Though fluent in Latin, Dante wrote most of his poetry and a great deal of his prose in his native Tuscan Italian. His fame in this art began to grow with the publication sometime between 1293 and 1295 of *La Vita Nuova*, "The New Life," comprised of poems written between 1283 and 1292 interspersed with brief prose explanations. This was followed by the writing between 1304 and 1307 of the four books of *Il Convivio*, "The Banquet," which, like *Vita Nuova*, was designed as a collection of Dante's poetry interspersed with prose explanations.

Dante had intended the *Convivio* to extend to fifteen books, but after finishing four, he found himself drawn to a new and greater work: *La Divina Commedia*, or "The Divine Comedy." The *Commedia's* first *cantica*, *Inferno*, "Hell," was written between 1304 and 1308; its second, *Purgatorio*, "Purgatory," between 1308 and 1312; and its third, *Paradiso*, "Heaven," between 1316 and 1321. The first two *cantica* were probably released to the public around the same time in 1314 or 1315. In 1321, Dante died, and so the *Paradiso* was revealed in its entirety after his death. The *Commedia* is his great contribution to world literature and is the pinnacle of medieval literature.

In addition to his major Italian works, Dante wrote three Latin prose treatises: *De vulgari eloquentia*, *De monarchia*, and *Questio de aqua et terra*. The first was written at the same time as the *Convivio*, between 1304 and 1305, the second around 1318, and the third in 1320. *De vulgari eloquentia* is a defense of his practice of writing poetry in vernacular Italian, echoing a similar defense in the first book of the *Convivio*, and the *Monarchia* is a political tract attacking papal pretensions to temporal power. The *Questio de aqua et terra* is a contribution to a philosophical debate engendered by the Aristotelian understanding of the order of the natural world. Apart from these major works, there are a large number of individual poems and letters, written in both Italian and Latin.

In all these works, Dante shows a tremendous erudition that belies his initial training as a notary. The source of his impressive knowledge may be pinpointed to the years between 1290 and 1293, when he attended the schools of the religious orders in the Florentine churches of Santa Croce, run by the Franciscan order, and Santa Maria Novella, run by the Dominican order. In both was taught the rigorous Aristotelian approach to philosophy, theology, and dialectic as synthesized by Thomas Aquinas and the other great scholastic thinkers of the thirteenth century. Dante's mastery of this knowledge combined with his rhetorical and poetic skill to result in the prodigious learning that characterizes all his works. This combination also enabled him to speak as an equal to many different classes of society, from the learned scholars of the universities to a layman ignorant of Latin.

DANTE AND POLITICS

Dante needed this rhetorical versatility for his intense engagement in the politics of Florence and Italy throughout his life. At this time, Northern Italy was divided into two main factions: the Guelphs (supporters of the Popes) and the Ghibellines (supporters of the Holy Roman Emperors). The Ghibellines had been driven out of Florence in 1266, and so Dante was naturally a Guelph. But the Guelphs who populated the Republic of Florence were themselves divided into two factions: the Black Guelphs, led by the Donati family, and the White Guelphs, led by the Cerchi family. Dante was a White Guelph and so was exiled from Florence along with the rest of the Whites in 1302. From this point, he led a wandering life until 1312, when he settled in Verona. He was not idle, for at first he schemed with his fellow White Guelphs to retake control of Florence; however, by the time of their utter defeat in July of 1304 at the battle of La Lastra, Dante had broken with them in frustration. At this point, his political ideology began to change from his inherited Guelph pro-papal politics to the pro-imperial politics of a Ghibelline.

The change in his political allegiance came to full flower in 1310, when the Holy Roman Emperor Henry VII came to Italy. Dante was as full-throated a supporter of the emperor as any. This initial exultation turned to severe disappointment, however, when Henry failed to unite Italy under his rule. The emperor faced fierce opposition from, among others, the city of Florence, which he unsuccessfully besieged in 1312. He died the year after, foiled in his ambitions. Foiled also were the ambitions and hopes of his supporters.

Dante then lived in the court of the Ghibelline lord Can Grande della Scala of Verona, whose court was renowned for its culture, its learning, and the remarkable generosity of its master. Politics once again intruded upon Dante's life, for Can Grande became locked in a ferocious dispute with Pope John XXII. During Henry VII's sojourn in Italy, Can Grande had been officially declared imperial vicar of Verona;

that is, his rule was now *de jure* rather than merely *de facto*, as had been the case earlier. However, the election of the new Holy Roman Emperor Ludwig of Bavaria in 1314 was never recognized by the Pope. So, in 1317, John issued the decree *Si fratrum*, proclaiming that with the imperial throne vacant and thus the empire under papal authority, no lord of any city was to proclaim himself imperial vicar.

The northern Italian Ghibelline lords, Can Grande among them, objected to this demand to subject themselves to the Pope and relinquish their authority, and they were thus excommunicated from the Church in 1318. Dante supported Can Grande and flouted the papal excommunication and interdict, as did most of the Veronese. That same year, however, he was invited to Ravenna by its lord, Guido Novello da Polenta, and so spent the last few years of his life in that city, surrounded by family and admirers. He was still not quite out of politics, however; in August 1321, he was sent to Venice as an ambassador. Upon his return, he came down with a fever and died during the night of September 13–14. All the poets of northern Italy competed to write his epitaph.

Out of Dante's mass of writing, two books provide the substance of the first vignette of the medieval atonement: the *Monarchia* and the *Paradiso*. And out of the fifty-six years of his life, five are brought into intense focus: 1316–1321. We will now focus in on the *Monarchia*, the year 1318, and the city of Verona.

CIRCUMSTANCES AND AUDIENCE
OF THE *MONARCHIA*

On March 31, 1311, Dante addressed a letter to the Florentine people: "Dante Alighieri the Florentine and undeserving exile to the most wicked Florentines in the city."[1] Written to rebuke them for their stubborn opposition to the emperor Henry VII's rule, it adopts the tone and rhetoric of the prophet Jeremiah, warning them of imminent destruction if they should continue on their current path. In this letter, we encounter in encapsulated form the argument that the *Monarchia* would later lay out in more level-headed splendor.[2] Rome is the justly ordained ruler of the entire human race since under its authority Christ was born and crucified; the troubles of the time were

---

1. Dante, *Epistola VI*, ed. P. Toynbee (Oxford: Clarendon, 1920). *Dantes Alagherii Florentinus et exul immeritus scelestissimis Florentinis intrinsecis.*

2. Dante, *Epistola VI*, 1. "The loving providence of the eternal king, who, even though he resides in his own heavenly goodness, does not refrain from looking down upon our ills, has placed the government of human affairs with the sacrosanct empire of the Romans, so that under the peace of so great a rule the mortal race might be at rest and everywhere lead a civilized life, as nature demands. Even if this is proved by the divine writings, even if antiquity maintains this by the means of reason alone, nevertheless, it is no mean thing promoting its truth that with the throne of Augustus empty, the whole world spirals downward, that the helmsman and rowers in the ship of Peter sleep, and that wretched Italy, alone, abandoned to private rule and devoid of all public direction, is struck by so great a shock of winds and waves that not only cannot words express it, but even the unhappy Italians themselves are hardly able to mourn it with tears. Therefore, let all those who with outrageous daring rise up against this very clear will of God now take heed with pale fright of the coming judgment of the stern Judge, if the sword of him who says 'vengeance is mine' has not fallen from heaven." *Aeterni pia providentia Regis, qui dum coelestia sua bonitate perpetuat, infera nostra despiciendo non deserit, sacrosancto Romanorum imperio res humanas disposuit gubernandas, ut sub tanti serenitate praesidii genus mortale quiesceret, et ubique, natura poscente, civiliter degeretur. Hoc etsi divinis comprobatur elogiis, hoc etsi solius podio rationis innixa contestatur antiquitas, non leviter tamen veritati applaudit, quod solio Augustuali vacante totus orbis exorbitat, quod nauclerus et remiges in navicula Petri dormitant, et quod Italia misera, sola, privatis arbitriis derelicta, omnique publico moderamine destituta, quanta ventorum fluctuumque concussione feratur verba non caperent, sed et vix Itali infelices lacrymis metiuntur. Igitur in hanc Dei manifestissimiam voluntatem quicumque temere praesumendo tumescunt, si gladius eius qui dicit 'mea est ultio,' de coelo non cecideit, ex nunc severi iudicis adventante iudicio pallore notentur.*

due to forsaking this lawful authority. Dante argues that the Florentines are placing themselves in opposition to Scripture, reason, and experience by their refusal to bow the knee to Henry VII, Holy Roman Emperor.

Dante's views on the matter were widely known. This letter was released publicly, and in any case, the fourth book of the *Convivio*, written in 1307, had made a similar argument. Thus, when in 1317 *Si fratrum* was promulgated by John XXII, Can Grande della Scala knew that he had in his court one of the foremost rhetoricians of the time devoted to his cause. What Can Grande needed was an argument that the Pope had no authority over the empire, especially an argument that would be persuasive to the university-educated clergy of Verona. They would need to decide in a very short time whether to obey a papal interdict. There is no evidence that Dante was commissioned directly by Can Grande to write, but he certainly had every reason to vigorously support his patron. He did so by writing in great haste the *Monarchia*, which probably came out in 1318.

The *Monarchia* is thus addressed principally to an audience of clergy and other *literati* educated in the rigorous Aristotelianism of the late medieval universities. What would impress this audience and persuade them that the claims of John XXII in *Si fratrum* were false? Dante chose to achieve this end by presenting them with a virtuoso display of Aristotelian logic, Roman history, and Thomistic theology. The *Monarchia* is above all a piece of finely crafted rhetoric, so its logic, history, and theology are not always up to a rigorous standard. It is also not very original; it borrows heavily from Dante's earlier writings on the subject as well as other Ghibelline authors. Still, with rhetorical flair and relentless logical precision accompanied by constant citations of biblical and classical authors, Dante argues that the Roman Empire has been shown to have been ordained by God alone, not the Pope, through rational necessity, the testimony of history, and the clear teaching of Scripture. Reading the *Monarchia* was (and is) an odd and intimidating experience.

Although it is not Dante's most popular work, its success as a political pamphlet may be confirmed by the strong support Can Grande did in fact receive from the clergy and other intellectuals of Verona after its publication, from the *Monarchia's* mild popularity with pro-imperial thinkers during the following two hundred years, and, above all, from the furious attacks launched upon it and its author by papal supporters. In 1328, it was condemned, and many of its copies burned by Cardinal Bertrand du Poujet, who had been sent to Northern Italy as papal legate by John XXII; only narrowly was Cardinal du Poujet dissuaded from exhuming Dante's body and subjecting it too to the flames. In 1329, the Dominican friar and dedicated Guelph Guido Vernani wrote his attack on the *Monarchia*, the *De reprobatione Monarchiae compositae a Dante*, "Rebuke of Dante's *Monarchia*." Vernani was the first of a long train of critics of Dante's book, which in addition to being officially banned in Italy was eventually placed on the papal *Index* of prohibited books in 1561, not to be removed until 1881.

Despised by the supporters of papal power, the *Monarchia* was naturally considered useful by partisans of the emperor. All the same, it was cited quite rarely until the fifteenth century, when it came back into fashion as a result of further disputes over papal authority. A 1461 translation of the *Monarchia* into Italian by Marsiglio Ficino, in the Florence of Cosimo de' Medici, was part of such an assault upon papal pretensions. In another use, in 1452, Alberico de' Roselli wrote a work for Emperor Sigismund that borrowed heavily from the *Monarchia*. All this was in the context of the furious attacks on papal power by humanist scholars such as Lorenzo Valla and Nicholas of Cusa, not to mention their royal patrons, who found in Dante an ally.

For all its pride of place at the head of a long line of challenges to temporal papal authority, the *Monarchia* is nonetheless primarily a political pamphlet. As such, its focus is on Verona in 1318. Its character as a pamphlet is illustrated by its being most widely read in the immediate aftermath of its publication; both of the epitaphs written for Dante in 1322 (by Giovanni del Virgilio and Bernardo Scannabecchi) mention it alongside the *Commedia* as one of his defining works. But it is in its role as political pamphlet—hastily written, intensely focused on its local audience, fiercely partisan—that its value appears for our book. For at the end of the second book of the *Monarchia*, Dante portrays the incarnation and crucifixion of Christ as the crowning glory of the Roman Empire and the seal upon its divine sanction. To the clergy and scholars of Verona, at any rate, Dante expected this to be persuasive. Let us see what this portrayal was.

The Doctrine of the Atonement
in the Monarchia

The second book of the *Monarchia* seeks to prove the divine authorization and natural lawfulness of the universal rule of the Roman Empire[3] by means of historical arguments. "Why have the nations raged, and the people meditated vain things? The kings of the earth have arisen, and the rulers have gathered together against the Lord and against his Christ."[4] So runs the opening to Psalm 2, referring to the Davidic king and, ultimately, to Christ himself. Dante places this passage at the opening of Book 2 of the *Monarchia* and refers to the emperor, who is also the Lord's anointed, as he explains further on in the introduction: "I am pained to see kings and rulers agreeing on only one thing—that they shall oppose their Lord and his Anointed, the Roman ruler."[5] He endeavors to break the bonds of ignorance and rebellion by the following chain of arguments: the Roman people were the most noble; they were helped by miracles; they sought the public good; nature outfitted them to rule; in the race between nations for world power, they won out; and their triumph in this duel between nations signaled God's favor. Finally, he makes two arguments from the Christian faith: Christ, the righteous savior of all mankind, was born under

---

3. *Imperium*, "Empire," here means not merely a historical state, whether the Roman Empire of antiquity or the Holy Roman Empire of the Middle Ages, but rather the abstract concept of rule. In Dante's argument, the Romans had lawful authority, *imperium*, over all mankind.

4. Dante, *Monarchia* 2.1.1, trans. Richard Kay. *Quare fremuerunt gentes, et populi meditati sunt inania? Astiterunt reges terre, et principes convenerunt in unum, adversus Dominum et adversus Cristum eius.*

5. Dante, *Monarchia* 2.1.3, trans. Richard Kay. *Cum insuper doleam reges et principes in hoc unico concordantes: ut adversentur Domino suo et Uncto suo, romano principi.*

Roman rule and registered in a Roman census; and Christ endured the punishment for Adam's sin under Roman rule.

"Up to this point," writes Dante, "our thesis has been demonstrated by arguments that are for the most part based on rational principles; from now on, however, it is to be proven in another way, namely from the principles of the Christian faith. For more than anyone else, those who claim to be zealous for the Christian faith are the ones that 'raged' and 'meditated vain things' against the Roman ruler."[6] He needs some arguments from faith that will especially appeal to his intended audience, the clergy of Verona. Two key elements of this faith are Christ's incarnation and crucifixion. Both took place under Roman authority yet benefited all mankind; therefore, Christians above all should accept that Rome's authority is universal.

"Christ ... wished to be born from the Virgin Mother under an edict of Roman authority, so that in that unique registration of the human race, the Son of God, made a man, might be enrolled as a man," Dante writes.[7] Christ's choice to submit to a Roman edict is proof of Rome's lawful right to rule. "Every unjust thing is approved unjustly; Christ did not approve anything unjustly: therefore, he did not approve an unjust thing," he reasons.[8] Moreover, as the representative human being, Christ naturally had to be officially registered by the divinely

---

6. Dante, *Monarchia* 2.10.1, trans. Richard Kay. *Usque adhuc patet propositum per rationes que plurimum rationalibus principiis innituntur; sed ex unc ex principiis fidei cristiane iterum patefaciendum est. Maxime enim fremuerunt et inania meditati sunt in romanum Principatum qui zelatores fidei cristiane se dicunt.*

7. Dante, *Monarchia* 2.10.6, trans. Richard Kay. *Cristus ... sub edicto romane auctoritatis nasci voluit de Virgine Matre, ut in illa singulari generis humani descriptione filius Dei, homo factus, homo conscriberetur.*

8. Dante, *Monarchia* 2.10.10, trans. Richard Kay. *Omne iniustum persuadetur iniuste; Cristus non persuasit iniuste: ergo non persuasit iniustum.*

authorized rulers of all mankind. In the next chapter, Christ's submission to Rome as universal ruler is likewise of greatest importance.

"Again: if the Roman Empire was not lawful, Adam's sin was not punished in Christ. But this conclusion is false; therefore, the contradictory of the antecedent from which this conclusion follows must be true," Dante begins.[9] The logic may be broken down as follows: the antecedent is "The Roman Empire was not lawful"; the consequent is "Adam's sin was not punished in Christ." The consequent is false, and therefore, the opposite of the antecedent must be true: the Roman Empire is indeed lawful (*de jure*). But why is the consequent false? Dante, addressing Christians who accept the authority of Scripture, cites Scripture to prove its falsity:

> By Adam's sin we were all sinners, for the Apostle says: "as by one man sin entered into this world, and by sin death, so death entered all men, in whom all have sinned." Accordingly, if satisfaction for that sin had not been effected through Christ's death, we would still be "children of wrath by nature," namely by our corrupt nature. But this is not the case, since the Apostle said *To the Ephesians*, when speaking of God the Father, "he has predestined us unto the adoption of children through Jesus Christ unto himself, according to the purpose of his will, unto the praise and the glory of his grace, in which he has graced us in his beloved son, in whom we

---

9. Dante, *Monarchia* 2.11.1, trans. Richard Kay. *Et si romanum Imperium de iure non fuit, peccatum Ade in Cristo non fuit punitum; hoc aute est falsum: ergo contradictorium eius ex quo sequitur est verum.*

have redemption through his blood, the remission of sins, according to the riches of his glory, which has super-abounded in us." Moreover, it is also not the case because while Christ was personally undergoing punishment, he himself said, in the *Gospel of John*: "It is finished." This proves the point because when a thing is finished, nothing remains to be done.[10]

The Scriptures proclaim that our sin has been forgiven through Christ's death and our status as children of God made sure, and therefore, Adam's sin must have been punished in Christ.

But here Dante runs into a problem: why does Adam's sin being punished in Christ require that the Roman Empire be lawful? While the argument works within the narrow confines of the syllogism, it needs further corroboration to make sense. Dante provides this:

> To see the consistency of the argument, one must understand that "punishment" does not simply mean "a penalty on one who causes an injury" but "a penalty inflicted on one who causes an injury by another who has the jurisdiction to impose such a penalty." Hence, unless the penalty is inflicted by a judge having ordinary jurisdiction, it

10. Dante, *Monarchia* 2.11.2–3, trans. Richard Kay. *Per peccatum Ade omnes peccatores essemus, dicente Apostolo "Sicut per unum hominem in hunc mundum peccatum intravit et per peccatum mors, ita in omnes homines mors, in quo omnes peccaverunt"; si de illo peccato non fuisset satisfactum per mortem Cristi, adhuc essemus filii ire natura, natura scilicet depravata. Sed hoc non est, cum dicat Apostolus ad Ephesios loquens de Patre: "Qui predestinavit nos in adoptionem filiorum per Iesum Cristum in ipsum, secundum propositum voluntatis sue, in laudem, et gloriam gratie sue, in qua gratificavit nos in delicto Filio suo, in quo habemus redemptionem per sanguinem eius, remissionem peccatorum secundum divitias glorie sue que superhabundavit in nobis"; cum etiam Cristus ipse, in se punitionem patiens, dicat in Iohanne: "Consummatum est"; nam ubi consummatum est, nichil restat agendum.*

is not a "punishment" but rather should itself be called an "injury."[11]

If Christ had not been punished by a judge with lawful right over him as a member of the human race, then he would not have been punished at all. This is the meaning of *iudex ordinarius*, a technical legal term derived from Roman Law that describes a judge who has been granted jurisdiction by a legitimate authority.

For Dante, it is manifestly the case that Christ *had* to have been punished for the sins of all mankind for them to be forgiven; therefore, the suffering he underwent *had* to have been a just punishment ordered by a lawful authority. As he continues:

> Therefore, if Christ had not suffered under a judge with ordinary jurisdiction, that penalty would not have been a punishment. And the judge could not have had ordinary jurisdiction unless it was over the entire human race, since the entire human race was being punished in that flesh of Christ, who, as the Prophet says, "was bearing our sorrows," or sustaining them. And Tiberius Caesar, whose vicar Pilate was, would not have had jurisdiction over the entire human race unless the Roman Empire existed lawfully.[12]

---

11. Dante, *Monarchia* 2.11.4, trans. Richard Kay. *Propter convenientiam sciendum quod "punitio" non est simpliciter "pena iniuriam inferenti," sed "pena inflicta iniuriam inferenti ab habente iurisdictionem puniendi"; unde, nisi ab ordinario iudice pena inflicta sit, "punitio" non est, sed potius "iniuria" est dicenda.*

12. Dante, *Monarchia* 2.11.5, trans. Richard Kay. *Si ergo sub ordinario iudice Cristus passus non fuisset, illa pena punitio non fuisset. Et iudex ordinarius esse non poterat nisi supra totum humanum genus iurisdictionem habens, cum totum humanum genus in carne illa Cristi portantis dolores nostros, ut ait Propheta, vel substinentis puniretur. Et supra totum humanum genus Tyberius Cesar, cuius vicarius erat Pilatus, iurisdictionem non habuisset, nisi romanum Imperium de iure fuisset.*

He concludes his argument by noting that Herod sent Christ back to Pilate rather than punish him himself, which was necessary because he did not have jurisdiction over all mankind. Dante here makes special note of the unwittingness of Herod in his performance of God's will, comparing it to the unwittingness of Caiaphas: "Herod did not comprehend the significance of what he did, just as Caiaphas did not when by divine decree he spoke the truth."[13] Still, it was necessary; if Herod had put Christ to death, the crucifixion would not have had the same salvific effect because it would not have been a punishment inflicted upon the whole human race by a judge who had lawful authority over it.

Dante uses the verb *satisfacere*, "to make satisfaction," to describe the effect of the atonement earlier; but it is clear that the effect is achieved by means of a punishment. The verb *punire*, "to punish," and its variants are found throughout the argument. Therefore, his doctrine of the atonement as manifested in the *Monarchia* is one that has at its center Christ enduring the penalty for sin on behalf of the whole human race as its unique representative—in other words, penal substitution.

As we have seen, then, Dante's final argument in Book 2 of the *Monarchia* for the lawful jurisdiction of the Roman Empire over the entire human race uses principles from the Christian faith. "Let those who pose as sons of the Church therefore cease to reproach the Roman Empire now that they see that the Church's bridegroom, Christ, thus approved the Empire at

---

13. Dante, *Monarchia* 2.11.6, trans. Richard Kay. *Herodes, quamvis ignorans quid faceret, sicut et Cayphas cum verum dixit de celesti decreto …*

the beginning and end of his life," he triumphantly concludes.[14] Christ is the representative of the human race, so at the beginning of his life, he is registered in the universal census of all mankind. Christ is the representative of the human race, so at the end of his life, he is punished by the universal authority set over all mankind.

THE RESPONSE OF GUIDO VERNANI

In 1329, there appeared the first of a long line of Guelph attacks on the *Monarchia*, the *De reprobatione Monarchiae compositae a Dante*, "Refutation of the *Monarchia* written by Dante." Guido Vernani, its author, was an obscure Dominican friar who lived in Rimini, although between 1310 and 1320, he was in Bologna and attended the university there. He wrote three commentaries on various works of Aristotle and three treatises defending the temporal authority of the Pope, the last of which was the *De reprobatione*. All three defenses of papal power were written within three years, between 1327 and 1329; all three were probably written to catch the eye of Cardinal du Poujet, who at that time was in Bologna. The cardinal's condemnation of Dante's *Monarchia* in 1328 may well have spurred Vernani to write the *De reprobatione* in a final effort to obtain an official position at du Poujet's court.

That Bologna was the place where Vernani intended his book to have its greatest effect is shown by its dedication to the notary Bonagrazia ("Graziolo") de' Bambaglioli. Bambaglioli was a chancellor of the Commune of Bologna, responsible for

---

14. Dante, *Monarchia* 2.11.7, trans. Richard Kay. *Desinant igitur Imperium exprobare romanum qui se filios Ecclesie fingunt, cum videant sponsum Cristum illud sic in utroque termino sue militie comprobasse.*

keeping the legal records of the city. More interestingly, however, he was a poet and, despite his being a staunch Guelph, an admirer of Dante. Bambaglioli had written a commentary on Dante's *Inferno* in 1324, one of the first to come out. Vernani's dedication was not so much in honor of the chancellor as it was a warning to him about the dangers of being overfond of an enemy of the Guelphs.

Vernani wasted no space giving Dante even perfunctory praise in an attempt to win over his dedicatee:

> There was a certain man who wrote many fantasies in poetry, a wordy sophist, gratifying many in his eloquence by means of hollow words. This man, through his poetic phantasms and figments, leading whores onstage (as the *Consolation* of the philosopher Boethius puts it), guides both learned and feeble souls by his sweet Siren songs to the destruction of salvific truth. But passing over his other works with revulsion, I wished to deal with a certain book of his that he wished to call *Monarchia*, since in it he seems to proceed in an orderly manner, yet mixing with a few truths many lies.[15]

The entire *De reprobatione* is written in a similar vein, by turns vindictive and mocking. However, it also strives to give the appearance of meticulousness by dealing systematically with

---

15. Guido Vernani, *De reprobatione monarchie composite a Dante*, ed. N. Matteini (Padua: Casa Editrice dott. Antonio Milani, 1958), 93. *Quidam fuit multa fantastice poetizans et sophista verbosus, verbis exterioribus in eloquentia multis gratus, qui suis poeticis fantasmatibus et figmentis, iuxta verbum philosophie Boetium consolantis, scenicas meretriculas adducendo, non solum egros animos, sed etiam studiosos dulcibus sirenarum cantibus conducit fraudulenter ad interitum salutifere veritatis. Pretermissis autem aliis ipsius operibus cum despectu, quoddam eius scriptum quod Monarchiam voluit appellare, quia in eo apparenter satis ordinate processit, cum aliquibus tamen veris multa falsa permiscens, volui perscrutari.*

Dante's arguments; Vernani first cites, then refutes, the poet. But it is when he encounters Dante's use of Christ's atonement that the spittle truly starts to fly.

Upon reaching the argument in the *Monarchia* that the Roman Empire was divinely instituted because Christ could only be rightfully punished by a judge with lawful jurisdiction over the whole human race, Vernani bursts out: "Here this fool raved most egregiously and, sticking his mouth in the sky, wriggled his tongue upon the earth."[16] Vernani's first point is that no earthly judge could have jurisdiction over original sin since the penalty for it was instituted by a divine—not a human—lawmaker. He then puts forward a ridiculous image:

> If this is so, then an earthly judge could punish a newborn infant with death since such a bodily death was rightly inflicted upon human beings due to sin by a divine law, according to that saying by the Apostle in the *Letter to the Hebrews* chapter 9: "It is laid down by law for human beings to die once."[17]

But this cannot be so since Adam's sin was against God, not against any human law code. "No human lawmaker in any of his laws ever instituted anything concerning this, nor did the gentiles recognize that sin, nor did Pilate judge Christ on account of it," Vernani insists.[18]

---

16. Vernani, *De reprobatione monarchie*, 108. *Hic iste homo copiosissime deliravit et, ponendo os in celum, lingua eius transivit in terra.*

17. Vernani, *De reprobatione monarchie*, 108. *Alioquin terrenus iudex statim natum puerum posset morte punire, quia mors corporalis talis peccati merito ex divino statuto hominibus est inflicta, dicente Apostolo ad Hebr. 9 cap.: Statutum est hominibus semel mori.*

18. Vernani, *De reprobatione monarchie*, 108. *Nec unquam aliquis homo legislator in suis legibus de hoc aliquid ordinavit, nec gentiles istud peccatum cognoverunt, nec Pylatus propter hoc iudicavit Christum.*

He then proceeds to explain what Christ's death was actually
for. Far from being a punishment upon Christ, it was an act of
obedience to God that was a fitting satisfaction for Adam's sin:
"In order that he might provide a full satisfaction for that sin to
God on behalf of the whole human race, it sufficed for Christ,
truly God and truly human, to be 'obedient to God the Father
up to death, even the death of a cross,' for the sake of the pres-
ervation of righteousness."[19] This obedience is what redresses
original sin and turns aside God's wrath. It is like the lesser act
of a martyr who, when forced even by private individuals to
choose between denying Christ and dying, chooses to die and
so obeys God and preserves righteousness.

As the martyr's act pleases God, so Christ's act pleased God.
Christ's death would have been just as efficacious, Vernani
argues, if this obedience had been occasioned by Christ being
slain by someone other than Pilate:

> If the Lord Jesus Christ, who did no sin himself nor con-
> tracted original sin, and so on account of these things
> ought not to have had to endure death, had been killed
> by anyone other than a judge for the sake of preserving
> that righteousness which he ought to have preserved out
> of obedience, in which he honored and glorified God the
> Father, he would have redeemed all mankind and made
> satisfaction for the sin of the whole human race.[20]

---

19. Vernani, *De reprobatione monarchie*, 108. *Ad hoc quod pro illo peccato Deo esset pro
toto humano genere plenarie satisfactum, sufficiebat quod Christus, verus Deus et verus homo,
pro conservatione iustitie esset 'obediens Deo patri usque ad mortem, mortem autem crucis'.*

20. Vernani, *De reprobatione monarchie*, 108–9. *Si Dominus Iesus Christus qui peccatum
personale non fecit nec peccatum originale contraxit, et propter hoc mortem sustinere non debuit
ab alio quam a iudice propter iustitiam conservandam quam ex obedientia servare debebat, in*

In other words, even if a common brigand had been the occasion for Christ's obedient death, it would still have turned aside God's wrath. This is the straightforward implication of the teaching of Anselm in his *Cur Deus homo*, which Vernani duly cites (although he does not quote) in the course of this section of his argument.

Vernani then explains how this death, even if at the hands of someone other than Pilate, benefits the sinner. Vicarious satisfaction is laid out in its full splendor:

> For that obedience and that life which he offered obediently and willingly to the Father, and the death which he endured for the sake of the Father's honor, was most graciously received by the divinity as being of such high worth that God considered it a complete satisfaction for the injury of the whole human race. And for this reason, all those believing in Christ and who through baptism are assimilated into his death, according to the catholic faith, are believed to have satisfied God.[21]

This explanation is then backed up by another citation of *Cur Deus homo*. He goes on to conclude that he has now demonstrated that Dante's argument about Pilate punishing Christ's sin as the lawful representative of the ruler of the entire human race is false. It is false, namely, because not only is original sin *not* under the lawful jurisdiction of Pilate, but Christ's sacrifice

---

quo Deum Patrem honorabat et glorificabat, fuisset occisus, omnes homines redemisset et pro peccato totius humani generis satisfecisset.

21. Vernani, *De reprobatione monarchie*, 109. Nam illa obedientia et vita illa quam Patri obediendo voluntarie obtulit, et mors quam pro Patris honore sustinuit, in tantum fuerunt in divinitatis acceptatione gratissime, quod Deus reputavit sibi esse pro iniuria totius humani generis plenarie satisfactum. Et ideo omnes in Christum credentes et per baptismum configurati morti eius, secundum fidem catholicam, Deo satisfecisse creduntur.

on the cross was *not* a punishment but an act of sacrificial obedience to God. The divine wrath is propitiated not because the
correct punishment has been meted out but because a great act
of obedience has counterbalanced the weight of original sin.

Vernani concludes by further countering Dante's assertion
that Christ's death was not an unlawful injury but a lawful punishment. He states, "And what silently or secretly is implied—
that what the judge inflicted was not an injury—is wholly false
since the greatest injury was brought upon Christ."[22] Scorn then
suffuses the final sentence: "Now that vile and contemptible
argument was not worthy of such a response, but I wrote it
for the benefit of those reading."[23]

The learned Dominican friar's anger when encountering
this part of Dante's argument is worth noting because there is
a real doctrinal difference that he correctly observes between
the atonement as vicarious satisfaction, as taught by Anselm,
and the penal substitutionary atonement portrayed in the
Monarchia by Dante. Vernani's response, however, is conde-
scending and pedantic; Dante was fully aware of the teaching of
Anselm and saw no contradiction between the two versions of
the atonement. More to the point, he did not expect his audience, equal at least in learning to Vernani, to see any contradiction. But to see this clearly, we will need to cast our eyes from
the *Monarchia* and the city of Verona in 1318 to the *Paradiso*
and the heavenly sphere of the planet Mercury in the jubilee
year 1300.

---

22. Vernani, *De reprobatione monarchie*, 109. *Et quod tacite vel occulte implicatur, quod
ex quo iudex erat, non erat iniuria, omnino falsum est, quia iniuria maxima Christo illata est.*

23. Vernani, *De reprobatione monarchie*, 109. *Tali autem responsione illud vile et derisibile
argumentum non erat dignum, sed propter utilitatem legentium ista scripsi.*

CHAPTER 3

DANTE ALIGHIERI, PART II

Penal Substitution and
Satisfaction in the *Paradiso*

More prosaically, of course, we are still in Verona between the years 1316 and 1318. The *Commedia* as a whole was written between 1306 and 1321, and the *Paradiso* between 1316 and 1321. We know that *Canto* 5 of the *Paradiso* was written before 1318 because Dante cites a line from it in the *Monarchia*. The focus of this section will be *Cantos* 6 and 7, so it is probable that we are in not only exactly the same place as the *Monarchia* but even the same time. Yet although written in the same place and at the same time, each work is distinct in its intended audience and its angle on the atonement. More importantly, the *Paradiso* explores the nuances of Christ's death on the cross in a subtler and more comprehensive way

53

than the *Monarchia*. As we will see, Guido Vernani's condescension in explaining to Dante the details of Anselm's vicarious satisfaction was exceptionally foolish.

This chapter will explore the *Paradiso* and its broader portrayal of the atonement. First, the doctrine of the atonement Dante puts forward in the *Paradiso* will be examined; then, we will investigate four fourteenth-century commentators on the *Paradiso* to see how they reacted to Dante's account. Last, we will conclude by looking at how two twentieth-century scholars responded to Dante's portrayal of the atonement. One of these is the indefatigable Jean Rivière.

The audience of the *Commedia* is much broader than that of the *Monarchia*. The latter is written in a Latin full of philosophical technicalities for a learned audience of university-trained clergy and laymen; the former is written in Italian for a lay audience who cannot read Latin. The latter is focused on Verona and the other northern Italian cities under Ghibelline control; the former, addressed to all Italian speakers wherever they may be. Dante strove in the *Commedia* to communicate the culture and ideas of "high" culture to a "low" audience.

Although Dante occasionally addresses his readers directly, more frequently, he is the one asking the questions of his guides and being taught. So he invites his readers to learn with him, as it were; and while in the *Inferno* and the *Purgatorio* his teacher is a medievalized Virgil, in the *Paradiso*, his teacher is his old love Beatrice. Dante's reader is intellectually challenged by the *Paradiso* more than either of the other *cantiche* of the *Commedia*, as befits the highest realm.

The *Commedia* as a whole, and the *Paradiso* in particular, is about the Christian faith: human redemption and the glory of God. While earthly politics comes into it, Dante's aim is to teach his audience about God's wisdom, his glory, and his love. The glories of heaven are so great that it is difficult to remember them on earth; and the final beatific vision at the end of the *Paradiso* is utterly impossible to describe: "Here power failed the lofty phantasy."[1] So in the *Paradiso*, Dante's aim is to guide his readers to love God and attune their will to his, and the effect of the closing beatific vision upon the poet is just that: "Already my desire and my will were revolved, like a wheel that is evenly moved, by the Love which moves the sun and the other stars."[2]

The *Paradiso* ends with glory and wonder, but throughout, it is filled with food for the reader's intellect. The mind must come to love God along with the will and heart. So, when Dante questions Beatrice about a strange thing that the shade of the emperor Justinian says in the heaven of Mercury, she gives him a detailed answer. That answer explains why God chose to redeem the human race by Christ's crucifixion. Understanding the nature of the atonement in the *Paradiso* is for Dante, and for his intended audience, a means of appreciating God's wisdom and glory.

The Doctrine of the Atonement in the *Paradiso*

In *Canto* 5 of the *Paradiso*, Dante and his guide Beatrice rise from the heaven of the moon, the lowest of the heavenly realms, to that of Mercury. In the heaven of Mercury appear the spirits of those who busied themselves with achieving worldly fame

---

1. Dante, *Paradiso* 33.142, trans. C. Singleton. *A l'alta fantasia qui mancò possa.*

2. Dante, *Paradiso* 33.143–45, trans. C. Singleton. *Già volgeva il mio disio e 'l velle,/ sì come rota ch'igualmente è mossa,/ l'amor che move il sole e l'altre stelle.*

and honor, thus not attending quite as they should to divine contemplation. They are assigned to the heaven of Mercury because that planet is frequently hidden from sight by the sun's rays, thus preventing the spirits there from boasting in their own glory. The travelers encounter a bright spirit shrouded in the light of its own happiness. The spirit invites Dante to ask it a question:

> O happy-born, to whom Grace concedes to see the thrones of the eternal triumph before you leave your time of warfare, we are enkindled by the light that ranges through all heaven; therefore, if you desire to draw light from us, sate yourself at your own pleasure.[3]

Encouraged by Beatrice, Dante asks the spirit who he is and why he is assigned to the heaven of Mercury.

Canto 6 begins with the response: *Cesare fui e son Iustinïano,* "I was Caesar and am Justinian."[4] Justinian, who ruled in Constantinople from 527 to 565, is the chief example in the heaven of Mercury of "good spirits who have been active in order that honor and fame might come to them. And when desires, thus deviating, tend thitherward, the rays of true love must needs mount upwards less living."[5] Justinian then describes to Dante the glory of the Roman Empire, its history, and the deeds of its rulers, and he condemns those who would

---

3. Dante, *Paradiso* 5.115–120, trans. C. Singleton. *O bene nato a cui veder li troni/ del trïunfo etternal concede grazia/ prima che la milizia s'abbandoni,/ del lume che per tutto il ciel si spazia/ noi semo accesi; e però, se disii/ di noi chiarirti, a tuo piacer ti sazia.*

4. Dante, *Paradiso* 6.10, trans C. Singleton.

5. Dante, *Paradiso* 6.113–17, trans. C. Singleton. *D'i buoni spirti che son stati attivi/ perché onore e fama li succeda:/ e quando li disiri poggian quivi,/ sì disvïando, pur convien che I raggi/ del vero amore in sù poggin men vivi.*

deny its divinely ordained authority. The pinnacle of its glory, as in the *Monarchia*, is the crucifixion of Christ:

> But what the standard that makes me speak had done before, and after was to do throughout the mortal realm subject unto it, becomes in appearance little and obscure if it be looked on in the hand of the third Caesar with clear eye and pure affection; because the living Justice which inspires me granted to it, in his hand of whom I speak, the glory of doing vengeance for its own wrath. Now marvel here at what I unfold to you: afterwards it sped with Titus to do vengeance for the vengeance of the ancient sin.[6]

Justinian tells Dante that the Roman Empire's greatest glory was crucifying Christ on the cross as vengeance for the sin of Adam.

Thus far the portrayal of the atonement is like that of the *Monarchia*; however, Justinian then presents to Dante a contradiction: after Tiberius (the *terzo Cesare*), God also granted Titus the glory of avenging the act of divine vengeance. Dante is stating here that the sack of Jerusalem in the year 70 was an act of God's wrath against the Jews for crucifying Christ, even though that crucifixion was also ordained by God as a just punishment upon sin. But as Justinian observes to Dante near the start of *Canto 6*, *ogne contradizione e falsa e vera*, "every

---

6. Dante, *Paradiso* 6.82–93, trans. C. Singleton. *Ma ciò che 'l segno ch parlar mi face/ fatto avea prima e poi era fatturo/ per lo regno mortal ch'a lui soggiace,/ diventa in apparenza poco e scuro,/ se in mano al terzo Cesare si mira/ con occhio chiaro e con affetto puro;/ ché la viva giustizia ch emi spira,/ li concedette, in mano a quel ch'i' dico,/ gloria di far vendetta a la sua ira./ Or qui t'ammira in ciò ch'io ti replico:/ poscia con Tito a far vendetta corse/ de la vendetta del peccato antico.*

contradiction is both false and true."[7] Nevertheless, this contradiction will need to be unpacked—for Dante, and for the reader.

At the start of *Canto* 7, Beatrice detects Dante's doubt over this contradiction. It is worth bearing in mind at this point the context of Justinian's dictum quoted above:

> One nature and no more I held to be in Christ, and with that faith I was content; but the blessed Agapetus, who was the supreme pastor, directed me to the true faith by his words. I believed him, and what he held by faith I now see as clearly as you see that every contradiction is both false and true.[8]

The theological truth that Christ is one person in two natures (i.e., divine and human), not in one nature, is key to Beatrice's explanation. Justinian once (according to Dante's mistaken sources) held to the position opposed to that enunciated at the Council of Chalcedon, namely, that after the incarnation there still exist two distinct natures in the person of Christ. However, he had come to the realization under Pope Agapetus's (535–536) tutelage that the teaching of two natures after the incarnation, although contradictory, was also true. Beatrice uses this reality of Christ's two distinct natures to explain how Titus justly avenged the just vengeance.

Beatrice begins, "By my judgment, which cannot err, how just vengeance could be justly avenged, has set you pondering; but I will quickly free your mind, and do you listen, for my

---

7. Dante, *Paradiso* 6.21, trans. C. Singleton.

8. Dante, *Paradiso* 6.14–21, trans. C. Singleton. *Una natura in Cristo esser, non piùe,/ credea, e di tal fede era contento;/ ma 'l benedetto Agapito, che fue/ sommo pastore, a la fede sincera/ mi dirizzò con le parole sue./ Io li credente; e ciò che 'n sua fede era,/ vegg' io or chiaro sì, come tu vedi/ ogne contradizione e false e vera.*

words will make you the gift of a great doctrine."[9] She then proceeds to outline the key to her explanation:

> By not enduring for his own good a curb upon the power that wills, that man who never was born, in damning himself damned all his progeny; wherefore the human race lay sick down there for many centuries in great error, until it pleased the word of God to descend where He, by the sole act of His eternal love, united with Himself in person the nature which had estranged itself from its Maker.[10]

Human nature in its entirety was condemned and alienated from God by the sin of Adam. The remedy for the lostness of mankind was the incarnation, where the Second Person of the Trinity, the Son, assumed human nature. Beatrice then solves the contradiction:

> Turn your sight now to that which now I say: this nature, which was thus united to its Maker, was, when it was created, pure and good; but by its own self it had been banished from Paradise, because it turned aside from the way of the truth and its proper life. The penalty therefore which the Cross inflicted, if it be measured by the nature assumed—none ever so justly stung; also none was ever of such great wrong, if we regard the Person

---

9. Dante, *Paradiso* 7.19–24, trans. C. Singleton. *Secondo mio infallibile avviso,/ come giusta vendetta giustamente/ punita fosse,/ t'ha in pensier miso;/ ma io ti solverò tosto la mente;/ e tu ascolta, ché le mie parole/ di gran sentenza ti faran presente.*

10. Dante, *Paradiso* 7.25–33, trans. C. Singleton. *Per non soffrire a la virtù che vole/ freno a suo prode, quell' uom che non nacque,/ dannando sé, dannò tutta sua prole;/ onde l'umana specie inferma giacque/ giù per secoli molti in grande errore, fin ch'al Verbo di Dio discender piacque/ u' la natura, che dal suo fattore/ s'era allungata, unì a sé in persona/ con l'atto sol del suo etterno amore.*

who suffered it, with whom that nature was bound up. Therefore from one act issued things diverse, for one same death was pleasing to God and to the Jews; thereat the earth trembled and Heaven was opened."[11]

The contradiction troubling Dante is solved by bearing in mind the two distinct natures of Christ united in his one person. The human nature was justly punished by the cross; the divine person who had assumed that nature, on the other hand, suffered a great *ingiuria*, "wrong," which was justly avenged by Titus.

"But now," observes Beatrice following this solution, "I see your mind from thought to thought entangled in a knot, from which, with great desire, it awaits release."[12] Solving one problem merely leads to another: the just vengeance can be justly avenged, well and good; but why did God choose *this* way, rather than another, to achieve our redemption? Beatrice responds:

> This decree, brother, is buried from the eyes of everyone whose understanding is not matured within love's flame. But inasmuch as at this mark there is much aiming and little discernment, I shall tell why that way was the most fitting.[13]

---

11. Dante, *Paradiso* 7.34–48, trans. C. Singleton. *Or drizza il viso a quel ch'or si ragiona:/ questa natura al suo fattore unita,/ qual fu creata, fu sincera e buona;/ ma per sé stessa pur fu ella sbandita/ di paradiso, però che si torse/ da via di verità e da sua vita./ La pena dunque che la croce porse/ s'a la natura assunta si misura,/ nulla già mai sì giustamente morse;/ e così nulla fu di tanta ingiura,/ guardanda a la persona che sofferse,/ in che era contratta tal natura./ Però d'un atto uscir cose diverse:/ ch'a Dio e a' Giudei piacque una morte;/ per lei tremò la terra e 'l ciel s'aperse.*

12. Dante, *Paradiso* 7.52–54, trans. C. Singleton. *Ma io veggi' or la tua mente ristretta/ di pensiero in pensier dentro ad un nodo,/ del qual con gran disio solver s'aspetta.*

13. Dante, *Paradiso* 7.58–60, trans. C. Singleton. *Questo decreto, frate, sta sepulto/ a li occhi di ciascuno il cui ingegno/ ne la fiamma d'amore non è adulto./ Veramente, però ch'a questo segno/ molto si mira e poco si discerne,/ dirò perché tal modo fu più degno.*

The investigation into the atonement changes from a focus on its *justice* to a focus on its *suitability*: *tal modo fu più degno*, "that way was more suitable," Beatrice will now argue. It is more suitable because it fits God's character; thus, to understand the answer she is about to give, it is necessary to be matured in the flame of God's love—in other words, to become so like God in love that you can comprehend the love that sent Christ to earth to die.

Beatrice first describes the nature with which mankind was first created and that by Adam's sin was lost:

> The Divine Goodness, which spurns all envy from itself, burning within itself so sparkles that it displays the eternal beauties. That which immediately derives from it thereafter has no end, because when it seals, its imprint may never be removed. That which rains down from it immediately is wholly free, because it is not subject to the power of the new things. It is the most conformed to it and therefore pleases it the most; for the Holy Ardor, which irradiates everything, is most living in what is most like itself.[14]

This nature, in other words, like the nature of the angels, comes from God directly, a spark from the divine fire. These sparks are impelled, as it were, by God's love to display his beauty visibly in creation. The natures "sparkled out" from the divine nature are thus not subject to decay or to the influences of the

---

14. Dante, *Paradiso* 7.64–75, trans. C. Singleton. *La divina bontà, che da sé sperne/ ogne livore, ardendo in sé, sfavilla/ sì che dispiega le bellezze etterne./ Ciò che da essa sanza mezzo piove/ libero è tutto, perché non soggiace/ a la virtute de le cose nove./ Più l'è conforme, e però più le piace;/ ché l'ardor santo ch'ogne cosa raggia,/ ne la più somigliante è più vivace.*

heavens and of nature as a whole (*le cose nove*, "the new things").
Mankind has (or had) the divine gifts of free will and immortality, things that also characterize God's nature. Therefore, the
creatures possessing these gifts are most pleasing to God since
they reflect most clearly the divine nature.

Beatrice then goes on to outline how these gifts were lost
and what was necessary to restore them:

> With all these gifts the human creature is advantaged,
> and if one fails, it needs must fall from its nobility. Sin
> alone is that which disfranchises it and makes it unlike
> the Supreme Good, so that it is little illumined by its
> light; and to its dignity it never returns unless, where
> fault has emptied, it fill up with just penalties against
> evil delight. Your nature, when it sinned totally in its seed,
> was removed from these dignities, even as from Paradise;
> nor could it recover them, if you consider carefully, by any
> way except the passing of these fords: either that God
> alone, solely by His clemency, had pardoned; or that man
> should of himself have given satisfaction for his folly.[15]

Sin makes the human race less like God, losing not only free
will but also immortality as punishment for freely choosing
to sin. To obtain these gifts once again, thus becoming once
more like its creator, mankind would have to make amends by

---

15. Dante, *Paradiso* 7.76–93, trans. C. Singleton. *Di tutte queste dote s'avvantaggia/
l'umana creatura, e s'una manca,/ di sua nobilità convien che caggia./ Solo il peccato è quel
che la disfranca/ e falla dissimile al sommo bene,/ per che del lume suo poco s'imbianca;/ e in
sua dignità mai non rivene,/ se non rïempie, dove colpa vòta,/ contra mal dilettar con giuste
pene./ Vostra natura, quando peccò tota/ nel seme suo, da queste dignitadi,/ come di paradiso,
fu remota;/ né ricovrar potiensi, se tu badi/ ben sottilmente, per alcuna via,/ sanza passar
per un di questi guadi:/ o che Dio solo per sua cortesia/ dimesso avesse, o che l'uom per sé isso
avesse sodisfatto a sua follia.*

suffering the penalties appropriate to the sin. The sin of Adam, infecting the whole human race, thus required one of two solutions to redress it: either that God, of his own *cortesia*, "clemency" or "courtesy," should forgive it, or that mankind should suffer the penalties sufficient to satisfy the demands of justice.

But as Beatrice notes, the latter was impossible to achieve, so God had to do something else:

> Fix your eyes now within the abyss of the Eternal Counsel, as closely fastened on my words as you are able. Man, within his own limits, could never make satisfaction, for not being able to descend in humility, by subsequent obedience, so far as in his disobedience he had intended to ascend; and this is the reason why man was shut off from power to make satisfaction by himself. Therefore it was needful for God, with his own ways, to restore man to his full life—I mean with one way, or else with both.[16]

The sin of Adam was pride, the desire to be like God; therefore, to satisfy the demands of justice, the human race would have had to humble itself to the same degree to which it had intended to raise itself up. This is, of course, impossible; being like God is so far above our capabilities, whatever our intentions were, that although we are judged by our intent, we do not have the ability to descend in humility as low as we intended to raise ourselves up. So God had to satisfy the demands of justice. But

---

16. Dante, *Paradiso* 7.94–105, trans. C. Singleton. *Ficca mo l'occhio per entro l'abisso/ de l'etterno consiglio, quanto puoi/ al mio parlar distrettamente fisso./ Non potea l'uomo ne' termini suoi/ mai sodisfar, per non potere ir giuso/ con umiltate obediendo oi,/ quanto disobediendo intese ir suso;/ e questa è la cagion per che l'uom fue/ da poter sodisfar per sé dischiuso./ Dunque a Dio convenia con le vie sue/ riparar l'omo a sua intera vita,/ dico con l'una, o ver con amendue.*

God acts in accordance with his character, which is typified by his "two ways," mercy and justice: *con l'una, o ver con amendue,* "with one of either, or with both." So God himself had to redeem mankind from sin, with either mercy or justice—or with both.

Both these ways, mercy and justice, were used in the redemption to restore mankind. Beatrice describes God's decision in this way:

> But because the deed is so much the more prized by the doer, the more it displays of the goodness of the heart whence it issued, the divine Goodness which puts its imprint on the world, was pleased by all its ways to raise you up again; nor between the last night and the first day has there been or will there be so exalted and so magnificent a procedure, either by one or by the other; for God was more bounteous in giving Himself to make man sufficient to uplift himself again, than if He solely of Himself had remitted; and all other modes were scanty in respect to justice, if the Son of God had not humbled himself to become incarnate.[17]

God takes delight in acting in accord with the fullness of his character, described by Beatrice here as the *divina bontà,* the "divine goodness." So both mercy and justice, which are both integral to "goodness," are used to lift mankind from the depths of sin. God is more merciful in descending to earth, becoming

---

17. Dante, *Paradiso* 7.106–120, trans. C. Singleton. *Ma perché l'ovra tanto è più gradita/ da l'operante, quanto più appresenta/ de la bontà del core ond' ell' è uscita,/ la divina bontà che 'l mondo imprenta,/ di proceder per tutte le sue vie,/ a rilevarvi suso, fu contenta./ Né tra l'ultima notte e 'l primo die/ sì alto o sì magnifico processo,/ o per l'una o perl'altra, fu o fie:/ ché più largo fu Dio a dar sé stesso/ per far l'uom sufficiente a rilevarsi,/ che s'elli avesse sol da sé dimesso;/ e tutti li altri modi erano scarsi/ a la giustizia, se 'l Figliuol di Dio/ non fosse umiliato ad incarnarsi.*

incarnate, and dying on the cross than if he had merely forgiven sin by his own power. But if he had forgiven sin by his own power, he would not have been acting in accord with justice, which is also part of his character. He therefore would not have taken delight in the redemption to the same degree or acted in a way that best displayed his character.

Thus ends Beatrice's discourse to Dante in *Canto* 7 on the nature of the redemption. As we have seen, the portrayal of the atonement in the *Paradiso* has two parts. The first is like that of the *Monarchia*: namely, that Christ's death on the cross was a punishment (a *giusta vendetta*, "just vengeance") for the sin of Adam. However, by introducing a contradictory statement on the effects of the crucifixion, how it pleased both God and the Jews, Dante introduces a nuance to his portrayal that is not emphasized in the *Monarchia*: God's *giusta vendetta* was inflicted upon the human nature of Christ, not his divine nature.

The second part is unlike the *Monarchia*. In the *Paradiso*, the question of why God chose the crucifixion to redeem mankind is answered with an emphasis upon God's character. The crucifixion was *degno*, "suitable" to express God's goodness, incorporating as it did both his mercy and his justice. The way in which it suited his justice, however, is expressed using the language and concepts of vicarious satisfaction. Christ, to redress the sin of Adam, performed an act of humility and obedience to God that equaled the intended sin. *Non potea l'uomo ne' termini suoi mai sodisfar*, "Man, within his own limit, could never make satisfaction," writes Dante; therefore, Christ would, and did.

Tutti li altri modi erano scarsi a la giustizia, se 'l Figliuol di Dio non fosse umiliato ad incarnarsi, "All other modes were scanty in respect to justice, if the Son of God had not humbled himself to become incarnate," Dante proclaims. Christ's humiliation in obedience to God is what saves; his act of obedience provides the *giuste pene*, "just penalties" that *rïempie, dove colpa vòta*, "fill up where sin has emptied." The penalties spoken of here are not punishments but acts of penitential obedience, like those we encounter in the *Purgatorio*: the gluttonous fast, the prideful are bowed low under heavy loads, and the avaricious have their eyes sewn shut. However, what is interesting is that Dante places both penal substitution and vicarious satisfaction together in the same place. He clearly saw no contradiction between them.

The Response of the Early Commentators

The staggering popularity of the *Commedia* from the moment of its dissemination is very well attested. From the idle scrawling of lines from the *Purgatorio* and *Inferno* in blank spaces in notarial documents in Bologna between 1317 and 1321 to the public performances of adaptations of the poem by street singers in market squares in the years immediately following Dante's death, the *Commedia* was taken at once into the heart of its audience. It appealed to all levels of society: the learned professors of Bologna and Florence took to lecturing on its subtleties, and the middle classes, no matter how small their libraries, made it their business to possess a copy.

This popularity also resulted in a remarkable phenomenon: commentaries, a genre usually reserved for classic texts and Scripture, were written in great number on the poem. Beginning with the notes on the *Inferno* by Dante's son Jacopo Alighieri in 1324, eleven commentaries were written within the first half of the fourteenth century. Many more were to be written by the time the century had ended. Composed in both Italian and Latin, they sought to expound the allegory and clarify the historical references in the *Commedia* to its broad audience. The eager reception of some of these commentaries (Jacopo della Lana's survives in almost eighty manuscript copies) testifies to the *Commedia*'s difficulty for many of its readers alongside its striking popularity.

The relevance of these commentaries to our present project is in how they reacted to Dante's portrayal of the atonement in the *Paradiso*. Did they, like Guido Vernani, angrily cite Anselm and dismiss the doctrine here as nonsense? By no means. Naturally, the early commentaries were written to establish Dante as a great spiritual and literary authority, and the later ones, to smooth the way for this great authority to operate among occasionally suspicious audiences, so their authors would have had no motivation to criticize. Still, one would expect a certain amount of explaining away to be done if the portrayal of the atonement were truly seen as odd and heretical. This was what occurred in other places—for example, Dante's seeming denial of the doctrine of the resurrection in *Canto* 13 of the *Inferno* in the wood of the suicides. But no: the dogma is exposited plainly as Dante wrote it, without any hesitation. The observations of four commentators are of particular interest and will serve to exemplify the responses: Jacopo della Lana, Andrea Lancia, Pietro Alighieri, and Benvenuto da Imola.

Jacopo della Lana wrote his Italian commentary in Bologna sometime between 1324 and 1328. It is uncertain which of the seven scions of the della Lana family named Jacopo present in the city during this time is to be identified as the author of the commentary, but what seems probable is that he was connected in some way with the University of Bologna. His commentary shows great learning in the liberal arts and theology, taking the typical approach of a scholastic theologian to his text. Jacopo della Lana pioneered the common approach of later Dante commentators of placing a prologue to each *canto*, called a *nota*, at the start of the respective commentary. Another fascinating—and quite relevant—aspect of della Lana's commentary is its openly Ghibelline sympathies. In *Canto* 6 of the *Paradiso*, this partisanship is especially visible, as might be expected, but more to the point, the *Monarchia* is cited at length in the opening *nota* to *Canto* 7—cited not in its original Latin but in della Lana's Italian paraphrase. The doctrine of the atonement in the *Monarchia* was thus very early on identified as identical to the one in the *Paradiso*.

Jacopo della Lana explains Justinian's cryptic comment about the deed of the *terzo Cesare* in *Canto* 6.81 in this way:

> He says that what the aforesaid eagle had done before and all that it would do in the successors of Tiberius was counted as nothing in comparison with what it did in the hand of Tiberius. For Tiberius undertook the vengeance for the sin of Adam; that is, under the rule of Tiberius, Christ died and was crucified. And through such a death, as has many times been said, the human race was reconciled with the Creator.[18]

---

18. Jacopo della Lana, *Commento della Jacopo della Lana bolognese*, as found in the Dartmouth Dante Project, dante.dartmouth.edu, Paradiso 6.81. *Dice che ciò che avea fatto la detta aquila e tutto ciò che avea a fare in li successori di Tiberio, tutto era scuro quasi nulla a comparazione di quello, che in mano a Tiberio fece, cioè ch'esso Tiberio fece la vendetta del*

This is plain exposition, without extraneous comments, as is his usual practice. It is in the *nota* at the head of each *canto*, however, that della Lana is more original. And in the *nota* to *Canto* 7, he connects Beatrice's resolution of Justinian's riddle with the *Monarchia*:

> As Aristotle demonstrates in his *Politics*, it is reasonable that the world ought to be ruled by a single principle ... and it was the opinion of the author that this principle, that is, temporal rule, was the emperor of Rome, as he wrote in the first and second parts of his *Monarchia*.[19]

Unlike Guido Vernani, Jacopo della Lana had no concerns about the orthodoxy of the *Monarchia*'s portrayal of the atonement, which he identifies as the same as that of the *Paradiso*.

---

peccato di Adam, cioè sotto lo imperio di Tiberio fue morto e crocifisso Cristo per la quale morte, come più volte è detto, fue reconciliata la specie umana con lo Creatore.

19. Lana, *Commento della Jacopo della Lana bolognese*, Paradiso 7 nota. *Sì come prova Aristotile nella sua Politica, ragionevilemente lo mondo si dee reggere per uno principio ... e fue opinione dell'autore che tale principio, cioè li temporali reggimenti, fosse lo imperadore di Roma, sì come ello tratta nella sua Monarchia nella prima e nella seconda parte.* He continues: "Having named this empire as having judicial jurisdiction over temporal affairs, he demonstrates his point, among other ways, by this: the penalty which ought to be the vengeance upon any sin needed to be imposed upon the sufferer by a person who had authority, that is, by an ordinary judge; otherwise, that penalty would be not vengeance but a wrong done to the sufferer. The death of Christ, as was said, was a vengeance for the sin of the first parents and of their descendants, and such were all the inhabitants of the earth, so the vengeance must needs be imposed by an ordinary judge, which judge, he writes, was at that time Tiberius Caesar, and his vicar in Jerusalem was Pilate. And so, summing up his point, the penalty of Christ was a vengeance by the vicar of Tiberius Caesar, who was emperor of Rome, and thus, that the empire has judicial jurisdiction was confirmed by what happened to Christ." *E nominato tale imperio avere giurisdizione giudiziaria circa questi temporali sì 'l prova tra gli altri modi in questo. La pena, che dee essere vendetta d'alcuno peccato, fa bisogno ch'ella sia imposta al paziente da persona che abbia autoritade, cioè da giudice ordinario, altrimenti quella pena non sarebbe vendetta, ma sarebbe ingiuria del paziente. La morte di Cristo, sì come è ditto, fue vendetta del peccato de' primi parenti e delli suoi discendenti, li quali erano tutti quelli del mondo, adunqua è bisogno ch'ella fosse commessa da giudice ordinario, lo quale giudice elli scrive essere in quello tempo Tiberio Cesare, ed essere suo vicario in Jerusalem Pilato. Adunque concludendo a proposito, la pena di Cristo fu vendetta dal vicario di Tiberio Cesare, ch'era imperadore di Roma, e così lo imperio hae giurisdizione giudicatoria e per lo avvenimento di Cristo roborata.*

Several years after Jacopo della Lana wrote his commentary, in 1333, the Florentine notary Andrea Lancia wrote the Italian commentary known as the *Ottimo commento*, "the best commentary." Although the attribution to Lancia is not certain—the *Ottimo commento* is formally anonymous—its early date and the strong internal evidence backing it up make it more likely than not to be accurate. Part of this strong internal evidence is the tendency of the *Ottimo commento* to present Italian-language versions of classical texts with great gusto. Lancia was an active popularizer of the Roman classics, translating and adapting such texts as Ovid's *Metamorphoses* and Seneca's letters into contemporary Italian.

This "vulgarizing" aspect of the commentary suggests that its intended audience was made up of comparatively unlearned laypeople, the middle classes of Florence and elsewhere who so quickly fell in love with the *Commedia*. Lancia also incorporates much of the earlier commentary tradition on Dante, especially that by Jacopo della Lana, although he also does not hesitate to disagree with others' interpretations. He claims to have met Dante on several occasions, using this personal knowledge to clarify a number of puzzles in the text of the *Commedia*. He is also a stalwart defender of Dante's orthodoxy; in *Canto* 13 of the *Inferno*, whose subject is the wood of the suicides, he brusquely rejects the possibility that Dante could have actually denied the doctrine of the resurrection.[20] What does Lancia, then, have to say about Dante's portrayal of the atonement in the *Paradiso*?

---

20. Andrea Lancia, *Ottimo commento*, as found in the Dartmouth Dante Project, dante. dartmouth.edu, *Inferno* 13.91–102. "That a man of so great an intellect as was the Author, and thus of such great skill in the crafts of knowledge, both theology (especially this) and philosophy, as he was, which was shown openly through his words in every place—that this man should have been ignorant of the article on the resurrection is not to be thought,

As is his common practice, Lancia includes a great deal of
Jacopo della Lana's commentary—in this case, the connection
to the argument of the *Monarchia*, which is repeated verba-
tim in the *nota* to *Canto* 7 of the *Paradiso*. This need not be
repeated; however, before this, he explains how Beatrice solves
Dante's dilemma:

> Now one ought to consider that there are in the person
> of Christ two natures, divine and human. If we con-
> sider the penalty of the death of Christ with respect to
> his humanity, which was fallen from grace, and that this
> death was the cause of redemption, says Beatrice, nothing
> was ever so necessary, nor could a death penalty be ever
> so justly done, that is, suffering ever be so justly inflicted;
> and the Author holds with respect to the death of the
> incarnate Son of God, suffering a penalty on the cross,
> no wrong, no offense was so great an injustice. So, of this
> death, two things are able to be considered: on the one
> hand, the pleasure of God, who wished to purchase the
> human race; on the other, the wickedness of the Jews.[21]

---

which every young child and old woman knows through the frequent recitation that the
aforesaid article enjoys in church: *et expecto resurrectionem mortuorum." E non è da pensare
che uomo di sì alto intelletto, come fu l'Autore, anche di così grandi abiti di scienzie, e massime di
teologia, e di filosofia, come fu elli, sì come per li suoi detti manifestamente appare in ogni luogo,
egli avesse ignorato l'articulo della resuressione, lo quale articulo ogni fanciullo, e vecchierella sa
per lo frequente cantare, che del detto articulo si fa nella Chiesa: et expecto resurrectionem
mortuorum.*

21. Lancia, *Ottimo Commento, Paradiso* 7 nota. *Ora è da considerare nella persona di
Cristo due nature, divina ed umana. Se consideriamo la pena della morte di Cristo per rispetto
della umanitade, la quale era caduta da grazia, e per quella morte era la redenzione, dice
Beatrice, nessuna fu mai così necessaria, nè mai morte pena porse così giustamente, cioè dolore
così giustamente; e per questo rispetto tiene l'Autore, che la morte di Cristo fosse vendetta giusta
del peccato de' primi parenti. Se consideriamo la persona del figliuolo di Dio incarnato sofferire
pena in sulla croce, nulla ingiuria, nulla offesa fu mai tanto ingiusta. Dunque di questa morte si
possono considerare due cose: l'una il piacere di Dio, di volere ricomperare l'umana generazione;
l'altra [la] nequizia de' Giudei.*

Lancia also notes the vicarious satisfaction taught during Beatrice's answer to Dante's second unspoken question: why the crucifixion was fitting.[22] As in Jacopo della Lana's commentary, there is no concern with the juxtaposition of vicarious satisfaction with a penal understanding of the atonement.

The sons of Dante tended their father's legacy with great care, as exemplified by the commentaries on the *Commedia* written by Jacopo, Dante's third son, and Pietro, his second-born. While Jacopo wrote the earliest extant commentary (in 1322, in Italian), he only covered the *Inferno*; his older brother Pietro, on the other hand, produced a complete Latin commentary on all three *cantiche*. Pietro wrote the first version of his commentary in 1340, then revised it twice in the ensuing two decades, with the final revision being completed sometime after 1358. It is to this commentary that we now turn.

Pietro Alighieri was still in his teens when his father Dante was exiled from Florence, and with him was sentenced to death *in absentia*. He was at his father's side during his wanderings, eventually settling with him in Ravenna, where, according to legend, he found the final thirteen *canti* of the *Paradiso* hidden behind a wall after Dante's death. He studied law in Bologna during the 1320s, meeting the young Petrarch and absorbing much of the pre-humanist classical learning that was starting

---

22. Lancia, *Ottimo Commento, Paradiso* 7.85–87. "Here he shows that the sin of the first parents was so great and of such a kind that the human race had been removed from spiritual dignity as much as from the delights of Paradise; so, in order to be able to return to the state of grace, before returning, either all should have to be forgiven by the simple mercy of God, or through its own power, it should make satisfaction with as many good works as there had been evils it had done in disobedience." *Qui mostra, che 'l peccato delli primi parenti fu tanto e tale, che l'umana generazione fue rimossa dalle degnitadi spirituali, come da quelle del Paradiso deliziano: onde a potere ritornare in grazia, prima convenia ritornare in essa o per simplice cortesia di Dio perdonante in tutto, o per se medesimo, satisfaccendo tanto con buone operazioni, quanto aveva offeso disubbidendo.*

to burgeon there. He then moved to Verona, where he practiced law and held several responsible positions in the civic government. It was in Verona that he wrote his commentary.

In the third edition's *nota* to *Canto* 6 of the *Paradiso*, Pietro expounds the doctrine of the atonement implied in the *canto* by Justinian:

> In the eighteenth and last year of his [Tiberius'] reign, under his consul or vicar in Judea, Pontius Pilate, God wished to do and to have vengeance upon the humanity of his own son Christ. By means of the aforesaid Pilate, urged on by the Jews, Christ was crucified in his human nature, which was [God's] enemy on account of the transgression of the first man, and so he satisfied his wrath, which he used to have against it. On account of this nature, as the Apostle says, we all "were children of wrath," and, "condemned because of the fault of one man," as he says in the fifth chapter of the letter to the Romans.[23]

For Pietro, Dante's portrayal of the atonement involves the execution of God's enemy, that is, human nature as represented in the flesh of Christ. He then cites two verses from the letters of the apostle Paul to support the assertion that human nature was subject to God's wrath.

In the first edition of his commentary on *Canto* 7, Pietro, like his predecessors mentioned above, cites (and quotes extensively

---

23. Pietro Alighieri, *Paradiso* vol. 3, as found in the Dartmouth Dante Project, dante.dartmouth.edu, 6 nota. *Anno XVIII et ultimo sui imperii, sub Pontio Pilato eius consule seu vicario in Iudea, Deus voluit facere et habere vindictam in humanitate Christi sui filii a dicto Pilato instantibus Iudeis crucifixi de humana natura eius inimica propter prevaricationem primi hominis, et satisfaciendo eius ire quam habebat contra eam. Ex qua, ut dicit Apostolus, omnes Eramus filii ire* [Ep. Eph. 2.3], *et In condempnatione propter delictum unius, ut ait Ad Romanos, Vº capitulo* [Ep. Rom. 5.18].

from) the portrayal of the atonement in the *Monarchia*. He then expounds the meaning of Beatrice's answer to Dante's second question, about why this way was the most fitting:

> And so, wishing to satisfy the divine justice on behalf of mankind, so that mankind might be able to rise up to heaven lawfully and with strict justice, he wished to be incarnate and to make noble human flesh with deity. In this flesh and humanity of Christ the son of God, he was tormented and despised by reproaches and at the last suffered death on the cross between two thieves. He was humiliated for this reason, that he should merit to be attended by redemption for our sake, having preserved righteousness in his own stern duty.[24]

Note the reason for Christ's crucifixion: *justitia in suo debito rigore servata*, "preserving righteousness in his own stern duty." In other words, Beatrice says that Christ's obedience is what satisfies God's wrath and redeems mankind—vicarious satisfaction.

Benvenuto da Imola is the last of the commentators on Dante whom we will examine. Educated in Bologna, he lectured on classical works there from around 1360 until just after 1375, when, after a falling out with his colleagues, he moved to Ferrara to work under the patronage of the Marquis Niccolò d'Este. He wrote two compendiums on Roman history, the *Romuleon* and the *Libellus Augustalis*, as well as commentaries on Virgil, Lucan, and Valerius Maximus. He was a friend of

---

24. Pietro Alighieri, *Paradiso* vol. 1, 7.109–120. *Unde volendo divina justitia pro eo homine satisfacere, ut valeret ipse homo de jure et rigore justitiae ad coelum ascendere, voluit incarnari, et humanam carnem nobilitare Deitate, qua carne et humanitate Christi filii Dei cruciata et opprobriis vilipensa, et ultimo mortem in cruce inter duos latrones passa, humiliata est adeo, quod pro nobis redemptionem meruit consequi, justitia in suo debito rigore servata.*

Petrarch and Boccaccio, and moving in these circles, he was one of the heralds of the humanist movement. His Latin lectures on Dante, revised and gathered together by 1380 into his commentary, were first given in Bologna and helped make the *Commedia* into a standard work studied in the university curriculum.

In the commentary on Beatrice's second speech in *Canto* 7 on the reason why God chose to redeem humanity by means of the cross, Benvenuto makes the following observations. First, when Beatrice notes that God showed forth his goodness by using both his ways (i.e., justice and mercy) to redeem mankind, he cites a historical example of a human ruler doing just that:

> And note here that if it is permitted to compare the human with the divine, our own Zaleucus, the most just Italian lawmaker, held to this path since wondrously and equally he practiced justice and mercy, so that he did not violate justice on account of mercy, nor mercy on account of justice. For when, as the Philosopher tells in the first book of the *Politics*, he had enacted a law that an adulterer should be deprived of both his eyes, he remained for a long time obdurate against his own son, who had offended against the law; finally, appeased by the prayers of all, he removed one eye from his son and one from himself. So too, that eternal judge, the most just lawmaker, for a long time severely enacted death against the guilty human race on account of the sin of the first parent, deceived by the woman; and finally, due to the prayers of many righteous and holy fathers, he practiced justice

and mercy by humbling his own Son in the incarnation and passion.[25]

The case to which Benvenuto refers is that of Zaleucus, a (possibly legendary) seventh-century BC ruler of Locri in the south of Italy. Benvenuto is a little muddled: the reference to Zaleucus is in the second book of Aristotle's *Politics*, and the incident involving his son is told in the *Memorable Deeds and Sayings* of the first-century AD Roman author Valerius Maximus, with whom Benvenuto was quite familiar. Still, the point stands: just as Zaleucus took his son's punishment upon himself, thus sparing his son's sight and acting both mercifully and justly, so too does God act both justly and mercifully by taking upon himself the punishment due to mankind for original sin.[26]

Second, at the end of Beatrice's account of the atonement, when she praises the *magnifico processo* by which the justice and mercy of God were both satisfied, Benvenuto writes:

> And she says well; for in the incarnation there appeared the power of the Father, the wisdom of the Son, the benevolence of the Holy Spirit. For there alone was owed a penalty for sin according to justice; and to forgive sin freely without a penalty was contrary to the justice of

---

25. Benvenuto da Imola, *Paradiso*, as found in the Dartmouth Dante Project, dante. dartmouth.edu, 7.109–111. *Et hic nota quod si licet comparare humana divinis Galengus noster italicus justissimus legislator hanc viam tenuit; quoniam mirabiliter et pariter usus est justitia et misericordia, ita quod non violavit justitiam propter misericordiam, nec misericordiam propter justitiam. Cum enim, ut narrat philosophus primo Politicorum, sanxisset legem ut adulter utroque oculo privaretur, filio proprio qui inciderat in legem, cum diu in rigore pertinaciter permansisset, tandem placatus precibus omnium eruit unum oculum filio alterum sibi; ita aeternus judex justissimus legislator diu severe egit contra genus humanum reum mortis propter peccatum primi parentis a muliere decepti; et finaliter precibus multis justorum et sanctorum patrum usus est justitia et misericordia Filium suum humiliando ad incarnationem et passionem.*

26. Valerius Maximus, *Facta et Dicta Memorabilia* 6.5 ext. 3.

God, who is Just without peer, and to not forgive was contrary to his compassion, who is Merciful without peer.[27]

Benvenuto quite agrees with Dante on the fittingness of Christ's death on the cross as a means of our redemption. It fits both God's justice and his mercy, and it fully displays his goodness.

As we have seen, then, the commentators on Dante's *Commedia* took no exception to his portrayal of the atonement as both penal substitution and vicarious satisfaction. This was not due to their ignorance of the *Monarchia*; all four knew of it, and three cited it explicitly in the context of the portrayal of the atonement in *Cantos* 6 and 7 of the *Paradiso*. So, while Guido Vernani condemned Dante's doctrine, Jacopo della Lana, Andrea Lancia, Pietro Alighieri, and Benvenuto da Imola did not. On the contrary, they reinforced it with citations of Scripture and the fathers, with classical *exempla* and plain logic. So the historical vignette of Dante's portrayal of the doctrine of the atonement is now complete. What remains now is to assess its significance. What are we to make of it?

Summing Up

How might we outline Dante's understanding of the atonement as portrayed in the *Monarchia* and the *Paradiso*? God's goodness, his *divina bontà*, as Dante puts it in the *Paradiso*, must be reflected in mankind's redemption. Not partially reflected, but wholly reflected: God's mercy and God's

---

27. Benvenuto da Imola, *Paradiso* 7.112–120. *Et bene dicit; nam in incarnatione apparuit potentia Patris, sapientia Filii, benevolentia Spiritus sancti. Nam peccato solum debetur poena secundum justitiam; et dimittere peccatum liberaliter sine poena erat contra justitiam Dei, qui est summe justus, et non dimittere erat contra misericordiam eius qui est summe misericors.*

justice must both be involved. This is more clearly stated in the *Paradiso*, where Beatrice's reason for God choosing the way of the cross to redeem mankind centers around the full display of God's goodness. Yet the *Monarchia* also depends upon God's goodness being shown forth in the economy of the redemption. God is just, so it is not fitting for sin simply to be forgiven; but God is also merciful, so it is not fitting for there to be no way of forgiveness offered at all. By redeeming mankind through the sacrificial suffering and death of Christ the Son of God, the God-man, on the cross, God unites his mercy and justice in such a way that both are displayed in their full glory.

Propitiation is explained in two ways. The solution to human sin involves the punishment of Adam's sin by the judicial execution of the representative of all mankind, that is, Christ. It also involves the redress of that first sin through a good deed that matches its evil in magnitude. Christ also provides this by means of his obedience to God and humiliation on the cross. Yet it should be emphasized that both these parts of the solution are fit together into one doctrine; Dante does not feel they contradict. The sacrifice of propitiation by which God's wrath is turned aside is both a punishment by a lawful authority inflicted upon a guilty party (Christ's human nature) and an act of obedient humiliation that redresses the evil done by sinful mankind in their first parent Adam. Human sin is consequently also expiated, and mankind enabled to lift itself up again to God's favor because the representative of all has been purged of sin.

This is Dante's doctrine of the atonement. It was supported and held to be unexceptional by his commentators. But what of the critique of Guido Vernani? How may it be answered? Vernani claims, after all, that Dante is quite mistaken in thinking that Christ was justly punished on the cross by a lawful authority. Propitiation, for Vernani, is strictly vicarious satisfaction—Christ's humble obedience is the pleasing aroma to the Lord that turns aside his wrath. Vernani insists that Christ's crucifixion was a wrongful injury inflicted upon an innocent victim. But as we have seen, if the learned Dominican had bothered to read the *Paradiso*, he would have discovered that Dante quite agreed with him. Both even use the same term (albeit one in Latin, the other in Italian): *injuria, ingiuria*; Christ's death was an *injury*. But what Vernani ignores is that for Dante, the *ingiuria* is inflicted against the person of the Son of God, while the punishment is imposed against the flesh assumed by the Son. But there is another important way in which Vernani entirely misses the point of Dante's argument in the *Monarchia*: he ignores Dante's conception of the hidden role of God's providence in the historical event of the crucifixion.

Bruno Nardi vs. Guido Vernani

To see how this is so, let us turn to a more contemporary voice: the great Italian Dante scholar Bruno Nardi. In an article published in 1965, Nardi addresses Vernani's argument.[28] Nardi points out that for Dante, universal monarchy is like the universal church: one of the two remedies for sin in the present age. To grasp Dante's portrayal of the doctrine of the atonement,

---

28. Bruno Nardi, "Discussioni dantesche. I. Di un'aspra critica di fra Guido Vernani a Dante," *L'Alighieri* 6, no. 1 (1965): 42–47.

one must first understand the broader framework of his argument for universal government.[29]

Nardi notes that the *Monarchia* as a whole is something of
a utopia in that a universal monarchy never existed in the past,
did not exist in Dante's time, and would probably never exist,
a fact of which Dante was well aware. Thus, "such institutions
are universal in conception, or, if you prefer, in aspiration, not
in the (quite different) historical reality."[30] Such a utopianistic
vision of the Roman Empire as the ruler of the entire human
race is also found (at least rhetorically) in Virgil's *Aeneid*, whose
influence on Dante was profound; and while such claims were
forcibly rejected by Vernani (as well as by Augustine in his *De
civitate Dei*), Dante took them more seriously. Nardi describes
Dante's thought like this:

> "No," responds Dante, "I also thought like this at one time;
> but when I had looked into it more deeply, I took into
> account, with derision and contempt for him who holds

---

29. Nardi, "Discussioni dantesche," 43. "I have spoken of the stupidity of Fra Guido
Vernani of Rimini in the harsh critique of Dante's argument I touched on just now, because
the first duty of one who fights against a particular thesis is to render an account of the
exact position of their adversary in its most important aspects. Now he, entirely enclosed
and armored up inside his own theological doctrines based on rather different foundations,
is unable to grasp the exact meaning of the thesis he takes as an adversary, and above all,
he does not understand at all in what sense and in what measure the 'temporal Monarchy,'
willed by God as one of the 'remedies against the sickness of sin,' arrives at the goal for which
it had been willed by God, even before the coming of Christ." *Ho parlato di stupidità di fra
Guido Vernani da Rimini nell'aspra critica dell'argomento dantesco ora accennato, perché il primo
dovere di chi combatte una certa tesi è quello di rendersi conto dell'esatta posizione dell'avversario
nei suoi fondamenti. Ora egli, tutto chiuso e catafratto in una sua dottrina teologico basata su
fondamenti del tutto diversi, non riesce a intendere il significato esatto della tesi che prende a
combattere, e soprattutto non comprende affatto in che senso e in che misura la «Monarchia
temporale» voluta da Dio come uno dei «remedia contra infirmitatem peccati» raggiunge la
scopo per il quale è stata voluta da Dio, anche prima della venuta di Cristo.*

30. Nardi, "Discussioni dantesche," 44. *Siffatti istituti sono universali nel concetto o, se
preferite, nelle aspirazioni, non nella realtà storica che è ben diversa.*

to this idea, that the force of arms is not the moving [i.e., primary] cause of historical events, but only the instrumental [i.e., secondary] cause. The true moving cause of human history is God, who makes use of human beings to put into action his own eternal decrees." The search for the moving cause of human events in the divine thought: behold what is at the root of Dante's utopia.[31]

For the practical and narrow-minded Vernani, such subtleties were too much.

So Vernani's fierce reaction to Dante's use of the atonement to make his argument merely demonstrates his own inability to grasp the argument. *Egli perde addirittura le staffe*, literally, "he really loses the stirrup," to use Nardi's evocative Italian colloquialism (which has the rough meaning in English of "he flies off the handle"), when faced with Dante's atonement in the *Monarchia.* "While spewing insults at Dante, he shows that he lacks the capacity to understand Dante's thinking, something that often happens to *bien-pensants* of his mental capacity," says Nardi, who is clearly having fun.[32]

Vernani's argument against Dante's atonement is that even if Christ had not been killed by a judge with ordinary jurisdiction, his sacrifice would still have been efficacious. To this Nardi responds:

---

31. Nardi, "Discussioni dantesche," 45. *No—risponde Dante—, questo pensavo anch'io un tempo; ma quand'ebbi guardato più a fondo, mi resi conto, con derisione e disprezzo di chi ciò pretende, che la forza delle armi non è la causa movente degli eventi storici, ma soltanto causa strumentale. La vera causa movente della storia umana è Dio, che si serve degli uomini per l'attuazione dei suoi eterni decreti. La ricerca della causa movente degli eventi umani nel pensiero divino, ecco quello che è alla base dell'utopia dantesca.*

32. Nardi, "Discussioni dantesche," 45. *Mentre vomita ingiurie contro Dante, si rivela incapace d'intenderne il pensiero, cosa che accade spesso ai benpensanti della sua levatura mentale.*

This brings to my mind what Baruccabbà says in Belli's sonnet:

> Therefore, continues Baruccabbà, "Since he came to die, / Someone had to kill him." Someone! Behold the opinion of this poor *bien-pensant* brother. It is this same banal *someone* that Dante cannot tolerate. To reduce the tragedy of the passion and death of the Son of God to, let us say, a murder during a quarrel or an act of bullying, is truly insupportable.[33]

To give some literary context: the nineteenth-century Italian satirist G. G. Belli wrote a number of sonnets about the Jews of the Roman ghetto, in one of which he discusses the old accusation that they killed Christ and so were worthy of Christian hatred.[34] Belli's fictional interlocutor, the ghetto Jew Baruccabbà, defends his people against the old charge by saying that if Christ was foreordained by God to die, then why blame those who did it? Using this quote from Belli, Nardi observes that it is precisely this indifference to the means of the death of Christ shown by Vernani that Dante opposes. Why does he do so?

---

33. Nardi, "Discussioni dantesche," 46. *Il che mi fa venire in mente quel che dice Baruccabbà nel sonetto del Belli: "Dunque, seguita a di Baruccabbà, / subbito che lui venne pe' mori, / quarchiduno l'aveva da ammazzà." Quarchiduno! Ecco il concetto di questo povero frate benpensante. E' proprio questo banale* quarchiduno *che Dante non tollera. Ridurre la tragedia della passione e morte del Figlio di Dio al banale caso, mettiamo, della sua uccisione durante un diverbio o in una sopraffazione, è davvero insopportabile.*

34. Lynn M. Gunzbert, *Strangers at Home: Jews in the Italian Literary Imagination* (Berkeley: University of California Press, 1992), 120–21. I have used Gunzbert's translation of Belli for Nardi's citation.

It is because he has meditated on Scripture longer than Vernani has and has noticed something important about Christ's passion:

> The "just penalty" for the ancient sin that was willed by God is the same that according to the account of the Gospels was inflicted by Pilate, the procurator of the Emperor Tiberius, in Jerusalem. But on this account of the Gospels Dante meditated for a long time while writing the *Monarchia*. Certainly longer than brother Guido Vernani. And one point of this account would make the greatest impression on him. It is the place where John narrates that Caiaphas, "since he was priest for that year," that is, while he carried out the highest office of the Hebrew religion, said: "It is better for you that one man should die for the people and not that the whole people should perish." And the evangelist adds: "Now he did not say this by himself, but ... prophesied." Caiaphas did not say this because he knew what he was saying, but "he prophesied," said that which was inspired by God, which is precisely the biblical meaning of the verb *profetare*. *He prophesied!* Therefore, in the drama of the trial, of the passion and death of Christ, he who moves and makes human beings speak is, for Dante, God himself.[35]

---

35. Nardi, "Discussioni danteschi," 46. *La «giusta pena» del peccato antico quale fu voluta da Dio è proprio quella che secondo il racconto dei Vangeli gli fu inflitta da Pilato procuratore dell'Imperatore Tiberio a Gerusalemme. Ma sul racconto dei Vangeli Dante ha meditato a lungo mentre scriveva la* Monarchia. *Certo più di fra Guido Vernani. E un punto di questo racconto ebbe a fargli la più grande impressione. E' il luogo là dove Giovanni (11, 49–53) narra che Caifàs, «cum esset pontifex anni illius», mentre cioè copriva la più alta carica della religione ebraica, disse: «Expedit vobis ut unus moriatur homo pro populo et non tota gens pereat». E il vangelista aggiunge: «Hoc autem a semetipso non dixit, sed ... prophetavit»; questo Caifàs non disse perché sapesse quel che diceva, ma «profetò», lo disse cioè ispirato da Dio, qual è appunto*

Nardi goes on to note Dante's mention of Herod's refusal to judge Christ, where the poet states that Herod did not relinquish his authority knowingly but did so by God's ordination to ensure that Christ would be executed by the proper authority. In any case, Christ himself supports Pilate's divine authority in his words, "You would have no power over me if it were not given to you from on high."

Nardi makes Dante's understanding that divine providence governs history the centerpiece of his refutation of Vernani. Christ had to be punished by God's ordained means, by Pilate, the representative of the Roman Empire.[36] God had so superintended human history that one of his temporary remedies for human sin, universal empire, played a key role in the redemption of all. A mere brigand could not have passed sentence like a judge, and a sentence was needed to demonstrate the iniquity of Adam's sin. God's divine superintendence of the crucifixion ensured that this public sentence occurred.

Nardi then goes on to describe the differences between Dante's conception of history and Vernani's:

> For brother Guido Vernani, he does not discern in the drama of the passion and death of Christ anything other

---

il significato biblico del verbo profetare. Prophetavit! Nel dramma dunque del processo, della passione e morte di Cristo, chi muove e fa parlare gli uomini è per Dante Dio stesso.

36. Nardi, "Discussioni danteschi," 47. "Pilate was not the someone of Baruccabbà; he was the representative of the supreme earthly authority prepared by God himself because the Roman Empire contributed on its side to the Redemption of mankind from original sin, which was not a private and individual fault like a theft or a murder but a public fault to be punished with a public sentence by a giusta corte [a "just court"], as Dante will say in Paradiso 7." Pilato non era il quarchiduno di Baruccabbà; era il rappresentante della suprema autorità terrena predisposta da Dio stesso perché l'Impero Romano contribuisse per la sua parte alla Redenzione dell'uomo dal peccato originale, che non è colpa privata e individuale come un furto o un omicidio, ma colpa pubblica da punire con pubblica sentenza da «giuste corte», come Dante dirà nel VII del Paradiso.

than a victim of the iniquity of the Jews and of the cowardice of Pilate; but for Dante, this tragedy reveals, like the ancient Greek tragedies of which he was unaware, the dominion of a divine and immutable fate over the contingencies and in the disjointed outward appearances of human events, transcending them and at the same time present to them.[37]

He concludes by stating that the high religious sense displayed by Dante fits well with his conception of the *Monarchia* as a utopia, not a mere political pamphlet; Vernani and other critics missing this point means that they also miss the deeper rationale behind Dante's understanding of the atonement.

Nardi is mistaken in thinking that the *Monarchia* is not a political pamphlet—it manifestly is—but he is correct in noting that it is not *merely* a political pamphlet. Dante's belief in universal monarchy was not simply a piece of Ghibelline propaganda but an almost religious millenarianism. Where he is most useful to our present discussion is in his perception of the role of divine providence in Dante's portrayal of the crucifixion. Dante did indeed, as Nardi observed, meditate long on the Gospel passion narratives, and one of their defining features is the sense that Christ, not his persecutors, is in complete control of events. How the trial and crucifixion of Christ are *arranged* has a vitally important significance to Christ's work on the cross.

---

37. Nardi, "Discussioni danteschi," 47. *Per frate Guido Vernani, nel dramma della passione e morte di Cristo non si scorge altro che una vittima dell'iniquità dei giudei e della vigliaccheria di Pilato; invece per Dante questa tragedia rivela, come le più antiche tragedie greche a lui ignote, il dominio di un fato divino e immutabile sule contingenti e in apparenza sconnesse vicende umane, transcendente e nello stesso tempo immanente ad esse.*

That Christ was crucified after a trial by a judge and placed between two criminals is important not only because it fulfills prophecy but also because it is necessary for the atonement to function properly. If Christ had been killed on the way to Jerusalem by a brigand, or had he died in Gethsemane after surrendering his will to God, his death would not have fulfilled the divine plan. Philip Hughes writes:

> Had Christ died privately in a garden (or in his bed), or even publicly by the hand of an assassin, the true significance of his death would not have been apparent. He might have been mourned as a good man or venerated as a hero. But something more than, so to speak, mere dying was required. A judicial process leading to his condemnation, while plainly innocent, as a common criminal and his public execution as such were a necessity, so that it might be seen that his death was the sacrifice of the innocent for the guilty. The cross, being both the symbol and the reality of the greatest possible shame, assures us, further, that the reconciling grace of God which flows from it reaches to the most wretched and depraved of sinners. Hence the rightness of the judgment that, had Christ died in the Garden of Gethsemane, "he could not have made atonement on the cross, and his whole life's work would have been frustrated."[38]

It is an ancient point, one made repeatedly in the homiletic tradition throughout Christian history, that Christ's death on the

---

38. Philip Edgcumbe Hughes, *A Commentary on the Epistle to the Hebrews* (Grand Rapids: Eerdmans, 1977), 185–86.

cross was efficacious symbolism of what was actually happening in spiritual terms. As the sixth-century bishop of Poitiers Venantius Fortunatus wrote in his sermon on the Apostles' Creed, "He was nailed to the cross in place of a brigand, and so Christ chose the highest punishment for this reason, that he might absolve mankind from original sin, which had been his highest torment."[39]

What Dante was doing, then, was using this vital symbolism to show that the Roman Empire was appointed by God to rule the whole world. It is important to remember that Book 2 of the *Monarchia* is interested in examining the signs by which God has indicated his will concerning the empire. So it is not the case that the crucifixion of Christ had to have been carried out by the Roman Empire *per se*, but the fact that it was carried out by the Roman Empire demonstrates a sign from God of its universal authority. Christ's crucifixion absolved mankind of sin because it was a sacrifice of propitiation and expiation; and the propitiation was achieved by means of a just punishment upon the human flesh deserving it. For Dante, this is the core reality of the atonement: Rome's role in the atonement is merely as an unwitting agent of God. But though unwitting, its agency is nonetheless also meaningful for Dante's political theory. The political conclusion is here subordinate to the theology, in which God directs all things to display his righteousness, justice, and glory.

---

39. Venantius Fortunatus, *Carmina* 11.1.26. *Aut ideo quia ante gravis latro in cruce configebatur, ergo ad hoc elegit Christus principale supplicium, ut hominem absolveret originali peccato quod erat principale tormentum.*

Jean Rivière and Dante

This is an important point because our friend Jean Rivière, that great champion of vicarious satisfaction, had some severe things to say about Dante's portrayal of the atonement. In a brief article he wrote in 1921, Rivière examines the *Monarchia*'s use of Christ's crucifixion as a historical curiosity.[40] He perceives Dante making the efficacy of the atonement dependent upon his own odd hypothesis about the Roman Empire and condemns it in an aside: "Regarding the idea of subordinating the value of our Redemption to a rather contestable theory, we are able without exaggeration to qualify it as a religious heresy, itself brought about by a philosophical heresy."[41] Rivière is being unjust here; as noted above, Dante is not "subordinating" the efficacy of the atonement to his theory about Rome, but rather the opposite. In any case, Rivière is not mainly concerned with this in his article. Instead, he looks at the place of the portrayal of the atonement in Dante's *Monarchia* in the history of the doctrine of the redemption.

He concludes that Dante did not represent mainstream theological thought; his portrayal of the atonement as penal substitutionary was "one of those singularities such as one often encounters in history and which are accountable only, until proof of the contrary, to the responsibility of their authors."[42] Let us examine his argument and then see if he was correct.

---

40. Jean Rivière, "Dante et le «châtiment» du Christ," *RevScRel* 1, no. 4 (1921): 401–6.

41. Rivière, "Dante et le «châtiment» du Christ," 404n1. *Quant à l'idée de subordonner la valeur de notre Rédemption à une théorie aussi contestable, on a pu sans exagération la qualifier d'hérésie religieuse, elle-même commandée par une hérésie philosophique.*

42. Rivière, "Dante et le «châtiment» du Christ," 406. *Une de ces singularités comme on en rencontre souvent dans l'histoire et qui ne sauraient engager, jusqu'à preuve du contraire, que la responsabilité de leurs auteurs.*

Rivière begins by noting the Protestant attachment to penal substitution:

> To better mark out at what point the divine justice is shown forth in the mystery of our Redemption, the first Reformers readily taught not only that the Christ suffered for us and bore the penalty of our faults but that he was literally punished in our place. This "theory of punishment" (*Straftheorie*) has remained, for a long time now, characteristic of Protestant orthodoxy.[43]

Nonetheless, he observes, this *Straftheorie* is an outsider to Catholic theology. Although on rare occasions some of the language of the fathers and of the medieval theologians approaches penal substitution, this phrasing is most often to be assigned to the needs of rhetoric. At no point do they erect a complete doctrine on the notion that Christ was punished in our place.[44]

One of the examples he uses of this appears in the thirteenth-century theologian Bonaventure's commentary on Peter Lombard's *Sentences*. Bonaventure writes, "For he is more greatly able to be placated through the punishment of the innocent than through the punishment of the guilty and unrighteous, and in such a way was Christ punished for our sins." Rivière notes a critical distinction, however, in Bonaventure's

---

43. Rivière, "Dante et le «châtiment» du Christ," 401. *Pour mieux marquer à quel point la justice divine s'est manifestée dans le mystère de notre Rédemption, les premiers Réformateurs enseignaient volontiers, non seulement que le Christ a souffert pour nous et porté la peine de nos fautes, mais qu'il a été littéralement puni à notre place. Cette «théorie du châtiment» (Straftheorie) est restée, depuis lors, caractéristique de l'orthodoxie protestante.*

44. Rivière, "Dante et le «châtiment» du Christ," 401. "But apart from these phrases being very rare, they were most often spoken *oratorio modo*, and the theologians refrained from erecting the teaching into a system." *Mais, outre que ces formules sont très rares, elles furent plutôt dites* oratorio modo, *et les théologiens se sont gardés d'en ériger en thèse la doctrine.*

teaching: "The Seraphic Doctor understands this as *concerning the divine pacification*, not *concerning the divine vengeance.*"[45] In other words, Bonaventure was applying the language of punishment in such a way as to avoid the notion that God was punishing Christ personally; he was pouring out his wrath on the Son, yes, but not punishing. Nonetheless, as unformed as this current was, and as careful as most medieval theologians were in applying the verb *punire* to Christ's suffering on the cross, there was an exception during the scholastic period: Dante.

Rivière outlines Dante's argument in the *Monarchia* and notes that for Dante, in this case, *satisfaction* means the same thing as *punishment*. He then pinpoints what makes this relevant for the history of the doctrine of the redemption:

> All that interests us here about this curious thesis is the theological principal on which it rests: to know that the Christ, to fulfill his role as Redeemer, had to receive a legal sentence of condemnation and to find himself punished, in the strictest sense, for our sins. It is true that in speaking thus about punishment, the author seems to envisage above all the exterior conditions of the redemptive act. But it is not to be doubted that the human formalities are for him the expression of an absolute ... Dante is indeed in the line of the future *Straftheorie*, save that he brings to it a confidence of affirmation and a

---

45. Rivière, "Dante et le «châtiment» du Christ," 402n1. *Moins rigoureux, saint Bonaventure acceptait de dire, sous le bénéfice de certaines distinctions, que le Christ fut «puni» de nos péchés. «Magis enim placari potuit per poenam innocentis quam per poenam rei et iniusti, et taliter punitus est Christus pro peccatis nostris.» Ce que le Docteur séraphique entend de poena divinae placationis, non de poena divinae ultionis (III Sent., Dist. xii, art. 1, qu. 2, sol. 2).*

virtuosity of application that we search for vainly in the spindly schoolmen of the Reformation.[46]

Rivière confirms that Dante's portrayal is, unlike that of Bonaventure, firmly penal substitutionary. He then goes on to look for possible sources for Dante: is he really so singular? He can find no parallels but suggests that since the teaching of Christ being punished for our sins was the special province of such later jurists as Hugo Grotius, Dante may have been drawing on similarly juridical circles. So Dante remains singular in his portrayal of the atonement. More to the point, one should not put too much historical emphasis on the poet with regard to the history of the doctrine of the redemption; his testimony does not outweigh that of Thomas Aquinas.[47]

So for Rivière, Dante's portrayal of the atonement in the *Monarchia* is a *singularité*. The poet may have been steeped in Aquinas and the scholastics, but he is sufficiently independent

---

46. Rivière, "Dante et le «châtiment» du Christ," 404–5. *Tout ce qui intéresse ici de cette curieuse thèse, c'est le principe théologique sur lequel elle repose: savoir que le Christ, pour remplir sa fonction de Rédempteur, a dû recevoir une sentence légale de condamnation et se trouver, à la lettre, puni pour nos péchés. Il est vrai qu'en parlant ainsi de châtiment l'auteur semble surtout envisager le conditions extérieures de l'acte rédempteur. Mais il n'est pas douteux que les formalités humaines sont pour lui l'expression d'un absolu … Dante est bien dans la ligne de la future Straftheorie, sauf qu'il y apporte une sécurité d'affirmation et une virtuosité d'application qu'on chercherait vainement chez les maigres scolastiques de la Réforme.*

47. Rivière, "Dante et le «châtiment» du Christ," 405–6. "Whatever may be the case, the prestige that attends the name of Dante ought not to make the historian change his opinion on the holding of this opinion … Is it not evident that the *Summa theologica* is more representative of Scholastic thought than the *Monarchia*, and, solely from the historical point of view, would not the method be strange that wishes to treat equally, or still better, to make as nothing by an *obiter dictum* of the latter a formal doctrine of the former?" *Quoi qu'il en soit, le prestige qui s'attache au nom de Dante ne doit pas donner le change à l'historien sur la portée de cette opinion … N'est-il pas évident que la Somme théologique est plus représentative de l'École que le De monarchia et du seul point de vue historique, la méthode ne serait-elle pas étrange qui voudrait équilibrer ou, mieux encore, annuler par un obiter dictum de celui-ci une doctrine formelle de celle-là?*

in his application of the details of Thomistic thought to be the originator of his own view—"Which is far from meaning that, in the present case, his spirit of initiative has happily served him."[48]

As we have seen, however, Dante's contemporaries did not, with the exception of Vernani, take exception to his portrayal of the atonement in the *Monarchia*. And in Vernani's case, the exception is gravely mistaken and fails to take Dante's argument into account. Since the commentators looked upon the *Monarchia*'s portrayal of the atonement with complacency, we might conclude that, historically speaking, Dante is more significant to the history of the doctrine of the redemption than Rivière thought. The scholastics' teaching on satisfaction seemed to flow quite easily into a penal substitutionary portrayal of the atonement.

Conclusion

The last two chapters have explored the portrayal of the atonement in two works of Dante Alighieri written at the start of the fourteenth century: the *Monarchia* and the *Paradiso*. One was a political pamphlet directed toward a clerical and learned audience, and the other was an epic poem written for an unlearned lay audience. In both, we see the keen mind of the poet wrestling with how Scripture portrays Christ's death and, more importantly, how it portrays God's character as revealed in that death. It is this focus on God's character that fills our next vignette, eight hundred years before Dante and in southern

---

48. Rivière, "Dante et le «châtiment» du Christ," 406. *Ce qui est loin de signifier que, dans le cas présent, son esprit d'initiative l'ait heureusement servi.*

France under barbarian kings. But before we move on, let us listen to the words of Dante's son Pietro:

> For all other men were debtors, and hardly anyone's virtue and humility were sufficient even for themselves; but Christ the sufficient human being was a perfect offering who was humiliated by much more, by tasting the bitterness of death, than Adam was prideful by enjoying the poisonous delight through eating from the old tree; and although God might have been able to proceed in another way, nevertheless, that way was more greatly suited to his divine righteousness. For by that way the devil was overcome by righteousness, not power: for the devil in his wickedness is a lover of power and a forsaker of righteousness.[49]

---

49. Pietro Alighieri, *Paradiso* vol. 3, 7.19–23. *Nam omnes alii debitores erant et vix unicuique sua virtus sufficiebat et humilitas; nullus ergo poterat hostiam offerre sufficientem nostre reconciliationi; sed Christus homo sufficiens perfecta fuit hostia, qui multo plus humiliatus est, amaritudinem mortis gustando, quam Adam superbivit per esum ligni vetiti noxiam delectationem perfruendo; et quamvis Deus alio modo procedere potuisset, tamen iste modus magis congruus fuit eius iustitie divine. Nam isto modo diabolus superatus est iustitia non potentia: diabolus enim sua perversitate amator est potentie et desertor iustitie.*

CHAPTER 4

CAESARIUS OF ARLES, PART I

Sin Offering in *Christus Victor*

T he second vignette belongs to the period of late antiquity, to the region of southern France, and to one genre: the sermon. We will focus on a sermon by bishop Caesarius of Arles, an endeavor that will be aided by an additional examination of two others by anonymous contemporaries. Each one explores the question of why God chose to carry out the redemption of humanity by means of the cross and the way in which the cross achieved this redemption. How did Caesarius's sermon portray the atonement, and what does this portrayal say about the general conception of Christ's atoning work at the outset of the Middle Ages? The next two chapters will seek to answer these questions.

This second vignette takes place at the beginning of the Middle Ages, thus providing us with a glimpse of the least "developed" understanding of Christ's work on the cross. It is closest to the church fathers, and the influence of these sermons (and of Caesarius of Arles) on medieval Christianity was significant. Sermons were the principal means of inculcating the faith in Christians of both high and low estate, and their characteristic style, language, and emphases are well represented by Caesarius. Moreover, sermons from this era, late antiquity, were one of the main conduits by which patristic teaching passed into the medieval world. Therefore, seeing how this was done through the narrow lens of one man, Caesarius of Arles, will be helpful in achieving the aims of this book.

We should emphasize that these sermons do not make up a complete account of the understanding of the atonement at the start of the Middle Ages. However, what this chapter will hopefully do is to bring to our attention texts dealing with the subject that are usually ignored in favor of the grand treatises of the fathers. Yet the teaching of the fathers was known to most people in the Middle Ages not chiefly through their formal treatises but through sermons drawn from these texts. And what this vignette shows is a doctrine of the redemption that not only views Christ's crucifixion through the lens of a victory over the devil but also sees it as a sacrifice of propitiation and expiation made to God that enables the devil to be defeated. This chapter will first introduce Caesarius and lay out his historical context. Then, the nature of the late antique sermon will be explored. Finally, his sermon on the atonement will be examined and its doctrine made plain.

THE EARLY LIFE OF CAESARIUS OF ARLES

From the late medieval world of Dante's Italy to the late antique world of Caesarius of Arles in Gaul: so our course takes us. The former is on the cusp of Renaissance humanism; the latter, near the end of the long twilight of ancient Roman learning. The former functions in a political milieu characterized by the counterbalancing forces of pope and emperor; the latter, in the milieu of the ancient Roman *civitas* and its relations with a sec-ular ruler. The former features a Christian theology dominated by complicated scholastic disputations and speculations; the latter, a Christianity passionate about the contemplative life and strict adherence to the orthodoxy of the fathers and the coun-cils. And who our main characters are changes quite signifi-cantly as well: Dante, a poet from the Florentine middle classes; Caesarius of Arles, a bishop from the Gallo-Roman aristocracy. We have already met Dante; let us now meet Caesarius and familiarize ourselves with his unfamiliar world.

Born around 470, Caesarius of Arles spent his childhood and early youth in the *civitas*, or city, of *Cabillonum*, modern Chalon-sur-Saône, in the region of Burgundy in modern France. His parents, whose names we do not know, were local aristo-crats and devout Christians. He was given the standard educa-tion available at that time in southern Gaul, learning to read and write in the sophisticated Latin style of the late Roman world. Caesarius displays in his writing an excellent command of the

Latin language and its standard rhetorical devices. He also exhibits an ability to adjust his Latin style based on his audience; in his sermons to the common people, he uses a simple and direct style, but in his letters to fellow aristocrats, he writes in the ornate and florid style typical of the time. This learning was to serve him well in his career.

When he was young, he left home and entered the monastery of Lérins, on an island south of Marseilles (modern Saint-Honorat). This monastery was famous for its rigorous asceticism drawn from eastern examples, its theological learning, and its supply of bishops and other clergy to the church of southern Gaul. If Caesarius was intent on pursuing an ecclesiastical career, this course of action made excellent sense. Cities wanted bishops who were learned, pious, and ostentatiously humble; a stay at Lérins guaranteed all three qualities. In 495, he was sent to the city of Arles in Provence, where his relative Aeonius was bishop. He was to carry the habits he had acquired at Lérins with him for the rest of his life.

When Caesarius arrived in Arles, he was welcomed into the circles of the ecclesiastical elite of the city. Caesarius was appointed by Aeonius as abbot of the men's monastery in Arles in 499, honing his growing reputation for ascetic piety as well as demonstrating his ambition for high office. His rapid rise through the ecclesiastical hierarchy was carefully shepherded by Aeonius until, in 501 or 502, the old bishop fell ill and died. Before his death, Aeonius had made clear that Caesarius was his desired successor. His episcopacy was to last forty years, until his death in 542. It was remarkably successful, leaving a spiritual legacy that would nourish future generations for a long time to come.

Caesarius the Bishop

Caesarius strove during his time as bishop to reform pastoral care and advance the discipleship of those under his charge, both clerical and lay. The bishop of Arles was the "metropolitan" bishop of the region of Provence, essentially the same rank as that of an archbishop, although the latter title had not yet come into general use. The role of a bishop in early sixth-century Gaul was as both a spiritual and civic leader. Bishops were expected, as good aristocratic patrons of their cities in the Roman style, to build new civic buildings, give generously to the poor, ransom captives from slavery, negotiate with higher secular authorities on behalf of their cities, and maintain local harmony. Metropolitan bishops were also expected to settle disputes among the lesser bishops under their charge and to call councils when necessary. Caesarius performed all these tasks in a political environment characterized by rapid shifts followed by long periods of order.

In the first half of the sixth century, Arles underwent two changes in government. When Caesarius took up the position of bishop of Arles in 502, Provence was ruled by the Visigoths under King Alaric II, grandson of the famed sacker of Rome. The Visigoths, though Arian Christians, let the orthodox Nicene church govern its own affairs without much hindrance. This was consonant with the rest of their policy, which left the civil administration of the old Roman Empire largely intact. In 507, however, the Franks and Burgundians under their kings Clovis and Gundobad invaded the Visigothic kingdom and defeated and killed Alaric at the battle of Vouillé. They did this despite the frantic diplomacy of Theodoric the Ostrogoth, king of Italy. Arles was besieged but not taken, and although accused

of treason by certain factions within the city itself, Caesarius
faithfully led his people through this trial. In 508, a relief army
sent from Theodoric defeated the besiegers, and Provence and
the rest of southern Gaul were placed under Italian jurisdiction.
Theodoric was now their ruler.

Theodoric portrayed himself as restoring Roman civiliza-
tion to a region of the old empire that had long been under the
barbarian yoke. Italian money flowed into Provence to repair
the ravages of war. Prosperity was nigh. And, in fact, this is
what occurred over the next twenty years or so. Ostrogothic
rule proved to be a boon for southern Gaul. In 511, the administration of Provence was assigned to the re-created position
of Praetorian Prefect of the Gauls, which was filled by Felix
Liberius, one of those remarkably competent, long-lived men
who seemed to proliferate in the sixth-century post-Roman
world. He based his rule in Arles, which had long been the
Roman administrative capital, and worked closely with
Caesarius its bishop. The *pax ostrogothica* that he oversaw
proved useful indeed to the bishop of Arles, who took advantage of this period of political stability to advance his reforms.

Caesarius's reform agenda may now be sketched. Coming
from a monastic background as he did, he sought to do two
things: encourage extraordinary holiness among the clergy and
encourage ordinary holiness among the laity. For the clergy, this
meant a monastic life, even if lived in the secular world and not
the monastery. Frugal living, preferably in some sort of clerical
community (*à la* Augustine); renunciation of personal posses-
sions; works of charity (e.g., redeeming captives and clothing
the poor); constant reading of Scripture and other spiritual
works to the exclusion of secular writing—all these and more

Caesarius urged his clergy to do. This represented an effort to make an ascetic life accessible to all clerics and make them better servants of their flocks.

As for the laity, Caesarius urged them to adopt as many of the monastic disciplines as were feasible for their station. Holiness was not just for a celibate elite but attainable for all Christians. In his sermons, the bishop of Arles told his parishioners to attend church daily, give alms, do no work on Sundays, and perform fasts and vigils. Most importantly, he promoted reading the Scriptures. His sermons rang with calls for his congregants to listen carefully to the reading of the Bible in church and then to reread the same passages themselves at home. If that were not within their powers because of the need to work long days, then they should memorize some key texts such as the Apostles' Creed and Psalm 50 and recite them as they walked behind their ploughs.

To help carry out this reform plan, he held four councils between 524 and 529, attended by a steadily growing number of bishops. Three of these councils dealt with such matters as reforming the lifestyle of the clergy and increasing the independence of rural parishes. The most famous of them, Orange, dealt mainly with the theological question of predestination. Orange was the high-water mark of Caesarius's power, and thereafter, his influence declined. Although its decisions were endorsed by the Pope, this endorsement was quite perfunctory. Rome during the sixth century was firmly in the Augustinian camp but in Caesarius's case was more interested in affirming its authority in Gaul and promoting a basic Augustinianism than in stirring up trouble with Gallic clergy. Pope Boniface, who sent a letter vaguely supporting the Council of Orange's decisions, urged Caesarius to use his own powers of persuasion to settle the matter. It was only later in the Middle Ages that Orange came to take on a higher profile.

In 536, his situation changed again; more than twenty-five years of Ostrogothic rule came to an end, and the Franks took over. Theodoric had died in 526, and his successors wavered between those who favored closer ties to the Eastern Empire, by now ruled by the emperor Justinian, and those who favored a more independent stance. In 535, Queen Amalasuintha, Theodoric's daughter and regent for his grandson Athalaric until his death in 534, was assassinated by her coruler, Theodahad. Justinian took this as a pretext for invading Italy, and by late 536, imperial forces had conquered Naples and were approaching Rome. The Gothic general Vitigis, who had just been crowned king to replace the ineffectual Theodahad, agreed to cede Provence to the Frankish king Childebert I to keep the Franks neutral and free up his forces for the war with Justinian. Thus, Arles came peacefully under the rule of the Franks, who, unlike the Arian Goths, were devout Catholics.

This was not a change for the better for Caesarius, however, for while under the Goths, he was the greatest prelate in the area; in the broader Frankish kingdom, he was but one of several important metropolitan bishops. Councils were now summoned by the Frankish kings, who as Catholics had more standing to interfere with ecclesiastical affairs. Caesarius's authority was thus diminished still further. Still, he remained a respected voice, and many of his clerical reforms were adopted more broadly. He died in 542. For the purposes of this book, of greater interest than his life as a whole is one aspect of his

reforms that had perhaps the greatest effect on later generations: preaching.

CAESARIUS OF ARLES AND THE
LATE ANTIQUE SERMON

Sermons were at the center of late antique Christianity. Gallic
bishops especially valued the sermon both as a means of
instructing the flock and as a demonstration of their authority. Indeed, lower clergy were generally forbidden from preaching sermons in their churches. This was because they did not
possess the theological education necessary to craft sermons
that could be trusted to be orthodox. Moreover, bishops, who
in fifth- and sixth-century Gaul were frequently liberally educated aristocrats, valued the opportunity to display their rhetorical skills and theological knowledge. Also, carefully crafted
sermons were an excellent—indeed, the primary—means of
inculcating Christian doctrine into the minds of the laity and
converting the unbelieving. It was the job of the bishop to
ensure that this would be done.

The power and prestige of the preached word were taken
as a given in fifth- and sixth-century Gaul. Bishops were frequently praised for their preaching. So Sidonius Apollinaris,
the late fifth-century aristocrat, poet, rhetorician, and (even-
tual) bishop of Clermont, wrote to the famed preacher Faustus
of Riez (c. 477):

> At times I, raucously applauding, heard your preaching,
> sometimes off the cuff, sometimes after long nightly labor
> as the situation demanded ... you were indeed the most
> learned in both the disciplines of spiritual and forensic

rhetoric, which while preaching you practiced in equal measure; we embraced your words with senses alert and ears tuned.[1]

Bishop Nicetius of Trier (c. 525–566) was likewise famed:"Who can disclose how bold he was in preaching, how dread-inducing in reasoning, how constant in upholding [truth], how wise in teaching?"[2]

Caesarius himself, as his biographer, friend, and ally Cyprian wrote, also had the reputation for being a great and eager expounder of doctrine:

Now in unfolding the Scriptures and in making clear its difficulties, who is able to tell of how great a grace shone forth in him? It caused him great joy if anyone prodded him to explain difficult things. And he himself very frequently urged this, saying to us, "I know that you do not understand everything; why do you not ask, so that you might be able to understand?"[3]

And his preaching reflected this facility and passion:

He taught from memory, as often as he was able, and always preached with a loud voice in church. In this work,

---

1. Sidonius Apollinaris, *Epistolae* 9.3.5. *Olim praedicationes tuas, nunc repentinas, nunc, ratio cum poposcisset, elucubratas, raucus plosor audierim … te inter spiritales regulas vel forenses medioximum quiddam contionantem, quippe utrarumque doctissimum disciplinarum, pariter erectis sensibus auribusque curvatis ambiebamus.*

2. Gregory of Tours, *Vitae Patrum* 17.3.4. *Quam fortis fuerit ad praedicandum, quam terribilis ad arguendum, quam constans ad sustinendum, quam prudens ad docendum, quis evolvere queat?*

3. *Vita Sancti Caesarii Episcopi* 5.40 (PL 67.1020). *In disserendis autem Scripturis et in elucidandis obscuritatibus, quanta gratia in illo emicuerit, quis poterit narrare? Ita ut haec ei summa jucunditas ferit, si illum aliquis, ut obscura dissereret, provocaret. Et ipse frequentissime incitabat, dicens nobis: 'Scio quod non omnia intelligitis: quare non interrogatis, ut possitis cognoscere?'*

so healthful and so conscientious was his careful fore-
sight that when he himself was unable due to illness to
perform that office, he empowered and instituted that
priests and deacons should preach in the church.[4]

He preached regularly, several times a week.

His subjects ranged from ethical matters to theological concepts. On doctrinal subjects, he preached on such things as the
Apostles' Creed, the Lord's Prayer, the theological difficulties
surrounding the hardening of Pharaoh's heart, the typology of
the Abrahamic narratives, the Exodus and the life of Moses,
the conquest of Canaan, and Elijah and Elisha. On ethical matters, he urged the frequent reading of Scripture; he condemned
men sleeping with their slave girls; he raged against such vices
as drunkenness, astrology, and bribery; and he commended
almsgiving and acts of penitence. These are just a few examples
of sermon subjects.

More importantly, as mentioned by Cyprian, Caesarius
encouraged priests and deacons to preach. This does not mean
that he encouraged them to write their own sermons. Instead,
he had them read sermons from more gifted preachers.[5] The

---

4. *Vita Sancti Caesarii Episcopi* 5.41 (PL 67.1021). *Docuit praeterea memoriter, quandiu potuit, altaque voce semper in ecclesia praedicavit, in quo opere tam pia atque salubris eius provisio fuit, ut cum ipse pro infirmitate iam non posset ad ipsum officium peragendum accedere, presbyteros et diacones imbuerit atque statuerit in ecclesia praedicare.*

5. *Vita Sancti Caesarii Episcopi* 5.41 (PL 67.1021). As Cyprian recalled him saying, "If the words of the Lord and of the prophets and apostles are read out by priests and deacons, why should not the words of Ambrose, of Augustine, of my own insignificant self, or of other holy men be read out by priests and deacons? The servant is not greater than his master. I believe that those who have been given the authority to read the Gospels are also permitted to read in church the homilies of the servants of God and the expositions of the canonical Scriptures." *Si verba Domini et prophetarum sive apostolorum a presbyteris et a diaconibus recitantur; Ambrosii, Augustini, seu parvitatis meae, aut quorumcunque sanctorum, a presbyteris et diaconibus quare non recitantur? Non est servus major domino suo. Quibus data*

policy of insisting that priests read a sermon as part of the lit-
urgy every Sunday was of vital importance to Caesarius. Instead
of hearing a sermon three or four times a year from an over-
worked bishop, the ordinary layman would be instructed in
the faith at least once a week. This was especially meaningful
for small parishes in villages or in the countryside, where the
majority of people resided.

To ensure that priests and deacons would be able to access
good sermons, Caesarius edited over two hundred sermons
and compiled them into several collections. Such collections,
or "homiliaries," were a common part of ecclesiastical libraries in the Middle Ages. Sermons by such luminaries as Peter
Chrysologus of Ravenna, Jerome, John Chrysostom, Orosius,
and, especially, Augustine were included in these homiliaries
and edited according to the needs of the compiler and his community. There were also hundreds of anonymous sermons;
some were collages of more famous preachers, and some, original texts by more humble clerics. It was in these humble texts,
not the grand treatises of the church fathers, that Christianity
was taught to and experienced by the vast majority of the laity
in the Middle Ages.

Caesarius crafted his own homiliaries to emphasize his
reform agenda. He included both his own sermons and those of
the fathers. However, he usually edited sermons that were not
his own to conform with his own style and doctrinal emphasis.
The style he preferred was the *sermo humilis*, "humble speech,"

---

*est auctoritas Evangelium legere, credo et licitum est homilias servorum Dei seu expositiones
canonicarum Scripturarum in ecclesia recitare.*

that Augustine had advocated for in his *De doctrina Christiana*. The homiliaries Caesarius created were thus comprised of sermons—both his own and those of others—edited to fit with this vision of accessibility. They were also organized so as to promote his vision of a holy Christian community including both clergy and laity. Priests and other bishops who made use of his sermons were thus equipped to instruct their congregations in what was necessary for their salvation and sanctification. Its audience was intended to include all levels of society, both urban and rural. It was also directed to people from many different cultural backgrounds: the city of Arles had a diverse population in Caesarius's day, comprising Gallo-Romans, Goths, Franks, Greeks, Syrians (people from the Levant), and others. The rural areas were not, of course, nearly so mixed; but there, Caesarius, a sophisticated urbanite, had to reach illiterate peasants deeply steeped in the ancient pagan traditions of the agricultural life. All the more reason, then, to make his sermons as accessible as possible. Later generations found his sermons useful for precisely this reason.

Caesarius of Arles thus had a significant influence on what Christians in the Middle Ages learned about their faith. What he thought about the work of Christ on the cross is therefore of great interest in illustrating what the medieval church thought about the atonement. One of his sermons is of particular interest to this subject. To this text, *Sermo XI* in the critical edition of Germain Morin, we now turn.

Caesarius of Arles and
the Atonement

It was important to Caesarius that those under his spiritual care would feel free to ask him anything they wanted about the Christian faith and the Scriptures. Many of his sermons begin by relating a question someone had asked him, or one he had detected simmering in his audience, and then providing the answer. It was a personal, pastoral approach. Caesarius wishes in *Sermo XI* to answer a question frequently posed to him: why did God not send Christ to simply destroy the devil by force, something he was surely able to do, rather than work salvation by suffering and dying due to the devil's schemes?

Caesarius begins by posing the question asked by his congregants:

A particular question occurs to many, dearly beloved brothers; pondering this matter sends many men of little understanding into a state of anxiety. For they say, "Why did the Lord Jesus Christ, the Power and Wisdom of the Father, work the salvation of man not by his divine power and sole authority but rather by his bodily humility and human struggle? For without a doubt, he would have been able by the heavenly power and majesty to overthrow the devil and to free man from his tyranny." Certain others ponder, "Why did he who is proclaimed to have given life in the beginning by his word not destroy death by his word? What reason was there that lost men should not be brought back by the same majesty that was able to create things not yet existing? Why was it necessary for our Lord Christ to receive so

harsh a period of suffering when he was able to free the
human race through his power? Why his incarnation?
Why his infancy? Why the course of his life? Why the
insults? Why the cross? Why his death? Why his burial?
Why did he take up all these things for the sake of man's
restoration?"[6]

The two questions posed deal with salvation from the perspective of mankind's captivity to the devil and to death; if our
problem is that we are enslaved to Satan and our own mortality, why could God not simply free us by his power? If Christ
is God, did he not have power over the devil? As creator of all
living things, could he not simply bestow life by speaking? Yet
rather than do these things with the power he surely possessed,
Christ instead underwent suffering and humiliation.

He then proceeds to answer the questions so eloquently laid
out, explaining why power alone would not have worked. The
answer, quite simply, is that the attributes of God's character
go beyond mere power.

Without a doubt, our Lord would have been able to triumph over the devil by his divine authority and to free
man from his rule. He would have been able, yes, but

---

6. Caesarius of Arles, *Sermo XI*, ed. G. Morin, CCSL 103 (Turnhout: Brepols, 1953) I,
54. *Multos, fratres carissimi, tangit ista suspicio; multos parvae scientiae homines in scrupulum
mittit huiuscemodi cogitatio; dicunt enim: Quare dominus Iesus Christus, virtus et sapientia
Patris, salutem hominis non potestate divina et solo est operatus imperio, sed humilitate corporea
et humana conluctatione; cum utique potuerit virtute et maiestate caelesti diabolum prosternere,
et hominem ab eius tyrannide liberare? Movet quosdam, quare mortem non verbo destruxit,
qui in principio vitam verbo dedisse praedicatur: quae fuit ratio, non eadem maiestate perdita
reparari, qua potuerunt nondum extantia procreari. Ut quid enim opus fuit Christo domino
nostro tam duram passionem excipere, qui genus humanum per potentiam potuit liberare? Ut
quid incarnatio, ut quid infantia, ut quid cursus aetatis, ut quid contumelia, ut quid crux, ut
quid mors, ut quid sepultura ad hominis reprarationem suscepta sunt?*

reason resisted, justice did not give its permission; and these are more important to God than all power and might. These two attributes are praised even among men; how much more are they praiseworthy to God, who is the Creator and Judge of reason and justice![7]

God's goodness includes the attributes of *ratio* and *iustitia*; he would not exist without them, so how could power operate without them also being operative? God is *good*; he is not worshipful if he is not good. So our salvation must be accomplished in a way that leaves God's goodness intact.

Caesarius then expands on this point by setting up an imaginary scene in the divine council:

Now it was in the mind of God to restore man, who had been deceived by the devil, to eternal life. This then had to be kept in mind: compassion must not destroy justice; love must not destroy equity. For if he had finished off the devil and rescued man from his jaws by his majesty and power, there would indeed have been power, but there would not have been justice.[8]

The preliminary considerations expressed, the devil's potential defense against God's acting through mere power must be considered, and so here, Caesarius inserts a lengthy speech from

7. Caesarius of Arles, *Sermo XI* 2, 54–55. *Haec dicunt parvae scientiae homines. Potuerat sine dubio dominus noster auctoritate divina diabolum triumphare, et hominem ab eius dominatione liberare. Potuerat quidem: sed ratio resistebat, iustitia non sinebat, quae maiora sunt apud deum quam omnis virtus totaque potentia. Haec in hominibus laudantur: quanto magis in deo, qui rationis atque iustitiae et auctor est et exactor?*

8. Caesarius of Arles, *Sermo XI* 2, 55. *Fuit igitur in proposito dei hominem reparare, hominem a diabolo deceptum aeternitati restituere. Hic iam considerandum est, ne misericordia iustitiam perdat, ne pietas destruat aequitatem. Si enim maiestate et potentia sua diabolum perculisset, et hominem de eius faucibus eruisset, erat quidem potentia, sed non erat iustitia.*

Satan. The Bishop of Arles will have nothing to do with a mere "devil's advocate": the devil himself will advocate for his position.[9] The devil points out that both he and mankind have the same gift of free will from God and therefore are held responsible for rebelling against God in the same way. Adam and Eve did not have to listen to the tempter, yet they did anyway by their own choice and so fell into the same lot as their adversary. There is nothing here of seeing humanity's predicament as simply a captivity to Satan. Certainly, this is a big part of the problem, but the reason for the captivity is equally as important: namely, the original sin of Adam and Eve. Humanity is enslaved to the devil by its own choice.

---

9. Caesarius of Arles, *Sermo XI* 2, 55. The speech runs as follows: "O Lord, you are just and true; you made man in your goodness, you who created me as well as a good, not an evil, angel. You gave to me as much as to man the free power of the will; you gave the law with this threat of judgment: if we touched something forbidden, we would die the death. I ruined myself at the very beginning by a voluntary envy; then I persuaded man to do a wicked deed. I persuaded—I did not force; for I was not able to force one having the freedom of his own will. I was listened to more than your word was preserved. We received by your judgment sentences befitting our merits: I the eternal word sent into evil; man was sent with me to death and terrible punishment. Man joined himself to me by his own will; he separated from you not unwillingly but by the same will: he is mine. Together we are destined for punishment; if he is torn away from me, it is not justice but violence, it is not grace but an injury, it is not compassion but plunder. Why should man, who did not wish to live when he had the ability, be made alive unwillingly? I presume to say this, O Just Judge: it is not fitting for there to be unequal sentences in the same case. Ultimately, if it pleases you that man be saved against all justice and reason, we ought both to be saved—both he who perished and I who was ruined." *Domine, iustus es et verus: fecisti in bonitate tua hominem, qui et me ipsum aliquando bonum angelum creasti, non malum. Dedisti tam mihi quam homini liberam arbitrii facultatem: dedisti legem cum interminatione sententiae, si ille attigisset inlicitum, morte moreretur. Me ipsum primum voluntario livore perdidi; deinde suasi homini malum. Suasi, non inpuli: quia nec poteram cogere habentem voluntatis propriae libertatem. Ego magis auditus sum, quam tuus sermo servatus est. Accepimus dignas meritis nostris te iudicante sententias: ego in maledictionem aeternam, ille in mortem mecum poenamque terribilem. Mihi se homo propria voluntate coniunxit; a te eadem voluntate, non invitus, distraxit: meus est. Pro peccato pariter destinati sumus in poenam: si avellitur a me, non est iustitia, sed violentia; non est gratia, sed iniuria; non est misericordia, sed rapina. Homo qui noluit vivere cum posset, quare vivificatur invitus? Praesumo dicere, iuste iudex: non decet in una causa dispares esse sententias. Postremo, si hoc placet, ut sola indulgentia, cessante omni iustitia atque ratione, homo salvetur, debemus ambo salvari, et ille qui periit, et ego qui perdidi.*

Even the enslavement to the devil, however, is subordinate to the real problem: God's wrath. *Accepimus dignas meritis nostris te iudicante sententias*, states the devil: "We received by your judgment sentences befitting our merits." God the Judge, not the devil, is ultimately responsible for humanity's punishment. The "captivity" to the devil should be seen not as something brought upon us unjustly by Satan but rather as something that reflects our just sentence from the divine judge. We are captive to the devil in that we are tied to him in a common damnation. As we will see, of course, there is also a sense in which the devil is God's agent in our punishment; yet in this speech, that agency takes second place to the common fate. If we are forgiven, so too must the devil be forgiven.

Yet this did not take place because God did not and does not act through power alone. God, after all, is good. So Caesarius concedes:

Should that speech of the devil not have seemed to God to have the appearance of being just and reasonable, since He did work and still works all things justly and reasonably? And so, in order that this criminal voice should not have any place and that all the deeds of God should be consistent with justice and reason, that very Strength came from heaven; it came not to tear man away from the devil through power but rather only after it had preserved equity in all things. This is just as the Lord Himself reminded John the Baptist at the time of his baptism—when John wished to decline—saying:

"Without delay; for thus it is fitting for us to fulfill all justice."[10]

Caesarius uses the example of Christ being baptized to illustrate his point about power giving way to justice; the Lord Jesus did not have to be baptized since he was without sin. Yet he did so because it was necessary to remain true to *iustitia*. This word, *iustitia*, "justice," also refers to "righteousness," and it is not always easy to distinguish when the different meanings occur. In this case, perhaps righteousness is better, as the following passage will make clear.

Caesarius continues by explaining what "fulfilling all justice" means. For him, "fulfilling all *iustitia*" means that Christ, by living a righteous life, resisting the devil by righteous means and living sinlessly during the time of his life on earth, uplifted the human flesh that ordinarily would sin.[11] He defeated sin in

---

10. Caesarius of Arles, *Sermo XI* 3, 55. *Nonne ista vox diaboli quasi iusta et velut rationabilis videretur in deum, qui omnia iustitia ac ratione et operatus est et semper operatur? Ut ergo haec vox scelerata locum non haberet, et omnia dei gesta iustitia ac ratione constarent, venit virtus illa de caelo, venit non per potentiam hominem a diabolo divellere, sed servata in omnibus aequitate, sicut ad Iohannem baptistam tempmore baptismatis excusantem dominus ipse memoravit dicens: 'sine modo: sic enim oportet nos implere omnem iustitiam.*

11. Caesarius of Arles, *Sermo XI* 3, 55–56. "Therefore, for this reason our Lord and Savior came 'in the likeness of sinful flesh,' as the apostle teaches, and endured all things without sin; so that thus, with justice having been fulfilled, he might condemn sin in his flesh since his flesh was taken up without sin from a sinful substance. That encounter in the desert orchestrated by the Spirit proves this, when the devil was conquered not by divine majesty but by the memory of a command, by fasting, and by a lawful response. The many different tests of the Pharisees also prove this, by whom the Lord was often challenged. When he benefits the ungrateful, when he does not resist an injury, when by his patience he overcomes an insult, by his goodness conquers ill-will, all justice is necessarily fulfilled, and every sin is condemned." *Pro hac ergo causa dominus et salvator noster venit 'in similitudinem carnis peccati,' sicut docet apostolus, et sustinuit omnia sine peccato; ut sic impleta iustitia damnaret in carne peccatum, dum de substantia peccatrice caro suscipitur sine peccato. Probat hoc illa congressio in deserto facta cum spiritu, ubi non divina maiestate diabolus vincitur, sed recordatione mandati, sed ieiuniis, sed responsione legali. Probant hoc etiam Pharisaeorum diversa temptamenta, a quibus saepe dominus laces situs est. Dum ingratis benefacit, dum iniuriae non resistit, dum vincit patientia contumeliam, vincit bonitate malitiam, impletur utique omnis iustitia, et damnatur omne peccatum.*

the same sort of flesh that was condemned to be infected by it. Caesarius states:

> Because of this, the same Lord preached, "The Prince of this world comes, and he possesses nothing in me." This is the first victory: that the flesh, assumed from a sinful race, stands forth as having no part in a misdeed; and so in that same flesh sin was condemned, in which it had believed itself able to reign; the same flesh, which at one time sin had conquered, conquered sin. For if divinity alone had conquered, the devil would not have been in great confusion, and it would not have inspired confidence in bodily men that it would conquer.[12]

If God's power alone had crushed the devil, there could be no trust that the sinful human race would have been saved since it remained sinful. The first stage of our salvation was thus achieved by "fulfilling all justice" since Christ lived a righteous, sinless life and so sanctified the flesh he took up. But the second stage of our salvation also involves "fulfilling all justice."

The second stage is the culmination of Christ's life on earth, his death on the cross. How is the cross a function of Christ "fulfilling all justice?" Caesarius now proceeds to explain the meaning of the cross in detail: "Let us see what the cross might want in itself, how the sin of the world is remitted upon it, how death is destroyed and the devil triumphed over."[13] He begins

---

12. Caesarius of Arles, *Sermo XI* 3, 56. *Inde ipse dominus praedicabat: 'Venit,' inquid, 'princeps huius mundi, et in me nihil habet.' Prima ergo victoria est, expertem delicti carnem praestare sumptam ex gente peccatrice: ut in ipsa damnaretur peccatum, in qua regnare posse se crediderat; immo ipsa nunc vinceret, quae victa fuerat aliquando: quia si divinitas sola vicisset, nec diabolo fuisset magna confusio, et corporeis hominibus vincendi fiduciam non dedisset.*

13. Caesarius of Arles, *Sermo XI* 4, 56. *Iam videamus quid sibi velit crux, quomodo in ipsa solvitur mundi peccatum, quomodo mors destruitur, et diabolus triumphatur.*

by outlining Christ's innocence and the effect of the success of the first stage of "fulfilling all justice." The Lord Jesus did not deserve the cross since he had led, alone among all mankind, a sinless life. So, the prophecies in the Old Testament predicting the execution of a sinless man came to pass. And just as Christ led a sinless life, even when subjected the devil's temptations, so too did he not sin during his death.[14]

Caesarius then goes on to contrast Christ's innate power with his refusal to use it as shown by his actions during the passion.[15] Rather than use this power, he submitted to suffer-

---

14. Caesarius of Arles, *Sermo XI*, 4, 56. "The cross is certainly not deserved, insofar as it pertains to the form of justice, unless by sinners; for both the law of God and of the world is recognized to have decreed the cross for guilty men and criminals alone. Therefore, with the devil hurrying about working through Judas, through the kings of the earth, and through the princes of the Jews, who 'came together as one' to Pilate 'against the Lord and against his Christ,' Christ was condemned to death; an innocent man was condemned, just as the prophet says in the Psalm: 'But the righteous man, what has he done?' And again, 'They will seek against the spirit of the righteous and will condemn innocent blood'; the man guilty of not even a trivial sin is condemned since the serpent was able to leave no trace in this rock. He patiently endured both insults and blows, the thorny crown and scarlet robe, and the other mockeries which are contained in the Gospel. He endured this without any guilt, so that filled with patience, as 'a sheep to the sacrifice,' he might come to the cross." *Crux certe non est debita, quantum ad iustitiae formam pertinet, nisi peccatoribus: nam et lex dei et lex saeculi reis et criminosis crucem decrevisse cognoscitur. Circumcursante igitur diabolo, operante per Iudam, per reges terrae, per principes Iudaeroum, qui 'in unum convenerunt' ad Pilatum 'adversus dominum et adversus Christum eius,' damnatur Christus ad mortem; damnatur innocens, sicut propheta dicit in psalmo: 'Iustus autem quid fecit?' et iterum: 'Captabunt in animam iusti, et sanguinem innocentem condemnabunt;' damnatur nullius ne levis quidem peccati reus, quia nullum potuit serpens facere in hac petra vestigium. Suscepit patienter et contumelias et colaphos, coronam spineam et vestem coccineam, ceteraque ludibria quae in evangelio conteinentur. Suscepit hoc absque ulla culpa, ut saginatus patientia, ut 'tamquam ovis ad victimam' veniret ad crucem.*

15. Caesarius of Arles, *Sermo XI* 4, 56. "He received this in a dignified manner who would have been able to inflict injury upon his enemies. He endured very powerful forces, as David sings, 'as a man without help,' who would have been able to avenge himself by his divine majesty. For he who withered the fig tree to its roots by his word would much more easily have immediately withered all flesh, which was reckoned as grass, if he had wished to resist. For if even those who had come to capture him retreated backwards when they were questioned with a gentle speech—that is, 'Whom do you seek?'—and they were made like dead men, what would he have done if he had wished to resist?" *Suscepit hoc dignanter, qui poterat referre in adversarios iniuriam. Praepotentes sustinuit, ut canit David, 'velut homo sine adiutorio,' qui divina se poterat maiestate vindicare. Nam qui arborem ficus verbo radicitus*

ing. Why? Caesarius here makes the point that if Christ himself declined to use his power to avoid the passion, there must
be some larger reason that merits the attention of those who
follow him. He then states that larger reason:

> But he fulfills the mystery of the cross, for which pur-
> pose he also came into this world; so that by means of
> the cross, by means of a salvific justice and reason, the
> note of our indebtedness to sin might be canceled, the
> enemy power be captured after being enticed by the bait
> of the cross, and the devil lose the prey he used to hold.[16]

The cross is the epitome of God's justice and reason as
displayed in the salvation of humanity. What it does is both
abolish sin and defeat death and the devil. How does it do
these two things? Caesarius answers:

> Now, it is necessary for this to be believed to have been
> done in this way. Christ the Lord, without any guilt,
> without any blame, underwent a penal sentence; the
> innocent man is crucified without sin. The devil is made
> guilty by the death of an innocent man; the devil is made
> guilty by bringing the cross upon a righteous man who
> owed nothing. The death of Christ benefitted man; what
> Adam owed to God, Christ paid by undergoing death,
> having been made without any doubt a sacrifice for the

---

arefecerat, multo facilius, si increpare voluisset, omnis caro, quae faenum aestimata est, protinus
aruisset. Si enim et illi, qui ad capiendum eum venerant, blando interrogati sermone, id est, 'quem
quaeritis?' abierunt retrorsum, et facti sunt velut mortui, quid factum fuisset, si increpare voluisset?

16. Caesarius of Arles, Sermo XI, 4, 56. Sed inplet mysterium crucis, propter quod et ven-
erat in hunc mundum; ut per illud peccati chirographum solveretur, et inimica potestas velut hamo
crucis inescata caperetur, et salva iustitia atque ratione praedam diabolus quam tenebat amitteret.

sin of men and for their race, just as the blessed Paul taught: "Christ," he says, "loved us and handed himself over for us as an offering and sacrificial victim to God in a pleasing aroma."[17]

The devil is defeated because he had Christ executed even though he was innocent of any wrongdoing. Thus, he brought condemnation upon himself. However, the death of Christ, though unearned, was nonetheless a benefit to humanity. Adam, and all humanity after him, owed God a death because of their willful sinfulness; Christ, by dying in human flesh, paid what Adam and his progeny owed to God. More specifically, Christ was a sacrifice for sin, a sacrifice made to God himself—not to the devil or any other power but to God, who alone had been sinned against and who alone could remit that sin. What was the nature of this sacrifice, and why was it necessary?

Caesarius states that the sacrifice for sin was one of propitiation:

> For that original sin was not easily able to be forgiven unless a sacrificial victim had been offered for the fault, unless that holy blood of propitiation had been poured out. For the saying of the Lord at the time of the Exodus remains in force now: "I will see the blood, and I will

---

17. Caesarius of Arles, *Sermo XI* 5, 57. *Hoc autem ita factum credi necesse est. Christus dominus sine reatu aliquo, sine culpa aliqua, sententiae poenali subiacuit, sine peccato innocens crucifigitur. Fit reus diabolus innocuo moriente: fit reus diabolus crucem iusto indebite inferendo. Mors Christi profecit homini: quod debebat Adam deo, Christus mortem suscipiendo persolvit, factus utique sacrificium pro crimine hominum eorumque progenie, sicut beatus Paulus edisserit: 'Christus,' inquit, 'dilexit nos, et tradidit se ipsum pro nobis oblationem et hostiam deo in odorem suavitatis.'*

protect you." For that figure of the lamb points to this passion of the Lord Christ.[18]

The blood of the sacrificial lamb, Christ, was necessary to protect humanity from the wrath of God as personified in the angel of death from the Exodus. Here is the attribute of *iustitia* that Caesarius insists must be part of God's salvation plan since it is a part of God's character. Sin, not the devil's power, is the problem for humanity; thus, it is sin that must be dealt with first. And sin can only be dealt with by the shedding of blood since without the shedding of blood there can be no forgiveness.

The Bishop of Arles then explains how this sacrifice of propitiation fits into the broader scheme of the devil's unjustly bringing death upon Christ and so being defeated:

> When blood is paid out for blood, death for death, and a sacrificial victim for a fault, even so did the devil lose what he was holding. It is now rightly said to him: "O enemy, you do not have that on account of which you had a legal case. The first Adam sinned, but I, the last Adam, did not receive the stain of sin; let my righteousness benefit the sinner, let my death, imposed upon me unowed, benefit the debtor. You are no longer able to hold man in endless death, for he conquered, overcame, and crushed you through me. You were not truly conquered through power but by justice; not by domination but rather by equity." Thus, the enemy vomited up what he had gulped

---

18. Caesarius of Arles, *Sermo XI* 5, 57. *Nec enim facile dimitti poterat illud originale peccatum, nisi oblata fuisset hostia pro delicto, nisi propitiationis sanguis ille sacer fuisset effusus; quia nec vane iam tunc in Exodo dictum constat a domino: 'Videbo sanguinem, et protegam vos.' Illa enim figura agni hanc designabat Christi domini passionem.*

down, and justly there was taken away from him what he used to hold since unjustly he dared to infringe upon that which under no arrangement was his concern.[19]

Satan lost his right to hold humanity in captivity because humanity was no longer liable for sin. By killing Christ, he performed the very sacrifice that was necessary to absolve mankind, thereby destroying his right over his erstwhile companions in a common damnation. Caesarius then shifts the emphasis to the devil's wrongdoing by killing an innocent man, thus losing his rights over humanity. There is therefore a twofold effect of the cross: on the one hand, it is the cause of humanity's forgiveness by God, and on the other, the cause of the devil's condemnation. In all of this, God acts with *iustitia*, not power. The devil has no reason to complain.

Caesarius then concludes with an admonition to his flock to strive to live up to the gift of salvation given to us.[20] The attributes of God displayed in Christ's sacrifice are justice

---

19. Caesarius of Arles, *Sermo XI* 5, 57. *Dum erogatur sanguis pro sanguine, mors pro morte, hostia pro delicto, sic diabolus quod tenebat amisit. Cui recte iam dicitur: Non habes unde, inimice, causeris. Peccaverat primus Adam, sed ego Adam novissimus peccati maculam non recepi: ipsa te vicit caro per meam iustitiam, quam seductione feceras peccatis obnoxiam: iustitia mea proficiat peccatori, mors mihi indebite inrogata proficiat debitori. Tenere iam in mortem perpetuam non pote hominem, qui te per me vicit, superavit, elisit. Nec sane potentia victus es, sed iustitia; nec dominatione, sed potius aequitate. Sic vomuit quod obsorbuerat inimicus, et iuste ei tollitur quod tenebat, quia iniuste invadere ausus est quod ad se nullo ordine pertinebat.*

20. Caesarius of Arles, *Sermo XI* 6, 57. "Behold, dearly beloved brothers, how much I deem that a reason has been given for why our Lord and Savior freed the human race from the power of the devil not through power but through humility, not through violence but through justice. For this reason, let us, to whom the divine compassion gave so many benefits with no preceding merits of our own, labor as much as we are able with the help of that same divine compassion so that the grace of so great a love should not produce a judgment for us but a reward." *Ecce, fratres carissimi, quantum arbitror, reddita est ratio quare dominus et salvator noster non per potentiam, sed per humilitatem, nec per violentiam, sed per iustitiam genus humanum de postestate diaboli liberaverit: et ideo nos, quibus tanta beneficia ullis praecedentibus meritis praestitit divina misericordia, quantum possumus cum ipsius adiutorio laboremus, ut tantae pietatis gratia non nobis iudicium pariat, sed profectum.*

(*iustitia*) and humility (*humilitas*), summed up in the phrase *tantae pietatis gratia*, "the grace of so great a love." Because of the nature of our salvation, therefore, we should live lives that will take hold of that same salvation. If we do so, if we do not despise so great a grace, we will have our reward. If we do despise this grace, then we will receive judgment. The conclusion may echo the "semi-Augustinian" language of the Council of Orange, a compromise position in which baptism was received by grace alone, apart from works, while ultimate salvation was dependent upon our working toward sanctification after baptism, albeit always with God's grace helping us. However, this conclusion should be held tentatively given the hortatory nature of a sermon. Augustine, after all, in his own sermons emphasized the importance of living a holy life to attain ultimate salvation.

We have now examined the sermon of Caesarius on why Christ conquered Satan and rescued mankind through suffering rather than power. Like many of the Bishop of Arles's sermons, however, this one draws on earlier sources for the bulk of its material then edits them for a contemporary audience. What sources did he draw on, and how did he edit them? Answering these questions will tell us a good deal about the place of Caesarius's doctrine of the atonement in history.

CHAPTER 5

CAESARIUS OF ARLES, PART II

Expiation and the Devil's
Rights in *Christus Victor*

To discover the place of Caesarius of Arles's sermon on the atonement in the broader history of the doctrine, it is necessary to compare it with contemporary texts. This chapter will first explore two anonymous sermons from the fifth century on which Caesarius of Arles drew for his own sermon on the atonement. Then, it will sum up the nature of the doctrine of the atonement found in all three sermons. Finally, it will look at how Jean Rivière interacted with Caesarius's sermon and assess the accuracy of his engagement.

Two Easter Sermons from the
Eusebius Gallicanus Collection

Caesarius's atonement sermon explored above is an edited pas-
tiche of two sermons probably composed slightly earlier, in the
second half of the fifth century. These two sermons were part
of a collection of forty-three sermons deriving from Gaul and
frequently attributed (wrongly) to the fourth-century Greek
bishop Eusebius of Emesa. The influence of this Eusebius
Gallicanus collection on medieval Christianity cannot be under-
estimated; hundreds of manuscripts, dating from throughout
the medieval period, contain groups of sermons drawn from
this collection. Columbanus, Isidore of Seville, Paul the Deacon,
Thomas Aquinas, and Gratian are just a few of the theologians
who drew on these sermons for their own works. Many of the
sermons Caesarius edited for his homiliaries were edited versions of a Eusebius Gallicanus original, although the Eusebian
collection itself may have originated at about the same time as
Caesarius's own.

The two sermons that Caesarius used for his own atonement
sermon are listed in the critical edition as numbers eighteen and
nineteen, or "De Pascha VII" and "De Pascha VIII." They form
part of a group of twelve sermons on Easter that appear in the
Eusebius Gallicanus collection, a group that was especially popular among medieval preachers, appearing in a large number of
later homiliaries and other religious texts. They take at times
a rather different approach from Caesarius's to describing the
atonement. Rather than repeat the sermons word for word, as
I did with Caesarius's sermon above, I will instead summarize
and quote extracts. Let us see what they have to say.

EUSEBIUS GALLICANUS
SERMO "DE PASCHA VII"

"De Pascha VII" begins by invoking the feast on which it is preached.[1] Easter is a time for rejoicing, for it celebrates the new creation. Christ's resurrection was as important and joyous an occasion as the initial creation. The preacher then proceeds to recount Christ's descent into hell, his reemergence on the day of his resurrection, and its salvific significance. The account of the descent into hell includes a description of how it brought about our salvation. In this case, Christ conquered death, *Mors*, here described as an independent agent. For the moment, the devil is not mentioned as the chief adversary whom Christ tricked and defeated. So the preacher states:

> Death indeed had burst into paradise, but Life took up the mortal condition, overcame Hell, and crushed the death-dealing law, fulfilling that to which the prophet bears witness: "O death, I will be your death." And thus, the wickedness of death, which was rejoicing that it had conquered him just as if he were a common man, suddenly took fright at its prey. In its own kingdom it was

---

1. Eusebius Gallicanus, "Sermo XVIII: De Pascha VII," in *Collectio homiliarum. Sermones extravagantes I (Eusebius 'Gallicanus')*, ed. F. Glorie, CCSL 101 (Turnhout: Brepols, 1970), 213. "It is well that we have learned that this Lord's Day of the Resurrection is the first day of the week after the world's Creation; for just as at that time there was a new joy, so now, after so many years, on the same day of the week there shines forth a gentle Beginning. This Day was happy indeed when it gave birth to the primal light, but it is happier now when it restores from Hell the very Creator of light; then, it emerged out of base material, but now, it is chosen for glory. And for this reason, with the prophet, 'Let us rejoice and be glad in it,' since happier are those days in which we are converted than those in which we are born." *Bene novimus primum esse ab origine mundi hunc resurrectionis dominicum diem; sicut enim in eodem nova nunc gaudia, ita dudum in hoc ipso tenera rerum fulsere principia. Felix quidem dum ex se primam pareret lucem, sed nunc felicior dum ipsum ex inferis reddidit lucis auctorem; tunc est inchoatus ad rudem materia, nunc est electus ad gloriam. Et ideo, cum propheta, 'exsultemus et laetemur in eo,' quia iucundiores sunt illi dies quibus conversamur, quam illi quibus nascimur.*

bound by one whom it thought was its own debtor, it was condemned by its own guilty victim, it was subjugated by its own captive. And so Damnation was tied up and ensnared by its own snares; while it was deceiving, it was tripped up; while it was slaying, it was blotted out; while it was devouring, it was eaten up.[2]

Christ was innocent, so death acted wrongly by taking him. Moreover, by bringing into its own realm one who was greater than itself, death was the more easily conquered. This is typical *Christus Victor* language, eloquently expressed.

The focus then shifts to expressing how great God's love toward humanity was revealed to be through the passion and resurrection. Mankind is portrayed as the object of God's love and the victim of death and the devil. Christ's death and resurrection provide proof of God's regard for humanity and its inherent dignity and worth.[3] God loves his creation, mankind;

---

2. Eusebius Gallicanus, "De Pascha VII" 2, 214. *Irruperat quidem mors paradisum, sed vita expugnavit infernum, legemque mortalem suscepta mortalitatis conditione calcavit, implens illud quod propheta testatur: 'O mors, ero mors tua.' Ac sic mortis iniquitas, quae se tamquam hominem vicisse gaudebat, expavit subito praedam suam, et in suo regno a suo, ut putabat, debitore constricta est, a suo condemnata reo, a suo est subiugata captivo. Ideo suis laqueis illigata et irretita perditio: dum deciperet supplantata est, dum interficeret exstincta est, dum devoraret assumpta est.*

3. Eusebius Gallicanus, "De Pascha VII" 3, 215. "Let the confused jealousy of the ancient Trickster weep and tremble; let the devil discern humanity rising again, almost happier and more noble, whom he had laid low by a mortal wound in the first parents. Behold, Grace restored truly greater things than creation had conferred. Indeed, there is a very great sign of divine love toward men when during the beginning of the world the servant received 'the image and likeness of his God'; but it is truly greater that now the Creator God has assumed the person and form of the servant ... Indeed, it is a great thing given to me from God that I understand myself to be his work, but it is so much more that I see how he handed himself over as my ransom and how the same redemption was made by a rich gift so that man might seem to be as strong as God." *Lugeat et intremiscat confusa antiqui supplantatoris invidia; cernat diabolus hominem, quem mortifero vulnere in primo parente prostraverat, paene felicius ac nobilius resurgentem. Ecce gratia paene maiora restituit, quam factura contulerat. Maximum quidem circa hominem divini amoris insigne est, quod inter ipsa mundi principia 'imaginem ac similitudinem dei' sui servus accepit; sed paene amplius est,*

this love is demonstrated by our being created and blessed in the image of God. However, this love is even more clearly demonstrated by the fact that God took on the image of mankind to redeem us. God's gift of himself also shows forth the dignity of humanity in a way that even the creation and its initial gifts could not.

So far, the anonymous preacher has not touched on any of the themes that Caesarius was interested in expounding, but now, he turns to the subject that interested the Bishop of Arles. Why did God redeem humanity through suffering, not through power? This portion of the sermon is one that Caesarius drew on, for the anonymous preacher's answer is substantially the same as his own. First, he links Christ's victory with the necessity of a sacrifice for sin:

> Therefore, the lofty strength received our humanity that it might bestow its own divinity; it received both soul and body, and because the whole man was liable for sin and had to be redeemed, the whole man is assumed in order to be sacrificed. And thus, that immense Majesty offered a sacrifice from what was ours, but he paid our ransom from what was his.[4]

God took up human nature to sanctify it, but he also took it up to sacrifice it. The union of divinity and humanity in the person of Christ serves not only to defeat the devil and raise up

---

quod nunc personam et 'formam servi' deus auctor 'assumpsit' … Magnum quidem mihi est de deo, quod esse me sentio opus suum; sed multo plus est, quod transisse ipsum video in pretium meum, quandoquidem copioso munere ipsa redemptio agitur: ut homo deum valere videatur.

4. Eusebius Gallicanus,"De Pascha VII" 3, 216. *Suscepit ero virtus excelsa humanitatem nostram, ut tribueret divinitatem suam; suscepit et animam et corpus; et, quia peccato obnoxius totus homo redimendus erat, totus homo assumitur immolandus. Ac sic immensa illa maiestas 'de nostro obtulit sacrificium, de suo contulit' pretium.*

fallen humanity but also to set up the conditions necessary for an effective sacrifice for sin. How this works out is the subject of the remainder of the sermon.

The preacher then asks the question lurking in the minds of his congregants:

> But perhaps at this point someone may say in his heart, "Why is it that divinity humbled its own self? Was it not able through the strength and power of its own arm to free man—his own creation—from the power of the devil, so that it would not have been necessary for it to assume a human body, to experience the wounds of universal misery and of our condemned condition, to be affected by spitting and flogging, by insults and sorrows, or to be fixed to the beam of the cross?"[5]

The answer revolves around the necessity for God to display his *iustitia*, his justice or righteousness, in the redemption of humanity. Why did God assume human nature and suffer in it?

> The chief reason is that of justice, just as the Lord himself says: "Without delay; for thus it is fitting for us to fulfill all justice." For the first man had sinned by his own fault and fall of disobedience and by the movement of his own will, having been seduced by the devil and not forced, just as that same man says in Genesis: "The serpent seduced me." And so, while he was able to be redeemed by means

---

5. Eusebius Gallicanus, "De Pascha VII" 4, 216. *Sed forte hic aliquis in corde suo dicat: 'Quid est hoc, quod 'semetipsam' divinitas 'hummiliavit?' non poterat per virtutem et potentiam brachii sui liberare a potestate diaboli hominem suum, ut necesse non haberet humanum corpus assumere, ut necesse non haberet universae miseriae atque damnatae conditionis iniurias experiri, sputis ac flagellis, contumeliis ac doloribus affici, patibulo crucis affigi?'*

of compassion as a guilty man, he could not be freed by means of power as an innocent man.[6]

Mankind is not an innocent victim of the devil's wiles. He is a rebel against God by his own will and so needs forgiveness from sin.

Therefore, a sacrifice for sin was necessary, but the nature of this sacrifice had to meet certain requirements.

> It pleased God in accordance with his justice to offer up for the sake of the human race a man pure and immaculate, "separated from sinners." But such a man our land did not possess. One who was guilty of a similar sin would have been able neither to be of assistance to sinners nor to intervene on the behalf of slaves since he himself was bound by the laws of slavery. Therefore, he would have to come from another land, so that an absolved man might be able to be offered up for debtors, a righteous man for the wicked, an innocent man for sinners, a lamb for the goats.[7]

Just as in the law of Moses the animal sacrificed for sin had to be perfect, so the final sin offering for all mankind had to be perfect. Only Christ, the God-man, fulfilled this condition. But

---

6. Eusebius Gallicanus, "De Pascha VII" 5, 216–17. *Prima iustitiae causa est, sicut ipse dominus dicit: 'Sine modo; sic enim decet nos implere omnem iustitiam.' Peccaverat enim primus homo suo vitio et inoboedientiae lapsu et propriae voluntatis impulsu, seductus a diabolo, non coactus, sicut ipse homo in genesi dicit: 'Serpens,' inquid, 'seduxit me;' et ideo per misericordiam poterat quasi reus redimi, non debebat per potentiam quasi innocens liberari.*

7. Eusebius Gallicanus, "De Pascha VII" 5, 217. *Placuit deo secundum iustitiam suam pro humano genere offerre hominem purum et immaculatum, 'segregatum a peccatoribus.' Sed talem nostra regio non habebat. Non subvenire peccatoribus poterat simili peccato obnoxius, nec intervenire pro servis adstrictus legibus servitutis. Ex alia ergo regione venturus erat, ut posset offerri pro debitoribus absolutus, pro iniquis iustus, pro peccatoribus innocens, pro haedis agnus.*

why did a man have to be sacrificed? Because the guilty flesh had to be punished:

> From me he had what made him subject to crucifixion, from his own he had what made him able to be glorified; from me what made him subject to death, from his own what made him able to rise again. Therefore, from what was ours he gave a sacrifice for sin, from his own he gave the grace of forgiveness; from what was ours there exists whatever was condemned in his suffering, from his own there exists whatever amount of blessedness is conferred from his resurrection.[8]

Though innocent, Christ was still a descendant of Adam, and therefore, his human nature was subject to condemnation. But since the Son of God took up that same human nature, the condemnation could not stand, and humanity was redeemed and sanctified.

The preacher then concludes with a return to the theme of the conquest of the devil. Christ's innocence means that when unjustly condemned in Adam's flesh, he saved the rest of the human race.[9] Thus, the sacrifice for sin, though important, plays

---

8. Eusebius Gallicanus, "De Pascha VII" 5, 217. *De meo ergo habuit unde crucifigeretur, de suo unde glorificaretur; de meo unde caderet, de suo unde resurgeret. De nostro itaque dedit peccati hostiam, de suo indulgentiae tribuit gratiam; de nostro est quidquid in passione damnatur, de suo est quidquid beatitudinis ex resurrectione confertur.*

9. Eusebius Gallicanus, "De Pascha VII" 5, 218. "And therefore, he drove back the death owed by all men since he alone was released as owing nothing. And thus, through his undeserved suffering, since he did not possess his own sins, he redeemed the sins of others. Therefore, so great an Enemy of the human race was conquered by this justice and by this chain. For when man sold himself to that Enemy, just as it says, 'You were sold by your sins,' and through the transaction of sin man alone was owed to him, he laid hands on God, being deceived by his accustomed presumption, and, when he killed the free man, he lost the guilty man." *Et ideo repulit mortem omnibus debitam dum solus solvit indebitam. Ac sic per indignissimam passionem, quia non habebat peccata propria, redemit aliena. Hac*

a subordinate role in the redemption since the emphasis is on Christ's innocence and the devil's injustice. The atonement in "De Pascha VII" is both similar and dissimilar to Caesarius of Arles's own *Sermo XI*. Caesarius is concerned with explaining the mechanism whereby the sacrifice for sin worked, while the anonymous preacher wants to extol the goodness of God and to give his audience an impression of the drama of redemption. The fact that this is explicitly an Easter sermon, and therefore that the descent into Hell and the resurrection have a much larger place than the crucifixion, is surely important for explaining the difference in emphases. Still, the mechanism for atonement is roughly the same in both: mankind is sinful and therefore needs a sacrifice for sin to be offered up in order to be freed from the devil. Simply tricking death and the devil into seizing upon an innocent man and therefore losing their rights over humanity as a whole is insufficient. God's *iustitia* would not be fully displayed if humanity's sin were not atoned for.

EUSEBIUS GALLICANUS
SERMO "DE PASCHA VIII"

"De Pascha VIII" is much longer and displays a rhetorical flair that is lacking from both previous sermons. It includes references to Cicero, Quintilian, and Plutarch in addition to the church fathers and draws examples from natural philosophy and civil law. It is also, interestingly, vociferously opposed to Augustinian ideas of grace and free will, following the lead of

---

itaque iustitia victus est et hoc vinculo vinctus est humani generis tantus inimicus. Nam cum se illi homo vendidisset, sicut ait: 'Peccatis vestris vendidi estis,' et per peccati commercium solus illi homo deberetur, ille deum consuetudinaria praesumptione deceptus appetiit, et, dum occidit liberum, amisit obnoxium.

such Gallic churchmen as Faustus of Riez and Hilary of Arles in insisting upon humanity's ability to choose the good and God's righteousness being displayed in not compelling acquiescence to redemption. Caesarius was not averse to using and adapting the sermons of his theological foes (he put many of Faustus's sermons into his own collections) but made sure to edit them carefully. But let us see first what "De Pascha VIII" has to say about the atonement.

The sermon opens with an image of the redemption drawn from Jeremiah and commented on extensively by such church fathers as Ambrose, Jerome, and Augustine: the *perdix*, the partridge, steals eggs not her own and hatches them; however, when the chicks grow up, they recognize the voice of their true mother and fly to her.[10] The image is then explained: the treacherous partridge is the devil, who takes humanity captive; however, when God calls to them through his prophets or with his own voice, human beings return with joy to their true Father. The anonymous preacher then addresses a question from his congregation: "But you say at this point: 'Teach me how the world was made captive; explain the captivity to me so that I might be able to understand the redemption.'"[11] He then proceeds to explain the nature of the captivity.

---

10. Eusebius Gallicanus, "Sermo XIX: De Pascha VIII" 2, 223–24. "What do you say to these things, O man, O precious vessel of wisdom, O image of divinity and possessor of a noble reason? What do you take away from your Creator? Behold, even the savage animals understand why their own being is owed to their Creator, and they who do not have understanding are proven to have affection. The captive generation abandoned the clever persuader; the robber remains, deceived, and the plunderer remains, bereaved." *Quid ad haec dicis, homo, pretiosum vas sapientiae, imago divinitatis et possessor generosae rationis? Quid te creatori tuo subtrahis? Ecce etiam bruta animalia cognoscunt quid proprium debeatur auctori, et quae non habent intellectum, habere probantur affectum. Callidum pervasorum captiva generatio derelinquit; remanet praedo deceptus et raptor orbatus.*

11. *sed dicis hoc loco, 'Doce me quomodo captivus fuerit mundus: expone mihi captivitatem, ut intellegere possim redemptionem* (Eusebius Gallicanus, "De Pascha VIII" 3, 224).

Was the world made captive by the devil by force? In other words, does the imagery of the partridge stealing another's eggs determine the theology? No. The preacher describes our captivity as follows:

> If we should question our passions and wicked customs as to what the captivity of the soul might be, we come to know clearly what it is by these words: he who is delighted by wine-bibbing is made a captive to inebriation, which is the mother of vices; he who is busy with obscene things and with the allurements of the stinking flesh is oppressed by the yoke of foul luxury; he who is inflamed with the attire of foreign material by insatiable and ever-hungering throats is led away into the service of burning greed; he who is fed by the cruelty of bestial wrath is subdued to the rule of bloody rage. And so it is that the apostle says, "For whatever a man is conquered by, he is also its servant."[12]

The soul is made captive by its own sins.[13] The devil made humanity captive by persuading our first parents to sin against

---

12. Eusebius Gallicanus, "De Pascha VIII" 3, 224–25. *Si passiones nostras et pravas consuetudines interrogemus, quid sit animae captivitas, evidenter agnoscimus; verbi gratia: qui vinolentia delectatur, ebrietati, quae mater est vitiorum, captivus efficitur; qui obscenis et fetidae carnis illecebris occupatur, luxuriae turpis iugo premitur; qui habitu alienae rei avidis et esurientibus sempter faucibus inflammatur, in servitium arsurae cupiditatis abducitur; qui crudelitate bestialis iracundiae pascitur, cruenti furoris dominio subiugatur. Inde est, quod dicit apostolus: 'A quo enim quis vincitur, eius et servus est.'*

13. Eusebius Gallianus, "De Pascha VIII" 3, 225. "Therefore, the devil sentenced the whole world to a penalty by this method: the perversity of greed, the harmful transgression of a command, the forbidden presumption of food, the domination of superstition, the assault of error, the forgetting of truth, the confusion of ignorance, the lengthy persuasion of foolishness and the death-dealing custom of idolatry." *Hoc ergo genere diabolus universum addixerat mundum—cupiditatis depravatio, mandati inimica transgressio, cibi interdicta praesumptio, superstitionis dominatio, erroris impressio, veritatis oblivio, ignorantiae confusio, stultitiae longa persuasio, mortifera idolatriae consuetudo.*

God, thereby darkening the mind and enslaving the reason.[14] Thus, humanity's captivity is first to sin and then to the devil, who lured Adam and Eve into sinning and thereby condemning their offspring to captivity.

With this being the case, how was redemption to be attained? The answer, according to the anonymous preacher, is that mankind's sin needed to be expiated by Christ recapitulating the fall. He pictures God pondering within himself the proper remedy for humanity's predicament:

> Let us remake him by a second birth so that he who was born for the devil through the original debt would be reborn for God through the institute of baptism; and when he is brought forth once more, by the working of the Spirit through grace, let him owe nothing to his Enemy on account of his nature. Heedless of others, he thrust his wicked right hand into the old tree, so let us extend innocent hands upon the cross for his sake; the punishment was incurred through a tree, so let the guilt be redeemed through a tree. But he was deceived by the wickedly seductive sweetness of the forbidden taste; so let the food of temptation and the injury of vinegar and gall be expiated. But he is liable for his pride, by which

---

14. Eusebius Gallicanus, "De Pascha VIII" 3, 225. "That same captivity had seized greater spirits, had taken away counsel, and had ensnared good sense; and for this reason, they who had abandoned the Creator of reason rightly lost the freedom of their primal understanding. And thus, the devil dragged all human offspring, who were mastered in the first parent and led into captivity by charming seduction, to a keenness for his worship. He captured those whom he had deceived, and the shoot which he had spoiled at the root he possessed by its fruits." *Ista captivitas magis animas occupaverat, consilium tulerat sensumque laqueaverat; et ideo, qui deserverant rationis auctorem, merito primi intellectus perdiderant libertatem. Ac sic diabolus universam posteritatem in primo parente possessam, blanda seductione captivam, ad studia cultus sui traxerat: ceperat quos deceperat, et stirpem, quam in radice vitiaverat, in fructibus possidebat.*

the command was broken and by which he burned with his ambition to divine status; so let our own divinity humble itself to human nature for the sake of the proud man, let Majesty hand its own self over for the crime of treason. But the guilty man belongs to death, and it is fitting that what is owed be paid; so the condition of mortality ought to be assumed, and a death ought to be offered for a dead man.[15]

There are several points being made in this speech. First, Christ's death on the cross was a recapitulation of the fall, and by this means the fall of humanity is reversed. Thus, the new tree (the cross) is in place of the old tree (the tree of the knowledge of good and evil); the vinegar and gall of Christ's drink on the cross are in place of the sweetness of the fruit, "good to eat and pleasing to the eye." Second, part of Adam's sin was his intent to be like God—in other words, treason or *maiestas* in Latin. So, to redress this evil, God hands himself over for the crime of treason (the play on words is *maiestas pro crimine maiestatis*). What humanity owes for its crimes is paid by God in the person of Christ.

The preacher then turns to the subject of the defeat of the devil. God becomes man, taking up a lowly body, to ensnare the devil:

---

15. Eusebius Gallicanus, "De Pascha VIII" 4, 226. *Secundam ergo nativitatem tantum illius innovemus: ut, qui per originis debitum diabolo nascebatur, per baptismatis institutum deo renascatur; dumque regeneratur spiritu operante per gratiam, nil inimico debeat per naturam. Improbam dexteram vetitae arbori importunus ingessit, extendamus pro illo innocentes in cruce manus: per lignum poena est contracta, per lignum culpa redimatur. Sed prohibiti gustus maleblanda suavitate deceptus est; expietur delectationis esca, aceti et fellis iniuria. Sed superbiae, qua praeceptum soluit, qua in ambitum divinitatis exarsit, obnoxius est; in hominem se divinitas nostra humiliet pro superbo, tradat seipsa maiestas pro crimine maiestatis. Sed mortis reus est; hoc reddi convenit, quod debetur: mortalis est assumenda conditio, et mors est offerenda pro mortuo.*

Why, I say, did the son of God visit the earth in his own self? So that the dominion of the tyrant might be more strongly destroyed through the coming of the Emperor. God lay hidden in the lowly state of the form of a slave for these reasons: so that he might ensnare the artful deceiver by his own deceits in turn; so that he who used to hold mankind as liable for punishment on account of his crime of forbidden ambition, when he crucified the Lord, should stand out as one guilty of a greater crime. Thus, he would lose the authority of ruling when the humanity of the Redeemer subdued the guilt of deceived mankind; nor can he any more lay before mankind the injustice of an appetite for divinity after he had blindly stretched out his parricidal daring against God. And thus, the impunity and impiety of the savage robber began to be made captive.[16]

The devil is defeated by two means: first, he commits a greater crime than humanity committed and so loses his authority over them; second, humanity's guilt is removed by the sacrifice of expiation performed at the crucifixion, and so, just as the devil found nothing to condemn in Christ, he finds nothing to condemn in humanity.

---

16. Eusebius Gallicanus, "De Pascha VIII" 6, 227–28. *Quare, inquam, per se terrena, dei filius, visitavit? Ut fortius destrueretur tyranni dominium per imperatoris adventum. Sub abiectione formae servilis latuit deus: ut dolosum supplantatorem suis vicissim fraudibus irretiret; ut ille, qui pro crimine ambitionis illicitae obnoxium tenebat hominem, dum dominum crucifigit, maioris reus criminis appareret: ac sic auctoritatem dominantis amitteret, dum vincit culpam decepti hominis, humanitas redemptoris; nec possit ulterius obicere homini appetitae divinitatis iniuriam, postquam parricidalem in deum caecus extendisset audaciam. Ac sic captivi esse coepit impunitas, feri praedonis impietas.*

The nature of the devil's offense against God is then explained. The preacher uses an example drawn from Roman contract law, when the buyer is exempt from any claims from the seller due to a breach of contract.[17] Failure of a legal case due to *genere* occurs "if he should have exacted a payment of another thing and a better material than the written document of the legal case indicated."[18] The devil seizes his payment in the gold coin of the sinless Christ rather than the silver of a sinful man and so loses his case. He is defeated by his own greed.

Attention is then turned to some more reasons why Christ came in the likeness of sinful flesh:

> But again you say, "Why did God rescue mankind from the power of the devil by means of the weakness of the flesh and not rather through the power of his divinity?" Since the human condition, which was held by its enemy as liable for punishment due to the guilt of its transgression, had to be rescued not by power but rather for a price, it was necessary that love be mixed with justice. A wretched man was able to be redeemed through compassion, but a guilty man was not able to be freed through power. For by God's authority are innocent

---

17. Eusebius Gallicanus, "De Pascha VIII" 6, 228–29. "Let us see here in what way the devil ended up in a legal action: by kind [*genere*], without doubt. For man was owed to him through disobedience, yet he attacked God due to his pride; therefore, in this way he incurred more danger from a plaintiff, having been seduced by human appearance and having persecuted God in His humanity. So, because he impiously attacked an innocent man, he lost his debtor." *Videamus quo hic modo diabolus causa cecidit: genere sine dubio. Homo enim illi debebatur per inoboediantiam, ille deum appetiit per superbiam; sic ergo plus petendi periculum, humana specie seductus et deum in homine persecutus, incurrit, et, dum impie appetiit innocentem, perdidit debitorem.*

18. Eusebius Gallicanus, "De Pascha VIII" 6, 229. *Si alterius rei ac melioris materiae mercedem, quam scriptura continebat, exigerit.*

people helped, but by his intercession and humility are criminals helped.[19]

The captivity of humanity was due to its own sin, not the devil's power. Sin had to be dealt with first.

There is another reason why God saved humanity through weakness: the freedom of the will. This is a mark of the anonymous preacher's position on the controversy concerning grace and free will, indicating that he opposed Augustine's (and Caesarius's) arguments about the necessity of grace coming before any good works. It is a mark of the preacher's "semi-Pelagian" position that he accepts Augustine's arguments for original sin and the nature of humanity's crime (*maiestas*, treason) against God but then goes on an extended peroration on the free will of mankind.[20] The preacher insists that God cannot force anyone to seek salvation but awards it to those who seek it willingly.

---

19. Eusebius Gallicanus, "De Pascha VIII" 7, 229. *Sed iterum dicis: 'Quare deus hominem de potestate diaboli per infirmitatem carnis et non magis per virtutem divinitatis eripuit?' Quia humana conditio, quae per transgressionis culpam obnoxia tenebatur inimico, non imperio erat eruenda sed pretio, necesse erat ut pietati iustitia misceretur. Poterat miser per misericoridam redimi, non poterat reus per potentiam liberari: innocentibus enim auctoritate, criminosis intercessione et humilitate succuritur.*

20. Eusebius Gallicanus, "De Pascha VIII" 7, 229. "And so if mankind had been seduced by the sin of disobedience and the assent of a free mind, not coerced by the devil, it was necessary that he be invited back by the Creator of all reason and equity rather than dragged back by force; indeed, it would seem most vile that he who had fallen willingly should be raised up unwillingly. You see how the eagerness of the worthiest doctor seeks the permission of his patient. Captivity was taken up through free will; freedom should be restored through free will once more; for the Lord who opens the gate also awaits the agitation of the knocker." *Propterea homo, si inoboedientiae lapsu et liberae mentis assensu a diabolo seductus fuerat, non coactus: a totius rationis et aequitatis auctore invitandus erat, non attrahendus; iniquissimum siquidem videretur, ut, qui ceciderat voluntarius, erigeretur invitus. Vides quia dignatissimi medici studium, infirmi sui requirit assensum. Per liberum arbitrium est excepta captivitas, per liberum rursus arbitrium erat restituenda libertas: dominus enim, qui ianuam reserat, etiam sollicitudinem pulsantis exspectat.*

He goes on to insist that grace, far from coming *nullis pracedentibus meritis*, "with no preceding merits," as in the Augustinian formula used by Caesarius in his sermon, instead comes only to those worthy of it: "But what if man is freed only by the consideration of God and not by his own eagerness? Shall not grace then be obliged to be offered to one ungrateful for his redemption? Is grace not rather incapable of being offered to one unworthy of it?"[21] Therefore, Christ comes in the likeness of human flesh to save humanity through a gentle invitation, not power.

The preacher then turns to another reason for the nature of our salvation: justice must be done. Here he places a speech from the devil on which Caesarius drew for his own sermon. The anonymous preacher portrays the devil as saying:

> O righteous Judge of all things, man is indeed yours because he is your creation, but he began to be mine because of his guilt; yours through nature, mine through disobedience. For he preferred to listen to my seduction rather than your law; by the law he is owed to you, but by his crime he is owed to me; he is yours by creative act, mine by his own will, since he was able to keep your command but did not wish to do so.[22]

Here the speech of the devil focuses on humanity's willing choice to forsake the law of God. Force does not suit God's

---

21. Eusebius Gallicanus, "De Pascha VIII" 7, 230. *Quod si homo dei tantum intiuitu et non etiam suo studio liberetur: numquid offerenda erat gratia redemptionis ingrato? Non suffecerat, quod offerebatur indigno?*

22. Eusebius Gallicanus, "De Pascha VIII" 7, 230. *Iuste rerum arbiter: tuus quidem est homo per creaturam, sed meus coepit esse per culpam; tuus per naturam, meus per inoboedian-tiam, quia maluit audire seductionem meam quam legem; tuam tibi debetur iure, mihi crimine; tuus est opere, meus voluntate, quia potuit praeceptum tuum servare sed noluit.*

character in this circumstance. Note the difference from Caesarius's version of the devil's speech, however: there is no mention of the devil's punishment having to be removed also if humanity's is remitted. Free will is the point of departure here. The preacher then continues:

> Therefore, lest the devil should be able to make a complaint that he was wrongfully overwhelmed through the power of God, God engages a wise and clever counsel and with humility clashes with pride. He does not wrench a captive away from the devil prematurely but rather weighs out a price; and since with no captive, the devil charges too much, and since he would rather condemn his prey, God in the form of a sinner ensnares the provoker of sin. He tricks by means of the bait of his flesh the insatiable beast avid for human damnation; his humanity stirs up the one hungering in his direction, and his divinity strangles the one devouring.[23]

Christ's two natures, divine and human, work together to defeat the devil.

The sermon concludes with three sets of questions and answers about the nature of the atonement. First question:

> But you say, "Why was it necessary to such a degree that the same splendid and uncorrupt divinity should have

---

23. Eusebius Gallicanus, "De Pascha VIII" 7, 231. *Ne ergo per potentiam dei se inique opprimi posset diabolus calumniari, astutum et callidum deus consilium implicat et contra superbum humilitate confligit: non ei captivum praeripit, sed pretium; quod sine captivo praeponderaret et quod praedonem magis damnaret, appendit; incentorem peccati, in formam peccatoris illaqueat; humanae avidam perditionis inexplebilem bestiam, per escam carnis illudit; homo in se provocat esurientem, et deus praefocat devorantem.*

experienced the wounds of the human flesh? Why did he not rather take up some brilliant body of light?"[24]

First answer:[25]

> Not so: he did not receive a body of light due to the requirements of our redemption. Was it light that had sinned, so that he who would make expiation should have taken up the material of light? Therefore, by means of this created material he would have been able neither to pay the price of death nor to show forth the example of his resurrection. He would have contributed nothing reliable to me against my enemy if he had not triumphed in my body.[25]

This part deals with the necessity of God's incarnation due to the requirements of the sacrifice of expiation. The likeness of sinful flesh had to be sacrificed to satisfy the requirements for forgiveness, and the flesh itself had to be raised on the third day to bestow the gift of eternal life upon the rest of fleshly humanity.

Second question: "But you say, 'God would have been able to administer the campaign of our redemption more suitably through one of the angels.'"[26] Second answer: An angel could

---

24. Eusebius Gallicanus, "De Pascha VIII" 8, 231. *Sed dicis: 'Quid tantopere necesse fuit, ut splendida illa et sincera divinitas, humanae carnis experiretur iniurias? Quare non magis aliquoid speciosum lucis corpus assumpsit?'*

25. Eusebius Gallicanus, "De Pascha VIII" 8, 231. *Non ita est; non hoc recipiebat ratio redemptionis nostrae. Numquid lux ista peccaverat, ut materiam lucis expiaturus indueret? Per hanc itaque materiam creaturae, nec mortis conferre pretium, nec resurrectionis praeferre potuisset exemplum. Nihil mihi contra hostem meum fiduciae contulisset, si non in meo corpore triumphasset.*

26. Eusebius Gallicanus, "De Pascha VIII" 9, 232. *Sed dicis 'Potuisset deus per aliquem commodius angelorum, redemptionis nostrae administrare militiam!'*

not have performed the redemption because an angel is not
strong enough or of sufficient dignity to effect humanity's salvation on the cross.[27] Third question: "'Why,' you say, 'not through
a man?'"[28] Third answer:

> Because a creature would not have been able to absolve
> a creature; because it would have been impossible for a
> mere slave to bestow freedom upon his fellow slave; it
> would have been impossible for one capable of sin to
> forgive sins and for a servant of God to fulfill the func-
> tion of God. For the Lord of all the ages alone sufficed
> to be of use for the preceding, present, and future ages.
> It pertained to God alone to pursue death into Tartarus
> and to carry mankind rescued from death into heaven.[29]

A mere human being could not have saved all mankind from sin
and captivity to the devil because one who was sinful could not
save from sin. It was for God alone to save from sin. "Who but
God can forgive sins?" asked the Pharisees upon seeing Christ's
healing of the paralytic. The answer is that the God-man, the

---

27. Eusebius Gallicanus, "De Pascha VIII" 9, 232. "Not so: for it would have been
disorderly and indecent that a creature should repair what the Creator had put in place.
At the same time, the person of a single angel would not have been able to be capable of
the salvation of the whole world. Besides, as we said, the Enemy of the human race, when
the deed was done resulting in the Lord's death, was outlawed by the loss of his captive.
Therefore if an angel had endured death for the sake of humanity, the devil would not
have incurred as great a crime, nor would God have displayed so great a love." *Non ita est;
nam inordinatum et indecens erat, ut, quod factor condiderat, factura repararet. Simul persona
unius angeli valere non poterat totius mundi salutem. Praeterea, ut diximus, inimicus generis
humani, dum in necem domini agitur, captivi sui amissione proscribitur. Si ergo pro homine,
angelus pertulisset: nec diabolus tantum incurrerat criminis, nec deus tantum praetulerat caritatis.*

28. Eusebius Gallicanus, "De Pascha VIII" 10, 233. *"Cur," inquis, "non per hominem?"*

29. Eusebius Gallicanus, "De Pascha VIII" 10, 233. *Quia absolvere creaturam, creatura
non poterat; quia impossibile erat, ut conservus conservis tribueret libertatem; impossibile erat,
ut peccati capax, peccata donaret; et dei famulus, dei munus impleret. Prodesse enim praeteritis
saeculis, praesentibus, postfuturis, soli universorum saeculorum domino competebat. Dei, inquam,
solius erat ut mortem persequeretur in tartarum, et ereptum morti hominem portaret in caelum.*

Son of God enfleshed, was able to forgive sins. And here the sermon ends.

This sermon proclaims that Christ conquered the devil on the cross through two means: by snaring the devil in his own greed and cruelty, thereby descending into his stronghold to free his captives, and by making a sacrifice of expiation for mankind's sins. The two themes are intertwined, not introduced systematically. We must remember that a sermon was first and foremost a rhetorical exercise, after all. This sermon also focuses on God's character, specifically his *iustitia*: the devil cannot simply be defeated by force since God is just and righteous. Humanity cannot be saved through conquest since sin was entered into freely. We are not victims but rebels; we rebelled freely, and we must return freely. Therefore, Christ provides that opportunity for forgiveness by humbling himself on the cross. God is glorified by saving us, however, and his resurrection from the dead lifts fallen humanity to the heavens.

How does this portrayal of Christ's work on the cross compare with Caesarius of Arles's own portrayal? Like Caesarius, the anonymous preacher insists upon the dual role of the cross: defeating the devil and providing a way for the forgiveness of sins. In both, the devil is defeated by the expunging of humanity's sin in addition to forfeiting his claim through his own criminality. However, while Caesarius focuses more on the forgiveness of sins as the means of defeating the devil, the anonymous preacher of "De Pascha VIII" tends to extol the enticement of the devil by the bait of the cross and subsequent loss of rights due to his overreach. The anonymous preacher also extols the freedom of the human will as a cause for Christ's coming in humility rather than power—a point that Caesarius, staunch Augustinian that he was, thought was much less important. The Bishop of Arles drew on this sermon, however, because for all its differences in emphasis and theological outlook, it contains the same essential elements driving the crucifixion.

Summing Up

What was Caesarius of Arles's conception of the atonement, and how did he adapt the Eusebius Gallicanus sermons on which he drew? What was the common thread in all of them? And what does this say about the place of his sermon in the history of the doctrine of the atonement?

It seems clear that Caesarius was working from a viewpoint that saw Christ's victory over the devil as the primary image of the atonement. The question he portrays as being asked by his congregants assumes as much and is raised because if humanity's captivity to the devil is the only problem, why should power not suffice for rescue? "Without a doubt, he would have been able by the heavenly power and majesty to overthrow the devil and to free man from his tyranny," claims Caesarius's fictitious questioner. To be sure, answers the Bishop of Arles: if this were the only problem, power alone would have sufficed—"But reason resisted, justice did not give its permission." Why not? Why did God's *iustitia* and *ratio* not permit the devil to be overthrown through power alone? Because humanity had sinned and rebelled against God. Enticed by the devil, to be sure, but still choosing freely. Adam and Eve might have resisted Satan's charms, but they did not. "Man joined himself to me by his own will; he separated from you not unwillingly but by the same will: he is mine. Together we are destined for punishment," Caesarius has the devil say to God. If mankind is forgiven through mere power, so should the devil be.

So, to stay true to his character and not allow the devil to reproach him for inequity, God came down to earth and became incarnate, "not to tear man away from the devil through power, but rather only after preserving equity in all things." This meant dealing comprehensively with sin. There are two ways sin is destroyed and forgiven: through expiation and through propitiation. Through expiation, because Christ took up our flesh and lived a sinless life in it, thereby cleansing it from sin: "This is the first victory: that the flesh, assumed from a sinful race, stands forth as having no part in a misdeed ... the same flesh, which at one time sin had conquered, conquered sin." Then, on the cross, Christ offered up himself as a sacrifice of propitiation: "What Adam owed to God Christ paid by undergoing death, having been made without any doubt a sacrifice for the sin of men ... For that original sin was not easily able to be dismissed unless a sacrificial victim had been offered for the fault, unless that holy blood of propitiation had been poured out." With this blood sacrifice, humanity was able to be forgiven, and the devil lost his hold. To be sure, the devil also was defeated equitably because of his overreach in condemning a sinless man to death, but at the root of the atonement is dealing with humanity's sin to accomplish our redemption. "When blood is paid out for blood, death for death, and a sacrificial victim for a fault, even so did the devil lose what he was holding," proclaims Caesarius.

How is this adapted from the two Eusebius Gallicanus sermons? In both, as we have seen, the same question that exercises Caesarius's hypothetical congregant is asked; as in "De Pascha VII," "Why is it that divinity humbled its own self?" so in "De Pascha VIII," "Why did God rescue mankind from the power of the devil by means of the weakness of the flesh and not rather through the power of his divinity?" In both, the answer includes the necessity of dealing with humanity's sin. So "De Pascha VII" says, "The first man had sinned by his own fault and fall of disobedience and by the movement of his own will, having been seduced by the devil and not forced." In "De Pascha VIII," the anonymous preacher proclaims, "A wretched man could be redeemed through compassion, but a guilty man was not able to be freed through power."

In both, part of the just means by which God redeems mankind is a sacrifice for sin. In "De Pascha VII," that sacrifice is described in the language of the sin offering under Mosaic law: "It pleased God in accordance with his justice to offer up for the sake of the human race a man pure and immaculate." Moreover, this sacrifice was in some sense penal, but whether it was expiation or propitiation is left unsaid: "From what was ours, he gave a sacrifice for sin ... from what was ours, there exists whatever was condemned in his suffering." In "De Pascha VIII," the sacrifice is one of expiation: "Was it light that had sinned, so that he who would make expiation should have taken up the material of light?" And a little earlier: "Let the blood of the crucified and the wickedness of the one crucifying absolve the man; and let our own suffering redeem the man, even while it condemns the devil."

Precision should not be expected in sermons for Easter, as both the Eusebius Gallicanus sermons are, and they are at least as concerned with proclaiming the benefits of the resurrection as explaining the mechanism of the atonement. They want to encourage Christians to marvel at God and at his love for them. "Behold how much that tremendous love does for the sake of our salvation and healing!" rejoices the preacher of "De Pascha VII"; "De Pascha VIII" thunders, "It belonged to God alone to pursue death into Tartarus and to carry mankind rescued from death into heaven!" The conquest of the devil through the descent into hell and subsequent resurrection is what concerns the author of "De Pascha VII," while the conquest of the devil through tricking him into committing a greater fault than those he held in captivity and so losing his rights over them is the focus of "De Pascha VIII".

Not so for Caesarius, who in any case is writing not for Easter but to crisply lay out and clarify a key doctrine of the Christian faith for his congregants. It is the sacrifice for sin that is the foundation of his understanding of the atonement. There can be no forgiveness without the shedding of blood, which explicitly protects humanity from God's wrathful angel. There is nothing so explicit as this in the Eusebius Gallicanus sermons. There is also a sense in which the free will of mankind factors into his captivity but not into his salvation. Humanity is liable for sin because of freely choosing sin, but Christ does not come in the weakness of the flesh to gently recall sinners, as in "De Pascha VIII." Rather, the closing admonition insists that grace apart from any preceding works leads a man to baptism.

The Devil's Rights in Caesarius of Arles and the Eusebius Gallicanus Sermons

He also has a slightly different sense of the nature of the devil's rights over humanity. Take the hypothetical speech by Satan that appears in both "De Pascha VIII" and in Caesarius's own sermon. In both, Satan pleads to God that saving humanity by power would be unjust. However, in "De Pascha VIII," the devil dwells exclusively on his rights over humanity; the injustice would be in God taking from him what was lawfully his own. Compare C. S. Lewis's own version of the devil's speech in *The Lion, the Witch and the Wardrobe*:

> "You have a traitor there, Aslan," said the Witch ...
> "Well," said Aslan. "His offence was not against you."
> "Have you forgotten the Deep Magic?" asked the Witch.
> "Let us say I have forgotten it," answered Aslan gravely. "Tell us of this Deep Magic."
> "Tell you?" said the Witch, her voice growing suddenly shriller ... "You at least know the Magic which the Emperor put into Narnia at the very beginning. You know that every traitor belongs to me as my lawful prey and that for every treachery I have a right to a kill ... And so," continued the Witch, "that human creature is mine. His life is forfeit to me. His blood is my property."
> "Come and take it then," said the Bull with the man's head, in a great bellowing voice.

> "Fool," said the Witch with a savage smile that was almost a snarl, "do you really think your master can rob me of my rights by mere force? He knows the Deep Magic better than that. He knows that unless I have blood as the Law says, all Narnia will be overturned and perish and fire and water.
> "It is very true," said Aslan. "I do not deny it."

As the White Witch in Narnia had rights over traitors, so the devil in "De Pascha VIII" had rights over sinners. In both, the great enemy was a sort of *executor* of God's wrath.

> "Oh," said Mr. Beaver. "So *that's* how you came to imagine yourself a queen—because you were the Emperor's hangman. I see."
> "Peace, Beaver," said Aslan, with a very low growl.

That wrath must be dealt with so that it upholds God's character for the enemy to lose their rights. "'Work against the Emperor's magic?' said Aslan, turning to her with something like a frown on his face. And nobody ever made that suggestion to him again."[30]

But in Caesarius of Arles's account of the devil's plea, the injustice done to the devil if humanity should be wrenched from his grasp by force is rather different. For Caesarius, the devil is a fellow criminal, sentenced to the same sentence for the same crime by the great Judge. The plea is not that of God's hangman but rather that of a criminal angered at his coconspirator's exoneration: "It is not fitting for there to be unequal

---

30. C. S. Lewis, *The Lion, The Witch and the Wardrobe* (New York: Scholastic, 1987), 138–39.

sentences in the same case." A judge who declared one man guilty but another innocent for no reason, when both had manifestly committed the same crime, would be an unjust and inequitable judge. God is a just judge—he *must* be a just judge to be who he is—and so cannot allow this to happen. If humanity can be saved through power alone, so can the devil. And so, God decides to save mankind through a sacrifice that propitiates and a life that expiates. And thus is the devil defeated.

Caesarius is here echoing the formulation of Augustine found, for example, in the *De Trinitate*:

> Indeed, when in his death there was offered up the one most true sacrifice for us, whatever there was of the guilt due to which the principalities and powers justly held us in order to undergo punishment, he purged, abolished, eliminated; and in his resurrection, he called us, the predestined, to new life, he made righteous those he called, he glorified those he made righteous. So the devil lost his hold, in that fleshly death of humanity, [of] those whom he used to hold fast through a willing seduction, just as with a total right ...
>
> Also, for this reason, the devil believed himself to be greater than the Lord himself, in however much a degree the Lord yielded to him in his sufferings; since also it was understood concerning him what is read in the Psalm: "You diminished him a little less than the angels"; so that, working against us by wickedness as with an equal right, the Lord overcame him with a very great and lawful equity, having been murdered as an innocent man, and so he took captive captivity on account of the

sin that was done and freed us from a just captivity due to sin, with his righteous blood unjustly shed destroying the title-deed of death and redeeming sinners to make them righteous.[31]

Augustine, like Caesarius, blends together the two means of defeating the devil on the cross. The devil kills an innocent man, so losing his right to hold humanity captive; but the death of Christ the innocent man is also the sacrifice for sin that cleanses humanity from that sin due to which they were held captive. Both go together.

This joining of the two means of the devil's defeat has therefore a long pedigree in Latin theology. When even such an Augustine-skeptical preacher as that of "De Pascha VIII" uses similar formulations, we can see that this merger was not unique to one faction or another. All Caesarius was doing, then, was to state more explicitly and clearly than his Eusebius Gallicanus inspirations the way in which the sacrifice of propitiation and expiation defeated the devil. His formulation of the devil's rights over humanity was also more carefully presented, making clear that the devil was a fellow criminal, not a power with any kind of claim to counter that of God. This is a key point, one that was missed by a surprising source: Jean Rivière.

---

31. Augustine, *De Trinitate* 4.13.17 (PL 42.899–900). *Morte sua quippe uno verissimo sacrificio pro nobis oblato, quidquid culparum erat unde nos principatus et potestates ad luenda supplicia jure detinebant, purgavit, abolevit, exstinxit; et sua resurrectione in novam vitam nos praedestinatos vocavit, vocatos jurstificavit, justificatos glorificavit. Ita diabolus hominem, quem per consensionem seductum, tanquam jure integro possidebat ... in ipsa morte canis amisit ... Quocirca etiam ipso Domino se credebat diabolus superiorem, in quantum illi Dominus in passionibus cessit; quia et de ipso intellectum est quod in Psalmo legitur, 'Minuisti eum paulo minus ab Angelis:' ut ab iniquo velut aequo jure adversum nos agente, ipse occisus innocens eum jure aequissimo superaret, atque ita captivitatem propter peccatum factam captivaret, nosque liberaret a captivitate propter peccatum justa, suo justo sanguine injuste fuso mortis chirographum delens, et justificandos redimens peccatores.*

Jean Rivière on Caesarius of Arles

In his opening salvo against Joseph Turmel, *Le dogme de la rédemption chez Saint Augustin*, Rivière deals with the passage of *De Trinitate* cited above as well as others that say the same thing. He first observes that Augustine is careful not to assign to the devil any actual right over humanity that is anything other than that of performing God's just punishment: "Here we see that the devil's 'right' relies on sin and refers to the mission that requires him to punish."[32] Second, Christ's death has a dual function:

> A sacrifice first and foremost because it achieves before all else the destruction of sin; ransom follows because once sin has been destroyed, our enslavement no longer has a reason to exist.[33]

This dual function is carried out by the malice of the devil, who, albeit unknowingly, is acting as part of God's plan, as Rivière comments further:

> His insatiable malice (*avidus mortis humanae*)—and we may read into it, although it is not the point in this place, that it was served by that of the Jews of which he was the instigator—was the direct cause that allowed Christ to make use of his spirit of magnanimity even unto a sacrifice. And because it was unmerited with respect to God, this death became an act of flagrant unlawfulness

---

32. Jean Rivière, "Le dogme de la rédemption chez saint Augustin," *RevScRel* 7, no. 3 (1927): 445. *Où l'on voit que le « droit » du démon repose sur le péché et signifie la mission qui lui incombe de le punir.*

33. Rivière, "Le dogme de la rédemption chez saint Augustin (suite et fin)," *RevScRel* 8, no. 1 (1928): 32. *Sacrifice d'abord, parce qu'il s'agissait avant tout d'abolir le péché; rachat ensuite, parce qu'une fois aboli le péché notre esclavage n'a plus de raison d'être.*

with regard to him who only had a right over sinners; therefore, [it constituted] an abuse of power as a result of which he was able to be lawfully dispossessed. So the drama of Calvary gains a double result: that most importantly of reconciling us with God by the blood of a holy sacrificial victim; then, as a bonus, to show forth the divine justice with regard to Satan.[34]

As Rivière makes plain, then, in the mature understanding of Augustine, the crucifixion is chiefly a sacrifice for sin that is made to God, and then—and to a lesser degree—the means of luring the devil into forfeiting his rights over humanity. The sermon of Caesarius of Arles examined above puts forward the same concept, as one might expect of such a staunch Augustinian as the Bishop of Arles, although foregrounding the imagery of trapping the devil.

Rivière makes ample use of Caesarius's sermon in his second series of articles against Turmel, collectively entitled *Le dogme de la rédemption après saint Augustin*. However, this was written before the edition of Germain Morin was published and restored *Sermo XI* to Caesarian authorship, so in this publication, Rivière considered it an anonymous sixth-century sermon (the "Anonymous of Caspari"). He uses it alongside the Eusebius Gallicanus sermons examined above in the course

---

34. Rivière, "Rédemption chez saint Augustin (suite et fin)," 33. *Son insatiable malice (avidus mortis humanae)—et l'on sous-entendra, bien qu'il n'en soit pas question en cet endroit, qu'elle fut servie par celle des Juifs dont il était l'instigateur—fut la cause occasionnelle qui permit au Christ de développer jusqu'au sacrifice son esprit de magnanimité. Et parce qu'elle était imméritée au regard de Dieu, cette mort devenait un acte de flagrante illégalité chez celui qui n'avait de droit que sur les pécheurs, donc un abus de pouvoir à la suite duquel il put être régulièrement dépossédé. Ainsi le drame du Calvaire obtient un double résultat : celui tout d'abord de nous réconcilier avec Dieu, par le sang d'une victime sainte, puis, et comme par surcroît, de manifester la justice divine à l'égard de Satan.*

of his analysis of the doctrine of redemption taught by Gregory the Great and his contemporaries. Rivière argues that this sermon does not take sufficient care to establish that the devil in fact has no real right over humanity that is not subject to God's sovereignty and therefore represents *un indice manifeste de décadence théologique*, "a clear indication of theological decadence," from the Latin fathers like Augustine and Leo the Great. The devil's speech in particular he finds distasteful.[35] Granted that this is a sermon, and that rhetorical considerations are paramount, he still considers it a decline.

But not totally a decline: for as Rivière notes later in his series, this sermon has a full-throated conception of a sacrifice to God by which salvation is obtained. He observes:

> According to this text, it is clear that humanity's debt is understood as linked to God: *debebat Adam Deo*. We can even discern there that the discharge of this sentence is not an element but an effect of the sacrifice. *Quod ... Christus mortem suscipiendo persolvit factus utique sacrificium* [What ... Christ by undergoing death discharged, having been made indeed a sacrifice], writes the author. These two parts of the same sentence have indeed the

---

35. Rivière, "Le dogme de la rédemption après saint Augustin: deuxième partie: au temps de saint Grégoire," *RevScRel* 9, no. 3 (1929): 327–28. "There is here a new element, knowing that the devil would be able quite rightfully to complain on his own behalf if he should have been robbed by the way of power and not of 'justice.' And the idea of this possible complaint, even toned down, as with the last author [i.e., *Eusebius Gallicanus*], with the qualifications *QUASI iusta et VELUT rationabilis*, even reduced, as with Faustus, to the rank of a shadow of reason: *aliquid rationis*, constitutes nonetheless a noteworthy worsening of the system from which the great Latin fathers all carefully guarded themselves." *Il y a ici un élément nouveau, savoir que le démon pourrait à bon droit se plaindre s'il était déouillé par voie de pusiance et non de 'justice.' Et l'idée de cette réclamation possible, même estompée, comme chez le dernier auteur, des qualificatifs QUASI iusta et VELUT rationabilis, même réduite, comme chez Fauste, au rang d'une ombre de raison: aliquid rationis, n'en constitue pas moins une notable aggravation du système don't les grands Pères latins se sont tous soigneusement gardés.*

sense of stating two distinct facts, of which the logic and the grammar require that the first has its qualification and its cause in the second. Whether he fails or not to confuse it with the payment of the debt, the lines which follow right after show without any possible doubt—and it's the only point that matters here—that the just dispossession of the devil was the result of the sacrifice: *Dum erogatur sanguis pro sanguine, mors pro morte, hostia pro delicto,* SIC *diabolus quod tenebat amisit* [emphasis Rivière's: "When blood is paid out for blood, a death for death, a sacrifice for a fault, THUS the devil lost what he was holding"]. It is the expiatory sacrifice of Christ which, in the redemptive plan, is the center upon which all else depends.[36]

So the concept of a sacrifice for sin that takes on the weight of redeeming humanity from sin and the devil is certainly present and represents no diminution from the great fathers.

In 1943 (French scholars continued to produce during the war), Rivière wrote an assessment of the doctrine of the redemption in the writings of Caesarius of Arles, making use for the first time of Morin's (at that time) new edition of the sermons. The "Anonymous of Caspari" became firmly established

---

36. Rivière, "Rédemption après saint Augustin: deuxième partie," *RevScRel* 9, no. 4 (1929): 501–2. *D'après ce texte, il est clair que la dette de l'humanité s'entend par rapport à Dieu: 'Debebat Adam Deo.' On peut même y deviner que l'acquittement de cette peine n'est pas un élément, mais un effet du sacrifice.* Quod … Christus mortem suscipiendo persolvit factus utique sacrificium, *écrit l'auteur. Ces deux membres d'une même phrase ont bien l'air d'énoncer deux faits distincts, dont la logique et la grammaire exigent que le premier ait sa condition et sa cause dans le second. Qu'il faille ou non le confondre avec le paiement de la dette, les lignes qui suivent immédiatement attestent sans aucun doute possible—et c'est le point qui seul importe ici—que du sacrifice le juste dépouillement du démon fut le résultat:* Dum erogatur sanguis pro sanguine, mors pro morte, hostia pro delicto, SIC diabolus quod tenebat amisit. *C'est l'oblation expiatoire du Christ qui, dans le plan rédempteur, est le centre dont tout le reste dépend.*

as a Caesarian composition, allowing Rivière to include it in his assessment. Describing it as "a popular *Cur Deus homo* … that … deserves without doubt to be counted among the most interesting things that the new edition has restored to the bishop of Arles," Rivière nonetheless notes that its approach was different from that of Anselm in that its perspective emphasized humanity's rescue from the devil's dominion rather than humanity's reconciliation with God.[37]

Next, Rivière deals with a problem inherent in the notion that the devil has rights over humanity that God is obliged to respect. Caesarius's sermon seems to go along with the notion, implied more bluntly in "De Pascha VIII" in the Eusebius Gallicanus collection, that God is bound by a higher law than his own person in respecting the devil's rights. Yet he notes that this seems to be more an effect of rhetoric than otherwise.[38] So Rivière sees Caesarius of Arles, despite his overwrought rhetoric, maintaining that God is not bound

---

37. Jean Rivière, "La doctrine de la Rédemption chez saint Césaire d'Arles," *BLE* 44 (1943): 14. *Un 'Cur Deus homo populaire' … qui … mérite sans doute de compter parmi les plus intéressants que la nouvelle édition ait rendus à l'évêque d'Arles.*

38. Rivière, "Rédemption chez saint Césaire d'Arles," 16. "In effect, there is no reason to take literally these imperious words: *resistebat, non sinebat* [it was resisting, it was not permitting], which, at first glance, seem to compromise the freedom of the divine will, seeing as the principle is earlier stated that power preserves its own free way. As opposed to immovable obstacles that God encountered on his road, they are instead some additional considerations suitable for influencing his course of action. And the author does not fail to add that, if reason and justice have importance for human beings, for a much greater reason do they have importance for the perfect being *qui rationis atque iustitiae et auctor est et exactor* [who is the author and enforcer of both reason and justice]. It is with this meaning that the plan of our redemption was devised." *En effet, il n'y a pas lieu de prendre à la lettre ces verbes impérieux: resistebat, non sinebat, qui, de prime abord sembleraient compromettre la liberté des voies divines, puisque le principe est préalablement posé que la puissance gardait son libre jeu. A défaut d'obstacles absolus que dieu rencontrerait sur son chemin, il ne s'agit pas moins de considérations complémentaires propres à influencer le cours de son action. Et l'auteur ne manque pas d'ajouter que, si la raison et la justice ont leur poids devant les hommes, à plus forte raison devant l'Etre parfait qui rationis atque iustitiae et auctor est et exactor. C'est dans ce sens que le plan de notre Rédemption a été conçu.*

by reason and justice as if they came from outside of him and constrained him, but rather, is bound by his character and free choice.

Still, this free choice to follow reason and justice pertains to the devil's rights over humanity: "This worship of *ratio* and of *iustitia* that rules over the redemption of humanity and the 'decencies' that result from it are practiced with regard to the devil."[39] Rivière recognizes in this sermon a clear emphasis upon humanity's redemption as a rescue from the devil's (just) grip. The devil's speech, about which he in his earlier work expresses his displeasure, is proof of this: "Far from rising up against this complaint, our orator admits, albeit in quite subdued terms, that it has at least the semblance of being *quasi iusta et velut rationabilis* [as if just and as if reasonable]."[40]

The centrality of humanity's captivity to the devil in Caesarius's understanding of redemption is supported furthermore by how the atonement is carried out. First, Rivière notes that the description of Christ during the course of his life living righteously is described as resulting in the devil having nothing to condemn: "The significance of this 'justice' exceeds the moral order to affect the theological framework on which must be seen the rehabilitation of our race in the eyes of its enemy who was at first its conqueror."[41] Second, the crucifixion has as

---

39. Rivière, "Rédemption chez saint Césaire d'Arles," 17. *Ce culte de la* ratio *et de la* iustitia *qui préside à la Rédemption de l'humanité et les 'convenances' qui en découlent s'exercent par rapport au démon.*

40. Rivière, "Rédemption chez saint Césaire d'Arles," 17. *Loin de s'insurger contre cette plaidoirie, notre orateur admet, en termes d'ailleurs très atténués, qu'elle aurait au moins l'apparence d'être quasi iusta et velut rationabilis.*

41. Rivière, "Rédemption chez saint Césaire d'Arles," 18. *Mais la portée de cette 'justice' dépasse l'ordre moral pour atteindre le plan théologique, sur lequel il faut y voir la réhabilitation de notre race aux yeux de son ennemi qui fut d'abord son vainqueur.*

its chief end the defeat of the devil and the rescue of humanity from his grip: "No less than the incarnation, the passion itself aims at the same goal by another means, knowing the innocence of him who underwent the suffering … [there is] a clear allusion to the theory of the abuse of power."[42] Rivière reads Caesarius as placing at the center of the crucifixion's aims the defeat of the devil by means of tricking him into an abuse of power. There are other aspects noted, of course, but they are overshadowed by the devil's abuse of power.[43] In other words, while the notion of a sacrifice for sin that justifies humanity before God plays a foundational role in Caesarius's understanding of the aim of the crucifixion, it is ultimately less prominent than the imagery of the devil's abuse of power.

How does Rivière see this portrayal of the atonement fitting into the broader history of the doctrine of the redemption? He sees it as a representative of the sloppy thinking and speaking characteristic of too many authors coming after the fathers and before Anselm, against which the Archbishop of Canterbury reacted so fiercely.[44]

---

42. Rivière, "Rédemption chez saint Césaire d'Arles," 18. *Non moins que l'incarnation, la Passion elle-même tend au même but par un autre biais, savoir l'innocence de celui qui accepta de la souffrir … Allusion manifeste à la théorie de l'abus de pouvoir.*

43. Rivière, "Rédemption chez saint Césaire d'Arles," 19. "Not that the *mysterium crucis* [mystery of the cross] does not show forth other aspects. The author points out in the passage, citing Ephesians 5:2, a *sacrificium pro crimine hominum* [sacrifice for human crime]. He even adds that this sacrifice held a place that was in some way necessary in the divine decrees … but this theme of sacrifice soon is subsumed into the preceding theme." *Non pas que le mysterium crucis ne présente d'autres aspects. L'auteur y montre au passage, d'après Eph., V, 2, un sacrificium pro crimine hominum. Il ajoute même que cette oblation tenait une place en quelque sorte nécessaire dans les décrets divins … Mais ce thème du sacrifice ne tarde pas à retomber dans le précédent.*

44. Rivière, "Rédemption chez saint Césaire d'Arles," 20. "It is nonetheless clear that his modest *Cur Deus homo* is a historical milestone, although only in its fraught way of connecting the entire *ratio* of God's plan to the devil … There is without a doubt no better document than these ancient pages to illustrate the situation in the midst of which

Yet although we would be right to conclude, with Rivière, that Caesarius of Arles portrayed the redemption principally through the imagery of Christ's triumph over the devil, there is an important point to remember that mitigates Rivière's harsh criticism. Caesarius was drawing from two earlier sermons and making of them one whole, rather than constructing a rational treatise. We should therefore seek his understanding of the redemption in how he changed the emphases of his sources, not in the sermon as a whole. And what we find, in fact, is that Caesarius was careful to adjust his sources such that the understanding of the redemption in his sermon is closer to that of Augustine in *De Trinitate*. The devil in "De Pascha VIII" has rights as a conqueror, but Caesarius recasts these rights as being rather those of a fellow criminal. The crucifixion as a sacrifice for sin is also stated more bluntly (though Rivière acknowledges this), and its necessary place in the redemption and the conquest of the devil is made clearer. In short, while the sermon as a whole may be partially characterized by Rivière's strictures, its Caesarian changes may not.

---

the archbishop of Canterbury [Anselm] would one day find himself, and to explain the reaction on his part out of which the rational theology of the redemption was to come: *Sed et illud quod dicere solemus, Deum scilicet debuisset prius per iustitiam contra diabolum agere ut liberaret hominem … alioquin iniustam violentiam fecisset illi … non video quam vim habeat* [And as for that which we are accustomed to say, namely that God had first to act against the devil in justice to free humanity … even though he practiced unjust violence upon humanity … I do not see how it has force]." *Il n'est pas moins clair que son modeste Cur Deus homo fait date, pour ne chercher que dans ses relations problématiques avec le démon toute la ratio du plan de Dieu … Il n'est sans doute pas de meilleur documents que ces pages archaïques pour illustrer la situation en présence de laquelle devait se trouver, un jour, l'archevêque de Cantorbéry et justifier de sa part la réaction d'où la théologie rationnelle de la Rédemption allait sortir:* Sed et illud quod dicere solemus, Deum scilicet debuisset prius per iustitiam contra diabolum agere ut liberaret hominem … alioquin iniustam violentiam fecisset illi …, non video quam vim habeat.

Conclusion

The atonement as *Christus Victor* indeed dominated the imagery of the church fathers and is expressed clearly in the sermon of Caesarius of Arles and those of the Eusebius Gallicanus collection. Yet the triumph over the devil could not operate without a sacrifice of propitiation and expiation by which the sins of humanity were forgiven. The devil is defeated not only because he overstepped his bounds but also because as a result of his unjust action, Christ's sacrifice removes the cause of our bondage, namely, sin and God's wrath. The punishment to which humanity was condemned was removed by the God-man, Jesus Christ. As yet another anonymous preacher in late fifth-century Italy proclaimed:

> For the righteous man was condemned in place of the unrighteous man, and the penalty that was owed by sinners he himself received without sin, so that he might both take away the penalty and destroy the sins of those in whose place he was punished.[45]

---

45. Ps.-Aug., *Sermo* 238 4 (*PL* 39.2186). *Condemnatus est enim iustus pro iniustis, et poenam quae peccatoribus debebatur, sine peccato ipse suscepit ut illorum pro quibus punitus est, et poenam auferret, et peccata deleret.*

CHAPTER 6

HAIMO OF AUXERRE, PART I

Expiation and Propitiation in a Sacrificial Offering

T he third and final vignette belongs to the early Middle Ages, the region of central France, and the genre of biblical commentary. Around three hundred years after the death of Caesarius of Arles, we encounter the third and last figure featured in this book: Haimo of Auxerre (c. 820–875). Unlike Caesarius, who in his own time was a prominent authority figure and public actor and whom later generations remembered both as the author of many of his sermons and as a spiritual authority, Haimo was a monk who lived a quiet life of scholarly obscurity, a shadowy figure in his own time whose memory rapidly faded in later years until it was almost completely forgotten.

Yet his theological writings—sermons, but most especially biblical commentaries—were more important to Christians in the Middle Ages than those of his more well-known contemporaries like John Scotus Eriugena (c. 800–877) or Hrabanus Maurus (c. 780–856). Certainly, Hrabanus Maurus and Eriugena were more prominent in contemporary politics and more innovative in their learning, but it is Haimo whose commentaries were copied more than any other for use in the libraries of cathedrals and monasteries throughout Europe. It is Haimo's commentaries, too, that became popular in lay circles in the later Middle Ages, in which we find manuscripts belonging to wealthy merchants. The followers of Jan Hus treasured them and deployed them (as did their adversaries) in the theological controversies surging in Bohemia in the fifteenth century. Haimo's commentaries were popular across Europe throughout the Middle Ages.

The reason for concluding this book's investigation with Haimo is that it gives a view of what Christians living in what may be called the middle of the Middle Ages thought of Christ's work on the cross. Its genre, biblical commentary, is one that was of all genres the most crucial to transmitting and developing theological ideas in the medieval church. And it was written well before the great work of Anselm of Canterbury, *Cur Deus homo*, giving us a glimpse—hopefully, a surprising one—of the theological conditions leading up to Anselm's work. What it will show is that in the ninth century, the atonement was understood in a thoroughly theocentric fashion: Christ's death on the cross was a sacrifice of expiation and propitiation made by God to God, performed to reconcile God to mankind and mankind to God. It is this understanding that lies at the foundation of the medieval understanding of the atonement.

The next two chapters will carry out this study. This chapter will first outline Haimo's life and times, then give a brief account of the commentary tradition in the Carolingian era (780–900), then focus in on Haimo's own commentaries and how they went about their task of biblical exegesis. Finally, two sections from his commentaries on Romans and Hebrews, Romans 3:21–26 and Hebrews 9:1–10:18, will be examined, and what they have to say about the atonement will be laid out.

Life and Influence

Haimo of Auxerre was probably born sometime before 820 While still young, he was given as an "oblate" to the abbey of Saint-Germain in the city of Auxerre; that is, he was dedicated to the monastic life as a child and raised in the monastery. This practice, while a departure from the norms of the patristic age and abandoned in later centuries, was the usual way to populate a monastery in the Carolingian era. Haimo would have been carefully brought up and educated in both secular grammar and the Scriptures. He became a teacher of theology at Saint-Germain, and the product of this period of teaching was his remarkable output of commentaries. Unlike those of his more prominent contemporaries, these seem to be derived from lecture notes; the fact that they were quickly subsumed into the general oeuvre of the school at Saint-Germain, and their author forgotten, tends to confirm this idea. It seems that Haimo wrote his commentaries between 840 and 860. Around 865, he left Saint-Germain and became the abbot of the monastery of Cessy-les-Bois until his death around 875.

The city he resided in, Auxerre, and more specifically, the abbey of Saint-Germain, to which he belonged for most of his life, was one of the major ecclesiastical centers of the Carolingian world. Saint-Germain had special status as a royal abbey, whose abbots were appointed directly by the king and therefore not under the authority of the local bishop, although all bishops of Auxerre were consecrated, and many were buried, there. Charles the Bald, grandson of Charlemagne, was a particularly attentive patron, and two of his sons became abbots there. It was also an intellectual center; four scholars stand out between the years 835 and 893, each the student of the other: the Irishman Muretach (author of an important commentary on the Roman grammarian Donatus), who was at Saint-Germain between 835 and 840 before moving to Metz; his pupil Haimo; Haimo's student Heiric of Auxerre (fl. 850–880); and Heiric's student Remigius of Auxerre (841–908), whose wide learning in both Scripture and the classics represents the pinnacle of the scholarship produced by the clerics of Saint-Germain.

Remigius of Auxerre left Auxerre in 893 to teach in Reims, then in 900 went to Paris. He was the teacher of many clerics who would go on to become major powers in the church: for example, Seulfe, archbishop of Reims; Gerlan, archbishop of Sens; and Odo, abbot of Cluny. Everywhere he went, he brought the commentaries of Haimo and used them extensively in his teaching. His influence was thus an important reason for the wide dissemination of Haimo's commentaries by the end of the ninth century. It was not the only reason— the abbey of Saint-German in Auxerre had many connections with the broader scholarly world of the Carolingian empire— but Remigius's use of Haimo played an especially important role in the long afterlife of these works. In the twelfth century, much of Haimo's commentary was included in the great *Glossa Ordinaria*, the standard Scriptural commentary for the later Middle Ages made up of many sources, both patristic and early medieval. While (again) far from the only means by which Haimo's commentaries insinuated themselves into the spiritual bloodstream of the Middle Ages, this is the paradigmatic and most influential example. In short, Haimo's exegesis formed a substrate for all medieval exegesis, and that alone makes getting to know him a worthwhile exercise.

BIBLICAL COMMENTARIES IN
THE CAROLINGIAN ERA

Haimo worked at a time and place in which the Latin biblical commentary tradition was experiencing an extraordinary rejuvenation. With the encouragement and patronage of the Carolingian monarchs, a wide range of scholars from across Europe gathered at major royal centers like Orléans or famous monastic centers like Auxerre, Fleury, and Corbie. While other types of literature, such as poetry or commentaries on classical texts, were produced, the primary contribution of the Carolingian writers was to the genre of biblical commentary. Some were derivative—in certain cases, a patchwork of excerpts from a selection of the fathers—but many other commentators creatively used their sources to develop a new exegetical synthesis. This involved both adapting their sources to emphasize the theological and pastoral priorities of the individual authors and introducing original material.

Scholars from the British Isles, such as Alcuin of York and John Scotus Eriugena, were influential in this surge and

championed a more explicitly learned approach that pains-
takingly quoted and identified sources. Yet their role should
not be exaggerated: Spaniards like Theodolf of Orléans and
Claudius of Turin and Franks like Hrabanus Maurus were just
as instrumental and by no means always followed the insular
example. And they are just the tip of the iceberg; thirty-four different authors produced at least 130 separate exegetical treatises
between the late eighth and early tenth centuries.[1] It is a dizzy-
ing array of texts whose surface has barely begun to be scratched
by historians and theologians. Their survival in almost two
thousand manuscripts dating from every era in the Middle
Ages testifies to their importance to medieval Christianity as a
whole. Carolingian exegesis, both original and derivative, pow-
erfully shaped theological conceptions for later generations.

Although encouraged by royalty and sometimes commissioned by them, commentaries were directed primarily to the
clergy, whose education in the Scriptures was a major focus of
the energies of the so-called Carolingian Renaissance of the
eighth and ninth centuries. The Bible was at the center of the
Carolingian church; reform of the church meant, first and foremost, increasing the clerical understanding of the Scriptures.
The enthusiasm for biblical study created by this education
coursed through the clergy. So Hrabanus Maurus wrote to
Bishop Samuel of Worms (a friend from his time as a student
of Alcuin of York) in the prologue to his commentary on Paul's
letters:

---

1. C. Chazelle and B. van Name Edwards, "Introduction: The Study of the Bible and
Carolingian Culture," in *The Study of the Bible in the Carolingian Era*, ed. C. Chazelle and
B. van Name Edwards (Turnhout: Brepols, 2003), 2.

From when I first saw you and recognized the excellence
of your mind and perceived the sobriety of your habits,
I was always eager to love you with the intention of my
heart; and I chose to hold fast my sweetest friends. For
this reason, sometimes with words, sometimes also with
the writings concerning the study of the Holy Scriptures
(the reading of which was always sweet to me), I held a
conversation with you. But now that I have heard that
you wish to have a certain part of my labor, which I
worked out in a commentary on the Holy Scriptures so
far as I was able, and especially that one on the letters
of the blessed Apostle Paul, I have sent to Your Sanctity
a book of excerpts from the works of the holy fathers
on those same Letters, which I have lately completed at
the request of the monk (now deacon) Lupus, so that I
might satisfy your desire as well as bearing in mind the
profit of others who wish to be participants in our labor.[2]

Hrabanus is careful to call his commentary a *collectarium*, or
book of excerpts, from the fathers, but there is plenty of origi-
nality in his work. In any case, studying the works of the fathers
meant for the Carolingians reshaping their writings for the
present era. As this excerpt shows, such work was an integral

---

2. Hrabanus Maurus, *Enarrationum in Epistolas Beati Pauli PL* III.1273. *Ex quo vos
primum vidi, et cognovi ingenii vestri excellentiam, morumque temperantiam sensi, semper
vos cordis intentione amare studui, et dulcissimos amicos habere elegi; ideo aliquoties verbis,
aliquoties etiam scriptis de divinarum Scripturarum studiis, quarum lectio semper mihi dulcis
erat, collationem vobiscum habui. Nunc autem quia audivi quamdam partem laboris mei, quem
in expositionem sacrarum Scripturarum, prout potui, elaboravi, vos habere velle, et maxime in
Epistolas beati Pauli apostoli: transmisi sanctitati vestrae quemdam collectarium de sanctorum
Patrum opusculis in easdem Epistolas, quem nuper, rogante Lupo monacho atque tunc diacono,
confeci, ut vestro desiderio satisfacerem, et aliorum utilitatibus, qui volunt nostri laboris participes
esse, consulerem.*

part of how clerics learned their profession. Hrabanus and
Samuel clearly took great pleasure in studying the Scriptures
together, and the exchange of exegetical material in their more
mature years served the purposes of not only reaffirming their
friendship but also including others in the singular pleasure
of this study. The writing of commentaries, then, was a central part of Carolingian intellectual and ecclesiastical culture.
Haimo of Auxerre was hardly singular in his choice of subject,
even if his output was unusually vast.

Haimo of Auxerre's Commentary on the Letters of Paul

The last of Haimo's commentaries, written sometime around
860, is the Commentary on the Pauline Epistles. We know
it was written around this time because it used Hrabanus
Maurus's own commentary on Paul's letters, which was written around 840. It was by far the most popular of Haimo's
commentaries, disseminated throughout Europe during the
remainder of the Middle Ages with remarkable persistence. The
number of manuscripts in which it appears dwarfs those con-
taining the writings of other medieval theologians. Moreover,
this commentary was *used*: its readers extracted excerpts from
it with wild abandon, annotated it, made sermons out of it, and
integrated it into other exegetical works. It, therefore, more than
any other of Haimo's commentaries, some of which only appear
in a single extant manuscript, informed Christian opinion in
medieval Europe. Using this commentary for understanding
the medieval atonement therefore makes a good deal of sense.

Haimo's commentary on the letters of Paul is clearly written, easy to understand, and composed in a lively and engaging

style. This, alongside its convenient size and lack of excessive displays of erudition, accounts in large part for its popularity. Its style both engaged advanced readers and was comprehensible to beginners; it integrated a vast amount of patristic teaching into its exegesis in an accessible way. Haimo was originally a teacher of the monks at Saint-Germain, and its clear style and accessible format reflect the original classroom context of the commentary. The monk of Auxerre was interested in ensuring his students understood what they read in the Scriptures rather than being impressed with his scholarship (impressive though that was).

Its continued popularity attests to how it naturally lent itself to being a primer on biblical exegesis for even those not so deeply immersed in the Scriptures. There are a few aspects of his style that are worth considering: he writes like a grammarian; he writes at times like an encyclopedist; and he writes frequently in a dialogic form, inviting his readers to learn with him. These three aspects will now be explained, with examples drawn from his commentary on the first chapter of Romans.

Haimo's Exegetical Method

First, Haimo adapts his teacher Muretach's approach to expositing Latin grammar for biblical exegesis. This means that his biblical citations are often broken up by clarifying comments, he paraphrases frequently to explain the meaning, he highlights the intended meaning and not just the literal text, he carefully analyzes Paul's complex syntax, and he defines individual words and sometimes gives their etymologies. So, for example, in his commentary on Romans 1:7, we read:

Now it ought to be noted that the beginning of this
letter is extended by a lengthy and roundabout manner
of speaking, and on account of this, his phrasing ought
skillfully to be considered, together with the greetings of
the letters that subsist under the headings of three per-
sons. Therefore there is read through short sections and
in phrases: *Paul, a slave of Christ Jesus*, and so on, up to,
among whom you also are the called ones of Jesus Christ, and
here a phrase is placed in the middle, and finally there
is brought out, *To all those called to be saints who are in
Rome*, and here the phrase is completed; and he wishes
them good health, being tacitly understood in the third
person. For what follows, *Grace to you*, is outside the
greeting since it is in the second person that he ought to
speak after his first greeting.[3]

Here he takes the whole of Paul's introduction and examines
how it is constructed and to whom it is addressed, taking into
consideration his use of grammatical person. He also defines
words and gives them a technical grammatical term, or defines
their original Greek, as in two examples from the vice list of
Romans 1:29–30:

Insinuations. "Insinuation" [*susurro*] receives its name
from the sound of speaking since not to anyone's face

---

3. Haimo of Auxerre, *In Epistolam ad Romanos* PL 117.369. *Notandum autem quia ini-
tium hujus Epistolae longo circuitu distenditur, ac per hoc ejus distinctio solerter est consideranda:
simulque considerandum salutationes Epistolarum sub tertiis personis consistere. Legatur ergo
per commata ac sub distinctionibus:* Paulus servus Christi Jesu, *etc., usque,* In quibus estis et
vos vocati Jesu Christi, *ibique ponatur media distinctio, deinde inferatur,* Omnibus qui sunt
Romae, vocatis sanctis, *ibique fiat plena distinctio, et subaudiatur tertia persona, salutem optat.
Nam quod sequitur,* Gratia vobis, *extra salutationem est, quia secunda persona est ad quam
debet post salutationem primam loqui.*

but in their ear it speaks in order to destroy; and it is an "onomatopoeia," a name made from a sound …

The proud. The proud one is a seeker after a perverse highness, and he who wishes to greatly excel others. From this it is called by the Greek word "hyperephanos," that is, over-seeing.[4]

Or consider his commentary on Romans 1:10, where he breaks up the phrase with explanatory notes:

> *Beseeching how I might at last have at some time an easy path by God's will to come to you.* How I might, that is, "that I by some way," at last, or "in the end," or "hardly." He says rightly, Beseeching, if by some way, I might have an easy path by God's will to come to you. For there are certain men who by the permission of God—not by his will—seem to receive an easy path to evil, for instance when they hasten to carry out murder or some other wickedness. But the apostle accounts as nothing all easy paths that come without the will of God and assigns them no place.[5]

This is the patient voice of the grammarian, explaining a complicated text by breaking it up into pieces and then showing how

---

4. Haimo of Auxerre, *In Epistolam ad Romanos PL* 117.377–78. Susurrones. *Susurro de sono locutionis nomen accepit, quia non in facie alicui, sed in aure loquitur, detrahendo: et est onomatopoeia, nomen de sono factum … Superbos. Superbus est perversae celsitudinis appetitor, et qui praecellere vult alios. Unde Graeco vocabulo hyperephanos, id est super apparens vocatur.*

5. Haimo of Auxerre, *In Epistolam ad Romanos PL* 117.370. Obsecrans, si quomodo tandem aliquando prosperum iter habeam in voluntate Dei veniendi ad vos. *Si quomodo, id est si aliquo modo, tandem, ad ultimum vel vix. Bene dicit* obsecrans si aliquo modo prosperum iter habeam in voluntate Dei veniendi ad vos, *quoniam sunt quidam qui Dei permissione, non voluntate, prosperum iter videntur accipere ad malum, si quando homicidium aut aliquod festinent scelus perpetrare. Sed Apostolus omnia prospera quae sine voluntate Dei veniunt nihili pendit, et pro nihilo deputat.*

it all fits together. Haimo wishes his students to understand the minutia of the text precisely.

Second, Haimo enlivens his exegesis by inserting general comments on aspects of history, physics, and natural philosophy. For example, he gives a brief account of pagan idolatry under Romans 1:23.[6] Here we have not only an account of which gods were worshipped by which nations but also a brief note, as one might find in an ancient encyclopedia such as that of Pliny the Elder or Isidore of Seville, on the habits of the crocodile. The word of God describes the real world, after all, and these notes serve to reinforce the truth and applicability of Scripture.

---

6. Haimo of Auxerre, *In Epistolam ad Romanos PL* 117.374–75. "*And they exchanged the glory of the incorruptible God for the likeness of a corruptible image of man, birds, beasts and snakes.* Every creature which is able to be turned into something better or worse is corruptible. For instance: Man is corruptible since he is corrupted through old age, through weakness, and at the last when also he returns to dust through death. But the Almighty God, who is not able to be changed, whether for better or for worse, but always remains the same or uniform, alone is incorruptible. His glory and worship, which alone befits him who is God, men exchanged for the likeness of other men, as the Assyrians did, who worshiped the image of Bel the father of King Ninus in place of God, so too the Sidonians, who called him Baal; the Jews, Beelzebub; and the Philistines, Zebet. And they did this not only with the likeness of mortal and corruptible man but also with the likeness of birds, like the Romans who worshipped a goose and the Egyptians who worshipped a hawk; so too with the likeness of beasts, like the Egyptians who worshipped Apis, that is, a white cow; and with the likeness of serpents, just as the Babylonians who worshipped a dragon and the Egyptians who worshipped a crocodile, which is a watery serpent, swimming in water like a fish and feeding on land like a cow." *Et mutaverunt gloriam incorruptibilis Dei in similitudinem imaginis corruptibilis hominis, et volucrum, et quadrupedum, et serpentium. Omnis creatura quae mutari potest in melius aut in deterius corruptibilis est. Verbi gratia: Homo corruptibilis est quia corrumpitur per senectutem, per infirmitatem: ad extremum etiam quando per mortem redigitur in pulverem: Deus vero omnipotens, qui non potest mutari, aut in melius aut in deterius, sed semper idem et aequalis manet, incorruptibilis solus existit. Cujus gloriam et culturam, quae soli convenit ei qui Deus est, mutaverunt homines in similitudinem aliorum hominum, ut Assyrii, qui simulacrum Beli patris Nini regis pro Deo colebant; et Babylonii idipsum, quem vocabant Bel, Sydonii Baal, Judaei Beelzebub, et Philisthaei Zebet: et non solum in similitudinem hominis mortui et corruptibilis, sed etiam in similitudinem volucrum, sicuti Romani qui colebant anserem, et Aegyptii qui colebant accipitrem. In similitudinem quoque quadrupedum, sicut Aegyptii qui colebant apim, hoc est vaccam albam. In similitudinem etiam serpentium, sicut Babylonii qui colebant draconem, et Aegyptii qui colebant crocodilum, qui est serpens aquaticus, natans in aqua ut piscis, pascens in terra ut bos.*

Haimo's habit of including his readers in a dialogue, deriving in part from the original classroom context of the commentary, adds to the attraction of his oeuvre. He asks questions that naturally arise from the text, then answers them; he also addresses his readers and admonishes them. Haimo frequently "breaks the fourth wall" of his commentary and addresses his readers as if they were students in his classroom. Haimo of Auxerre delighted in teaching; this much is clear from his commentary on Paul, both in the liveliness of its exposition and in his clear passion for his students' accurate knowledge of the text. In this, we can catch a glimpse of the man at work and the atmosphere of his lectures and understand to some degree why his Scriptural exposition was so beloved. His passion and love for teaching shine in a note on Romans 1:12:

> Teachers are comforted by the progress of their students, namely, when they discover the stability of faith in them; and, on the other hand, students are comforted when the grace of the Holy Spirit is heaped upon them by the coming of their teachers, or when they understand that his knowledge and faith agrees with and is a participant with the knowledge and faith of their teachers.[7]

This quiet voice, from a man who avoided the limelight but worked faithfully to instruct his pupils in the Scriptures, reverberated throughout the Middle Ages in ways that are only now beginning to be understood.

---

7. Haimo of Auxerre, *In Epistolam Romanos PL* 117.371. *Consolantur magistri de profectu discipulorum, quando scilicet stabilimentum fidei reperiunt in illis: econtra consolantur discipuli dum adventu magistrorum cumulatur illis gratia Spiritus sancti, vel dum suam scientiam et fidem magistrorum scientiae aut fidei concordare et comparticipare intelligunt.*

It is fitting that such a man's conception of the atonement should be the final vignette of this book. It is in the commentaries and sermons of Haimo that we see the ground-level theology of medieval monks and clergy, their passion for the Scriptures, and their love for God and his gospel. What we find in Haimo, that great synthesizer of the patristic and medieval tradition, is that Christ's death on the cross is foundationally a sacrifice of expiation and propitiation made by God to God. To demonstrate this, in the rest of this chapter and the next we will look at the atonement in portions of Haimo's commentaries on two New Testament epistles: Romans and Hebrews.

THE ATONEMENT IN HAIMO'S COMMENTARY ON ROMANS

Romans 3:21–26 is key to understanding the doctrine of the redemption. Haimo's commentary spends a good deal of time on this section, so it is worth examining in detail what he has to say about it. In this case, as we will see, the atonement is viewed chiefly through the lens of expiation. The passage from Romans runs as follows:

> But now apart from the law the righteousness of God has been made known, to which the Law and the Prophets testify. [22] This righteousness is given through faith in Jesus Christ to all who believe. There is no difference between Jew and Gentile, [23] for all have sinned and fall short of the glory of God, [24] and all are justified freely by his grace through the redemption that came by Christ Jesus. [25] God presented Christ as a sacrifice of atonement, through the shedding of his blood—to be received by faith. He did this to demonstrate his righteousness, because in his

forbearance he had left the sins committed beforehand unpunished—[26] he did it to demonstrate his righteousness at the present time, so as to be just and the one who justifies those who have faith in Jesus.

Haimo's commentary uses the Vulgate, which has some slight differences with a modern translation like the NIV. The main difference is in the division of the phrase εἰς ἔδειξιν τῆς δικαιοσύνης αὐτοῦ διὰ τὴν πάρεσιν τῶν προγεγονότων ἁμαρτημάτων ἐν τῇ ἀνοχῇ τοῦ θεοῦ, "in the demonstration of his righteousness through the overlooking of preceding faults in the forbearance of God." Modern translations reflect the interpretation of the passage taking it to refer to God's delay of judgment upon sinners until Christ's passion, while ancient and medieval interpreters, at least in the Latin tradition, took it to refer to baptism, in which sins committed previously by the individual being baptized would be forgiven. This distinction should not be pressed too far because the modern interpretation was also noted by the medievals, as will be seen. But let us see what Haimo has to say about Romans 3:21–26 as a whole.

Haimo begins by clarifying what the *iustitia Dei*, the "righteousness of God," means, and he offers two interpretations.[8]

---

8. Haimo of Auxerre, *In Epistolam Romanos PL* 117.390. "The righteousness of God at the present time was revealed without the law: not the righteousness alone with which he himself is righteous, or with which he is made righteous who is in essence righteousness itself, but rather that with which he fills the impious when compassionately he makes faithful from unfaithful, from an adulterer and fornicator he makes a chaste and continent man, from unrighteous and sinner makes a righteous man and a lover of virtue. This righteousness was revealed in Christ and given *without the law*, that is, without observing the law, since no part of the law regarding mysteries and sacrifices is passed on to be observed; but he says: *He who will believe and be baptized will be saved.* That is, he will be righteous. We are also able to understand that same righteousness of God the Father as the Son, by whom and through whom we are made righteous, since without observing the law through the works of his deity he was revealed to be the Son of God." *Justitia Dei in praesenti tempore sine lege manifestata est: non ea solummodo qua ipse justus est, aut qua justificetur qui essentialiter ipsa justitia est, sed qua induit impium, quando misericorditer de*

First, the "righteousness of God" refers not to one of God's attributes but rather to that righteousness which he imparts to us to make us holy. Second, Haimo suggests that the "righteousness of God" refers to Christ, by whose work we are made righteous. Here we also see the fundamental union that Haimo insists upon between individual faith and the act of baptism in the achievement of salvation—"He who will believe and be baptized will be saved," quotes Haimo from the extended ending of Mark (16:16). This will come up again and is fundamental to his interpretation of the entire passage of Romans.

He then proceeds to explain how the Old Testament predicts our salvation through Christ, focusing again on baptism:

> *Having been testified about by the law and the prophets.* The righteousness of baptism, by which we are made righteous, is testified about through the law, when it is said, *In the last days the Lord will circumcise your heart,* that is, take away your sins, and will make you righteous through baptism. It is also borne witness to through the prophets, when it is said, *He will bear our iniquities, and he will carry our sins.* And elsewhere: *I will pour out upon you a clean water, and you will be cleansed from all your impurities.* And by this, Christ himself, our righteousness, has a witness from the law and the prophets.[9]

---

infideli facit fidelem, de adultero et fornicatore facit castum et continentem, de injusto et peccatore facit justum et amatorem virtutum. Quae justitia in Christo est revelata, et data sine lege, id est sine observatione legali, quia nulli lex secundum mysteria et sacrificia traditur jam observanda; sed dicit: Qui crediderit et baptizatus fuerit, salvus erit. Hoc est justus erit. Possumus etiam ipsam justitiam Dei Patris, id est Filium intelligere a quo et per quem justificamur, quia sine observatione legis per opera deitatis manifestatus est Filius Dei esse.

9. Haimo of Auxerre, *In Epistolam Romanos PL* 117.391. *Testificata a lege et prophetis. Justitia baptismatis, qua justificamur, per legem testificatur, dum dicitur:* In novissimis diebus circumcidet Dominus cor tuum, *id est auferet peccata tua, et justificabit te per baptismum.*

The act of baptism is one that cleanses us from both original sin and the sins committed before we are baptized—the standard patristic and medieval understanding of the nature of the sacrament. However, it is important to remember, as Haimo will shortly make clear, that baptism has this power because it is linked indissolubly with Christ's sacrifice and our individual faith. Note that the final comment in this section states that these prophecies, linked in the first few comments to baptism, refer in fact to Christ.

Next, he turns to the importance of individual faith in salvation and the object of that saving faith, Christ's passion:

> But the righteousness of God, that is, the justification by which we are made righteous by God, comes upon all the believing Jews and gentiles, through the faith of Jesus Christ, by which we believe him to be the Son of God the Father; and he gave a reason why he said, upon all who believe the righteousness of God will come, when immediately he adds: for there is no distinction, that is, there is no difference between Jews and gentiles, since as the Jews were found to be sinners, so also were the gentiles. And so it continues: For all have sinned and lack the glory of God, that is, all lack forgiveness and pardon for sins, Jews as much as gentiles; on account of which God ought to be glorified.[10]

Testificatur et per prophetas, dum dicitur: Ipse iniquitates nostras portabit, et peccata nostra ipse tollet. Et alibi: Effundam super vos aquam mundam, et mundabimini ab omnibus inquinamentis vestris. Ipse quoque Christus justitia, nostra testimonium, habet a lege et prophetis.

10. Haimo of Auxerre, In Epistolam Romanos PL 117.391. Justitia autem Dei, id est justificatio qua justificamur a Deo super omnes Judaeos et gentiles credentes venit. Per fidem Jesu Christi, qua credimus illum Filium Dei esse Patris, reditque causam quare dixerit: super omnes qui credunt justitiam Dei venturam, cum protinus subdit: Non est enim distinctio,

Belief is here front and center, as opposed to baptism, as in
the previous comment. All require true belief to be saved since
all are sinners, regardless of their works. "The faith of Jesus
Christ," a term much debated in modern theology, refers here
(and elsewhere for Haimo) to the individual Christian's faith in
the work of Christ, not to Christ's faithfulness in carrying out
the Father's plan of salvation. It is part and parcel of Haimo's
emphasis upon the connection between baptism and right faith
necessary for the individual's salvation to be achieved.

Haimo now embarks upon his most in-depth examination
of a passage in this particular section. The connection between
baptism and faith is made explicit:

> *Having been made righteous freely through his grace; through
> the redemption which is in Christ Jesus. Freely* he says, that
> is, without any preceding merits. For example, he who
> comes to baptism has done at no time anything good, is
> baptized, and at once is made righteous. Behold, freely
> he is made righteous through grace, that is, through the
> gift of God, and this, *through the redemption which is in
> Christ Jesus,* not in works of the law. Our own redemp-
> tion by which we are redeemed and through which we are
> made righteous is the passion of Christ; when it has been
> joined with baptism, it makes a man righteous through
> faith, and afterward, through repentance.
>
> For those two are so mutually joined that the one is
> not able to make a man righteous without the other. For
> the faith of the Lord's passion does not cleanse a man

---

id est nulla est differentia inter Judaeos et gentiles, quia ut Judaei peccatores sunt inventi, ita et
gentiles. Unde sequitur: Omnes enim peccaverunt et egent gloria Dei, id est indulgentia et
venia peccatorum indigent omnes, tam Judaei quam gentiles: pro qua glorificandus est Deus.

without the water of baptism unless perchance what is in martyrdom is received in place of baptism; nor is the water of baptism able to purify a man without the faith of the Lord's passion. Therefore, they are joined together, and thus, they will provide a complete redemption and a complete cleansing. Therefore, neither a Jew nor a gentile is made righteous by his own works since each is a transgressor of his own law: the Jew, namely, of the natural and written law, but the gentile, of the natural law. But [each is justified] with the redemption with which Christ redeems us by his blood and with faith; and with the water of baptism with which whosoever has been reborn, if he should immediately die, he will be saved to life, but if he should live, he ought to adorn his faith with works, *since faith without works is dead.*[11]

Several elements in this passage need to be enumerated. First, baptism is an example of our freely given redemption apart from works but is not its entire definition. It must be joined with Christ's work on the cross and put into action

---

11. Haimo of Auxerre, *In Epistolam Romanos* PL 117.391. Justificati gratis per gratiam ipsius: per redemptionem, quae est in Christo Jesu. Gratis *dicit, id est sine ullis praecedentibus meritis. Verbi gratia: Qui ad baptismum venit, nihil unquam boni fecit, baptizatur, statimque justificatur. Ecce gratis justificatur per gratiam, id est per donum Dei: et hoc per redemptionem* quae est in Christo Jesu, *non in operibus legis. Redemptio nostra qua sumus redempti, et per quam justificamur, passio Christi est quae, juncta baptismo, justificat hominem per fidem: et postmodum per poenitentiam. Ita enim illa duo mutuo sunt conjuncta, ut unum sine altero hominem non possit justificare. Nam neque fides Dominicae passionis sine aqua baptismatis hominem mundat, nisi forte in martyrio quod pro baptismate accipitur: neque aquam baptismi sine fide Dominicae passionis purificare hominem valet. Jungantur ergo simul sicque praestabunt perfectam redemptionem, perfectamque mundationem. Itaque neque Judaeus, neque gentilis suis justificatur operibus, cum uterque sit praevaricator suae legis: Judaeus videlicet naturalis et scriptae; gentilis autem naturalis. Sed redemptione qua Christus nos redemit suo sanguine et fide; et aqua baptismatis, qua quisque renatus, si statim obierit, salvabitur in vita: si autem vixerit, debet ornare fidem operibus,* quia fides sine operibus mortua est.

by individual faith. Second, baptism and individual faith in
Christ are tightly bound together. As Haimo makes clear, being
baptized is not a magic spell that saves us; it must be done to
someone having true faith to be effective. The same applies to
faith: without baptism, it does not work. This is typical patristic and Augustinian teaching, including the exception to the
rule that occurs when someone is martyred for the faith before
they can be baptized. In that case, their shed blood serves as
the waters of baptism for them. In any case, the point is that
salvation is achieved apart from works. That being said, once
one is baptized, one ought to show forth one's true faith by
doing works pleasing to God.

The atonement so far has only featured indirectly as the
object of the believer's faith and that which works in some
unsaid way to forgive sins. What is this redemption through
Christ's blood, exactly? Although this is not Haimo's focus in
this commentary, it will become clearer what he thinks about
Christ's sacrifice on the cross. He goes on:

> But it ought to be noted that he says, *through the redemp-
> tion which is in Christ Jesus.* For through redemption, cap-
> tives are redeemed who were taken captive by enemies.
> Now how is a man able to be taken captive, since God
> is everywhere? But he was taken captive in spirit by the
> devil when he subjected himself to the devil by trans-
> gressing the law of God and when he began to serve vices
> and idols. But this captivity was dissolved when the spirit
> returned to God and understood that it was sick, but

God was a physician; and the finished redemption was made clear in the shedding of Christ's blood.[12]

Here we have the atonement as a response to humanity's predicament, which is stated in terms of captivity to the devil. This captivity is a willing one, brought on by sin and the breaking of God's law. It is removed by individual repentance and faith in God, the great physician. Christ's blood plays an important role in this, but what it does is not yet obvious.

Haimo continues by explaining the next verse, in which the means by which the finished redemption was made clear is expounded:

Whom God the Father put forward as a propitiator through faith in his blood. God the Father put forward his Son, that is, he decreed and foreordained him as a propitiator and reconciler, so that he might make God the Father propitious toward us and easily appeased through the faith of his passion, or he placed him in the open before the eyes of all so that he might save all those believing in him, since when we believe in him and we confess his blood shed for us, without which we are not able to be made righteous, we are made righteous entirely.[13]

---

12. Haimo of Auxerre, *In Epistolam Romanos* PL 117.391–92. *Notandum vero quod dicit per redemptionem quae est in Christo Jesu. Nam per redemptionem captivi redimuntur qui ab hostibus captivatur. Quomodo ergo homo captivari potuit, cum Deus ubique sit? Sed captivatus est animo a diabolo, quando diabolo se subdidit praevaricando legem Dei, et quando vitiis et idolis coepit servire. Haec autem captivitas soluta est, dum animus ad Deum rediit, et se infirmum, illum vero medicum intellexit; perfectaque redemptio in effusione sanguis Christi patuit.*

13. Haimo of Auxerre, *In Epistolam Romanos* PL 117.392. Quem proposuit Deus Pater *propitiatorem per fidem in sanguine ipsius. Filium suum proposuit Deus Pater, id est decrevit et praefinivit propitiatorem et reconciliatorem, ut ipse nobis propitium faceret Deum Patrem et placabilem per fidem passionis suae, vel in promptu ante oculos omnium posuit, ut omnes salvaret in se credentes, quia dum in eum credimus, et ejus sanguinem pro nobis fusum confitemur, sine quo justificari non possumus, ex integro justificamur.*

Christ the Son of God is the propitiator of God, that is, one who makes God favorable toward humanity. The emphasis is still on faith as the means of salvation, however, so it is the individual's faith in Christ's passion that appeases God, not the passion itself; yet the passion enables this propitiation to take place. The passion instead begins to reveal itself, in Haimo's telling, as a sacrifice of expiation that cleanses us from sin since the shed blood of Christ makes us righteous in a way to which faith is incidental.

The meaning of righteousness is again treated in the next section, but alongside it, Christ's shed blood takes on a clearer meaning.[14] Haimo reiterates his twofold definition of righteousness in Romans but then goes on to explain the nature of Christ's passion in greater detail. First, we become righteous by means of the shedding of Christ's blood—in other words, expiation. Second, God handed over his Son to death for our sake—an echo of substitution, given that death here is clearly

---

14. Haimo of Auxerre, *In Epistolam Romanos PL* 117.392. "*For the demonstration of his righteousness;* understand 'to inferiors'. *At this time,* that is, in the latest age. Righteousness in this place is able to be understood in two ways: namely, either Christ himself who makes us righteous or the righteousness by which God the Father makes righteous those believing in his Son. Therefore, God the Father showed openly his righteousness, that is his Son, or since he makes us righteous by the shedding of the blood of his Son *at this time,* that is, from his advent up to the end of the age, since if he had not wanted to make us righteous, he would not have handed his Son over to death for our sake, he who did no sin. He also put him forward to come and suffer, *For the forgiveness of preceding faults,* that is of the original fault which we take from our parents before we are born, or of all the sins which we commit before baptism." Ad ostensionem justitiae suae; *subaudis ab inferioribus. In hoc tempore, id est in novissima aetate. Justitia in hoc loco duplici modo potest intelligi: videlicet vel ipse Christus qui justificat nos, vel justitia qua justificat Deus Pater credentes in Filium suum. Ostendit ergo manifeste Deus Pater justitiam suam, id est Filium suum, vel quia nos justificat in effusione sanguinis Filii sui in hoc tempore, id est ab adventu illius usque in finem saeculi, quia nisi nos justificare voluisset, ad mortem Filium suum pro nobis non tradidisset, qui non fecerat ullum peccatum. Proposuit etiam illum venire et pati propter remissionem praecedentium delictorum, id est originalium quae ex parentibus trahimus antequam nascamur, vel omnium peccatorum quae committimus ante baptismum.*

a punishment. Third, Christ's shed blood empowers the sacrament of baptism, by which our original sin from Adam and our sins committed before baptism are forgiven. The emphasis is on cleansing from sin as the means of forgiveness.

The final verses in this passage are treated briskly, with the emphasis once again upon faith and its centrality to salvation:

> *In the restraint of God*, that is, to show forth the patience of God, since when we sin we are not immediately punished, but we are awaited by his patience and endurance for repentance. Unless there was this restraint by God, at the time of the first man, there would have been an end to humanity through his judgment.

> *For the demonstration of his righteousness at that time*, understand in the latest time, that is, for this reason he foreordained his Son to be made a propitiator for us so that he might show forth his righteousness through him, and the compassion by which he awaits us unto repentance.

> *So that he might be righteous.* He is righteous who delivers what he promises. So also God the Father promised his Son to us, and in him, justification: since he clearly fulfilled it, sending him into the world through the mystery of the incarnation, by the faith of whose passion we are made righteous, washed by the water of baptism. And so it follows: *And making righteous him who from faith belongs to Jesus Christ*, that is, whatsoever man having faith; not, nevertheless, through the works of the law does he make him righteous, but through the faith of

Jesus Christ, since without the faith of him we are not
able to be made righteous.[15]

First, God's patience is explained as referring to his attitude
toward both the individual and humanity as a whole. Second,
Haimo now gives righteousness its third meaning in the passage,
as one of the attributes of God. This righteousness is demonstrated by Christ's foreordained suffering and the solution to
human sin being promised and provided by that suffering. Here
again, however, we have the focus of the redemption being the
importance of individual faith in Christ's passion rather than
the details of the atonement.

Haimo of Auxerre's commentary on Romans 3:21–26 displays how he integrated his understanding of Christ's death
as a sacrifice of expiation into a broader discussion of the role
individual faith plays in redemption and the nature of righteousness. This is not a systematic treatment of atonement but
an exposition of a passage of Scripture dealing mainly with
faith and righteousness. Nevertheless, Haimo's assumptions
about Christ's work on the cross may be discerned. First, note
that the devil only appears once, and the captivity into which
he leads humanity is one brought about by the sin of Adam.

---

15. Haimo of Auxerre, *In Epistolam Romanos PL* 117.392. *In sustentatione Dei, id est
ad patientiam Dei manifestandam, quia cum peccamus non statim punimur; sed eius patientia
atque sufferentia ad poenitentiam exspectamur. Quae sustentatio nisi a Deo esset, in primo
homine finis hominum per judicium fuisset. Ad ostensionem justitiae suae in hoc tempore,
subaudis novissimo, id est ad hoc praefinivit propitiatorem fieri nobis Filium suum, ut suam
justitiam ostenderet per illum, et misericordiam qua nos exspectat ad poenitentiam. Ut ipse sit
justus. Justus est qui quae promittit, tribuit. Ita et Deus Pater promisit nobis Filium suum, et
in eo justificationem: quod utique adimplevit, mittens illum in mundum per incarnationis mysterium, cuius passionis fide justificamur, abluti aqua baptismatis. Unde sequitur: Et justificans
eum qui ex fide est Jesu Christi, hoc est quemlibet hominem fidem Jesu Christi habentem:
non tamen per opera legis justificat illum, sed per fidem Jesu Christi, quoniam absque eius fide
non valemur justificari.*

In other words, there is no notion here that human beings are just victims of the devil's power. Our own sin is the problem, and that sin must be dealt with before we can be saved. Second, Christ's death cleanses us from sin in accordance with God's predetermined plan. The cross is neither a tragedy nor a trick played on the devil but a vital part of the divine plan of salvation that deals with human sin and reconciles humanity to God. The cross also brings about the propitiation of God by expiating human sin and being the object of a faith that pleases God.

Haimo's Commentary on Hebrews Chapter 9

The ninth and tenth chapters of the Letter to the Hebrews comprise the most sustained treatment in the New Testament of the sacrificial nature of Christ's death on the cross and its foreshadowing by the Levitical sacrifices of the Old Testament. What Haimo of Auxerre has to say about these chapters is therefore of great interest to us. His careful (and lengthy) treatment of these two chapters shows how Christ's death on the cross as a sacrifice of expiation and propitiation made to God by God lies at the center of Haimo's understanding of the atonement.

Rather than go phrase by phrase, as in the commentary on Romans analyzed above, I will summarize some parts due to the length of the passages in question. Hebrews 9 opens with a description of the tabernacle and its ceremonies, a description to which Haimo assigns spiritual meanings. Haimo then goes on to explain, following the text of Hebrews, that these ceremonies and the old law they represented were unable to ultimately reconcile humanity to God and forgive sin because they were a shadow of Christ's work. He writes:

> For this reason, the priest used to enter alone with the blood into the Holy of Holies: that he might teach that the kingdom of heaven was still inaccessible to mortals until Christ should come, who, having finished his passion, opened for us the gate of the heavenly kingdom, laying open the curtain, that is, heaven.[16]

Haimo then explains how the sacrament of baptism likewise fulfills the ritual washings of the old law.

After describing the tabernacle, the rite of the Day of Atonement, and their inability to cleanse sinners, the author of Hebrews proceeds to explain how Christ was the fulfillment of what they stood for. Haimo comments:

> *But Christ, standing forth as the priest of future goods, for a greater and more perfect tabernacle not made with hands, that is, not of this creation.* The priest of the Jews, who once a year used to enter with blood behind the curtain into the Holy of Holies and then pray for the people, represented Christ, just as has been declared now in many places, who with the blood of his passion opened heaven and entered into the hidden places of the heavenly homeland, where now he stands before the face of God the Father praying for us.[17]

---

16. Haimo of Auxerre, *In Epistolam Hebraeos* PL 117.881. *Ideo solus pontifex cum sanguine intrabat semel in Sancta sanctorum, ut discamus quia coeleste regnum inaccessibili erat adhuc mortalibus, quoadusque veniret Christus qui, expleta passione sua, aperiret nobis januam patriae coelestis, reserato velo, id est coelo.*

17. Haimo of Auxerre, *In Epistolam Hebraeos* PL 117.882. Christus autem assistens pontifex futurorum bonorum, per amplius et perfectius tabernaculum non manufactum,

Christ's blood is the entry key into heaven, just as the blood of a lamb was the entry key into the Holy of Holies. Haimo then explains that the words "of future goods" refer either to Christ's life, death, and resurrection, which at the time of the first tabernacle were in the future, or to the Christian's future bliss in heaven obtained by Christ's priestly intercession. The "greater and more perfect" tabernacle is the body of Christ.

Haimo then examines the significance of Christ's blood for our salvation and the reason why it is so superior to the blood of animals:

> Not through the blood of goats or calves but through his own blood he entered once into the holy places having uncovered eternal redemption, not with the blood of lawful animals, by which complete justification was not able to be given, but with the blood of his passion he entered into the heavenly homeland, he by whose blood all have been redeemed and completely justified, not by a temporary but by an eternal redemption. Concerning this redemption, it is said through Zechariah the father of the blessed John: He has visited us and has carried out the redemption of our people. But redemption pertains to captives, and we had been made captive, having been made captive by the devil in our first parent.[18]

---

id est non huius creationis. Pontifex Judaeorum qui semel in anno cum sanguine introibat intra velum in Sancta sanctorum oraturus pro populo Christum significabat sicut jam multis in locis declaratum est, qui cum sanguine passionis suae reserato coelo ingressus est secreta patriae coelestis, ubi nun assistit vultui Dei Patris, orans pro nobis.

18. Haimo of Auxerre, In Epistolam Hebraeos PL 117.883. Neque per sanguinem hircorum aut vitulorum sed per proprium sanguinem semel introivit in sancta aeterna redemptione inventa, non cum sanguine legalium animalium, a quo perfecta justificatio non poterat dari: sed cum sanguine passionis suae introivit in patriam coelestem quo sanguine omnes sunt redempti, perfecteque justificati non temporali, sed aeterna redemptione. De hac redemptione dicitur per

Here the devil makes a brief appearance as the one at whose instigation Adam and Eve fell into sin. However, the focus is on the blood of Christ as the means of redemption. The devil is not defeated save by his victims being cleansed from sin.

The argument of Hebrews then turns to the superiority of Christ's blood over the blood of animals, and Haimo comments:

> If the blood of irrational animals was able to cleanse our conscience according to the flesh, and, as it seemed at that time, if any unclean person was made holy who had been sprinkled with that blood, how much more was the blood of Christ able to cleanse our own soul and to fully make it righteous. But lest anyone should think that the full justification and cleansing comes forth from the sprinkling of that blood of the Law, the Apostle adds beneath that the cleansing of the flesh according to the law is given for that same flesh; as if he says, "the flesh indeed is made holy and is cleansed because of the command of the law, but nevertheless the soul is not expiated."[19]

For Haimo, Christ's blood cleanses the sinner from his sin in a way that the blood of animals shed according to the Law of Moses could not; namely, in the soul itself. He goes on:

Zachariam patrem beati Joannis: Visitavit nos et fecit redemptionem plebis suae. Redemptio autem ad captivos pertinet, et nos captivi eramus, captivati a diabolo in primo parente nostro.

19. Haimo of Auxerre, In Epistolam Hebraeos PL 117.883. Si sanguis animalium irrationabilium poterat mundare conscientiam nostram secundum carnem, et, sicut tunc temporis videbatur, sanctificabatur si quis immundus aspersus fuisset illo sanguine: multo magis sanguis Christi poterat mundare animam nostram et plenissime justificare. Sed ne quis putaret plenam justificationem et emundationem provenire aspersione illius sanguinis legalis, subintulit Apostolus carnis emundationem secundum legem per illum dari; quasi dicat: Sanctificatur quidem caro et mundatur propter legis praeceptum, sed tamen anima non expiatur.

He added, too, a different reason, through which he showed that the same blood of animals was not without stain, saying concerning Christ: *Who through the Holy Spirit offered his own self, without stain, to God.* The Holy Spirit, who filled that man in the virgin's womb, guarded him so that no sin from this world should pass into him and that he might be a sacrifice without stain in a pleasing aroma to God the Father. He will cleanse our conscience, that is our mind, from deathly works. Deathly works are sins, which slay the soul. For just as the spirit lives in its virtues, which are called the works of life, so it dies in its vices and sins and with them is dragged to the death of eternal damnation.[20]

Here we see Haimo explaining the nature of Christ's death on the cross as a sacrifice of expiation made to God. The Holy Spirit kept the incarnate Christ from sin, thus enabling him to be a sin offering ("in a pleasing aroma" is the biblical formula used also by Caesarius of Arles to denote a sacrifice of propitiation, as noted in the previous chapter) that was better than the worldly sin offerings of the old covenant. Such an offering cleanses the soul in a way that an offering of animals could not.

Haimo then goes on to connect this sacrifice with how it is applied to the Christian—namely, through faith and baptism.

---

20. Haimo of Auxerre, *In Epistolam Hebraeos PL* 117.883. *Addidit quoque differentiae causae, per quam demonstravit illum sanguinem animalium non esse immaculatum, dicens de Christo:* Qui per Spiritum sanctum semetipsum obtulit immaculatum Deo. *Spiritus sanctus, qui replevit illum hominem in utero virginali, custodivit eum ut absque peccato ab hoc mundo transiret, essetque immaculatum sacrificium in odorem suavitatis Deo Patri. Emundationem conscientiam nostram, id est mentem nostram ab operibus mortuis. Opera mortua sunt peccata, quae animam occidunt. Sicut enim anima vivit virtutibus, quae opera vitae appellantur, ita moritur vitiis et peccatis, simulque trahitur ad mortem aeternae perditionis.*

A sinner is cleansed through Christ's sacrifice by faith in that
sacrifice, repentance from sin, and baptism done in faith.
Furthermore, this cleansing allows the sinner to enter into
God's presence in the same way that the sacrifices of the old
covenant enabled the Israelite sinner to enter into the temple.

The argument of Hebrews then turns to a discussion of
Christ as mediator of a new covenant and the connection
between a covenant (using a will as an example) and the shedding of blood. Haimo explains the example of the will and the
necessity of a death to confirm it. He writes:

> In this way, the covenant of eternal life that we receive
> from Christ is not otherwise able to be made firm for us
> unless by his very death he should have confirmed it. For
> so great was our sin that there was no other way we were
> able to be redeemed and saved unless the only-begotten
> Son of God should have died for us. And since we had
> been made unworthy for that which had to follow what
> he himself promised, he himself was made a mediator
> for us by his death, so that through his unowed death
> he might take away what we owed.[21]

As the maker of a will had to die for the will's promises to be
made firm, so Christ's new covenant with us had to be made
firm with a death. Haimo explains the enacting of the new
covenant's promises by describing what it was that Christ's

---

21. Haimo of Auxerre, *In Epistolam Hebraeos PL* 117.884. *In hunc modum testamentum
vitae aeternae quod a Christo accepimus non aliter nobis firmum manere poterat, nisi ipse morte
sua illud roborasset. Tantum enim erat peccatum nostrum, ut aliter non potuissemus redimi et
salvari nisi unigenitus Dei Filius pro nobis moreretur. Et quia ad illud consequendum quod
ille promiserat indigni eramus, ipse nobis morte sua mediator factus est, ut per mortem suam
indebitam illam quae nobis debebatur auferret.*

death did: it enabled the promise of eternal life to be given to us, unworthy as we were of it, by taking away our sin. It also took away "what we owed," namely, our punishment—a hint at substitution.

He goes on to explain further how the new covenant is like a human will: until its writer is dead, it can be changed, but once the death has occurred, those who are the subjects of its promises have their inheritance irrevocably. He connects this reality of a human will to God's promises to his elect.[22] Haimo insists that the promises are confirmed for the elect alone, that is, those who were the subjects of God's predestination to salvation, by Christ's death. He then explains further what this promise entails for the elect: peace and forgiveness and an eternal inheritance, fulfilled ultimately after Christ's second coming.

The author of Hebrews next talks about the inauguration of the first covenant with blood (Heb 9:18–22). Haimo identifies how this foreshadowed Christ's sacrifice and the efficacy of his own blood:

---

22. Haimo of Auxerre, *In Epistolam Hebraeos PL* 117.884. "For this reason, the Apostle, wishing the covenant that Christ applied to us to have been made firm, said: *And so Christ is the mediator of the new covenant,* so that by his death—occurring for the sake of the redemption of those transgressions that had not been able to be taken away and destroyed in the old covenant but were destroyed through his passion—they who were called with an eternal calling might receive the promise of an eternal inheritance. For he does not speak here of the general calling about which the Lord says: *Many were called, but few have been chosen,* but that about which the same great preacher speaks, saying about the elect of God that those whom he foreknew he also predestined, and those whom he predestined he also called, and those whom he called he also justified, and those whom he justified he also glorified." *Quapropter volens Apostolus firmum esse testamentum, quod Christus nobis dimisit, dicens: Ideo, inquiens,* Christus Novi Testamenti mediator est, *ut morte sua interveniente in redemptionem illarum praevaricationum, quae non poterant auferri et deleri in priori testamento deletae sunt autem per eius passionem, ut repromissionem aeternae haereditatis accipiant illi qui vocati sunt aeterna vocatione. Nam non loquitur hic de generali vocatione de qua Dominus ait:* Multi sunt vocati, sed pauci electi, *sed illa de qua idem egregius praedicator loquens, ait de electis Dei quod praescivit, hos et praedestinavit et quos praedestinavit, hos et vocavit, et quos vocavit, illos et justificavit, et quos justificavit, illos et magnificavit.*

All those things are given figuratively. For the bull that was usually the sacrifice of the priest indicates Christ, who, standing forth as the true priest, offered the bull, that is himself, to God the Father on the altar of the cross. He is that bull whom the loving father slaughtered upon the return of the prodigal son. The goat, too, that was offered for sin indicates the same Christ, who was offered as a sacrifice for sinners, according to that which the same apostle elsewhere says: *He who knew not sin, God the Father made to be sin for us*, that is, a sacrifice for sin.[23]

Here we have a clear statement that Christ's death on the cross was a sacrifice for sin made by God to God. The cross is the altar upon which the bull for the final sin offering was slaughtered. By this means was sin forgiven and the promise to the elect made sure.

Haimo then goes on to explain how the cleansing blood and the water sprinkled upon the tabernacle and the people as a whole with the branch of a hyssop signify the cleansing blood of Christ and the water of baptism, respectively. The scarlet wool is the love of Christ and of God that led to the crucifixion, and the hyssop branch indicates either Christ's humility and strength that purges us from sin or our repentance that does the same. Following the argument of Hebrews, he then notes how the shed blood of Christ both confirms the new covenant and cleanses us from sin, as in Christ's words at the Last Supper:

---

23. Haimo of Auxerre, *In Epistolam Hebraeos PL* 117.885. *Omnia ista in figura agebantur. Nam vitulus ille, qui plerumque hostia sacerdotis erat, Christum significabat, qui verus sacerdos existens, vitulum, hoc est semetipsum obtulit Deo Patri in ara crucis. Iste est vitulus quem pius pater mactavit pro reversione filii prodigi. Hircus quoque qui pro peccato offerebatur eumdem Christum significabat, qui pro peccatoribus oblatus est, juxta quod idem apostolus alias ait:* Eum qui non noverat peccatum, Deus Pater pro nobis peccatum fecit, *hoc est hostiam pro peccato.*

"This is the blood of the new covenant for the forgiveness of sins." More typological meanings for the tabernacle's contents are put forward: the tabernacle itself, the dwelling place of God, is the individual believer, and the vessels of the tabernacle are the believers in their various church offices, including that of apostle. All are cleansed by the blood of Christ. Moreover, this blood is greater than the blood of the animal sacrifices of the Old Testament because it removes the guilt of greater sins like murder as well as the guilt of lesser sins.

All this follows the argument of Hebrews closely, explaining in Haimo's clear method what the text of Scripture is talking about and how it applies to the Christian's life and doctrine. Haimo then turns along with Hebrews to Christ as the great high priest who enters into the Holy of Holies:

> The Holy of Holies prefigured what Christ entered into once. But we say that Jesus enters in according to his humanity. For according to his divinity, he is everywhere and fills everything. He entered not into things made by human hands but into that very heaven created by the command of God. Nor is this the only difference, but also, the last priest is the first creator, so that he might appear before the face of God for our sake, that is, so that he might show forth his own self to the power of the Father and make him propitious toward us. And so John says: *We have an advocate with the Father, the righteous Jesus, and he is the propitiation for our sins.*[24]

---

24. Haimo of Auxerre, *In Epistolam Hebraeos* PL 117.887. *Sancta sanctorum praefigurabant quae Christus semel introiit. Introire autem dicimus Jesum secundum id quod homo est. Nam secundum id quod Deus est, ubique est, et omnia implet, nec in manufactis hominum introiit sed in ipsum coelum, jussione Dei creatum. Nec hanc solam differentiam ostendit, sed*

Here we come to a passage denoting the heart of Haimo's understanding of propitiation. Christ's sacrificial death on the cross enabled him to enter into heaven as fully human, there to stand before God interceding on our behalf and so making God favorable toward us. This is closely bound up with his sacrifice on the cross since without the blood shed on it, he could not, as the final high priest, enter into God's presence.

He continues by commenting on the insistence by the author of Hebrews that Christ's death was only necessary once rather than multiple times as under the old covenant:

> For not that he offers himself many times, as the priest enters into the Holy of Holies every year with the blood of another; otherwise he would have to suffer many times from the beginning of the world. Christ did not for this reason enter into the Holy of Holies, that he might many times offer up his own self in the same way that the priest of the Jews used to enter into the Holy of Holies every year, nor with the blood of another, but with his own blood, since he himself who is priest and sacrifice offered himself once upon the altar of the cross; and truly rising from the dead now does not die, death will no longer rule over him: it is not necessary to die any more since his single passion suffices enough for the salvation of all those who believe.[25]

---

etiam pontificem proximum primum factorem, ut appareat, inquit, vultui Dei pro nobis, hoc est, ut seipsum exhibeat potentiae paternae nobisque illum propitium reddat. Unde Joannes dicit: Advocatum habemus apud Patrem Jesum justum, et ipse est propitiatio pro peccatis nostris.

25. Haimo of Auxerre, In Epistolam Hebraeos PL 117.887. Neque enim ut saepe offerat semetipsum, quemadmodum pontifex intrat in Sancta sanctorum per singulos annos in sanguine alieno; alioquin oportebat eum frequenter pati ab origine mundi. Non est Christus ad hoc ingressus in Sancta sanctorum, ut saepe semetipsum offerat quemadmodum pontifex Judaeorum ingrediebatur in Sancta sanctorum per singulos annos, neque cum sanguine alieno, sed cum suo, quoniam ipse qui sacerdos est et sacrificium, semel seipsum obtulit in ara crucis: ac

Again, Christ is the great high priest who offers a sacrifice of himself upon the cross, which acts as an altar of sacrifice. His passion thus destroys death and enables those who believe to live forever.

The final few verses of Hebrews 9 deal with Christ's second coming and its relation to his first. Haimo notes:

> *But now once at the culmination,* that is, at the end, *of the ages,* in the new age, *for the destruction of sin he appeared through his own sacrifice,* that is, through his own body that he made a sacrifice for sin. Once, he says, at the end of the ages he appeared for this reason, to destroy sin through his own sacrifice. And rightly at that time did he appear, when there were many sins, to show the riches of his grace; for if it were done in the beginning, perchance no one would have believed. And this occurred once at the culmination of the ages, through his own blood rather than through another's.[26]

Haimo again describes the atonement as a sacrifice of expiation that takes away sin; this sacrifice consists of Christ's physical body and blood. This sacrifice is also a demonstration of his grace that leads many to faith in him. He then explains how Hebrews compares every human's death and judgment

---

vero resurgens a mortuis jam non moritur, mors illi ultra non dominabitur: nec est necesse ut amplius moriatur, quoniam ad salutem omnium credentium satis sufficit una passio eius.

26. Haimo of Auxerre, *In Epistolam Hebraeos PL* 117.887. *Nunc autem semel in consummatione, hoc est in fine saeculorum, in novissima aetate, ad destructionem peccati per hostiam suam apparuit, hoc est per corpus suum quod fecit hostiam pro peccato. Semel, inquit, in fine saeculorum ad hoc apparuit, ut per hostiam suam destrueret peccatum. Merito tunc apparuit, quando multa erant peccata, ut ostenderet divitias gratiae suae. Si enim in principio fieret, fortassis nullus crederet et hoc semel in consummatione saeculorum, per proprium sanguinem, non per alienum.*

with Christ's death in the present age and his future coming.[27] Christ's once-for-all sacrifice is again defined as a sin offering made by Christ himself to take away sin.

Haimo continues by specifying the meaning of the phrase "taking away the sins of many" as referring only to the elect:

> But it ought to be noted that he was offered up to take away the sins of many and not of all, since not all will have believed. This is what the Lord himself says to the apostles: *This is my blood of the new covenant, who for you and for many will be poured out for the forgiveness of sins.*[28]

Hebrews concludes its ninth chapter by referencing the second coming of Christ in judgment to save those who believe in him, and Haimo comments:

> As if it were saying, "Indeed, the first time he appeared through his sacrifice, that is, through the mortal body, since he was a sacrifice for sin, but he will appear for a second time without a sacrifice for sin since now there

---

27. Haimo of Auxerre, *In Epistolam Hebraeos PL* 117.887. "*And just as it has been ordained for men to die once, but after this the judgment: thus also Christ was offered up one time to take away the sins of many; the second time he will appear without sin to those awaiting him for salvation.* Just as it was instituted and decreed for human beings that they should only be able to die once, but afterward to receive judgment, that is in accordance with what each one does in the body, whether good or evil: thus also Christ was offered up one time by his own self to take away the sins of many, nor is he able to die any more, but nor do we have need of anything more." Et quemadmodum staturum est hominibus semel mori, post hoc autem judicium: sic et Christus semel oblatus est ad multorum exhaurienda peccata; secundo sine peccato apparebit exspectantibus se in salutem. *Sicut hominibus statutum et decretum est, ut non possint mori nisi semel, postea autem accipiant judicium, hoc est prout unusquisque gessit in corpore sive bonum, sive malum: sic et Christus semel oblatus est a semetipso ad multorum tolenda peccata, nec potest amplius mori, sed nec indigemus.*

28. Haimo of Auxerre, *In Epistolam Hebraeos PL* 117.887. Notandum autem ad multorum tollenda peccata illum esse oblatum, et non ominium, quia non omnes credituri sunt. Tale est quod et ipse Dominus apostolis ait: Hic est sanguis meus novi testamenti, qui *pro vobis* et pro multis effundetur in remissionem peccatorum.

will not be a sacrifice for sin as there was in the first." For he will no longer be able to die. For just as each one of us receives after death in accordance with his works, so Christ, having conquered death and having obtained the kingdom, *will appear for a second time to those waiting for him for salvation,* so that he might justly vindicate his own, who justly endured suffering from others.[29]

The atonement only occurs once in Christ's pre-resurrection body since Christ's post-resurrection body is not capable of death. Instead, Christ will come as a victor over death and as king of the earth. Haimo cites Revelation 1:7 to clarify the nature of Christ's second coming:

> *Every eye will see him, even those who pierced him.* That is, therefore, he appears for a second time without sin, now not to be seen in the likeness of sinful flesh and not bearing the sins of others in his body upon the tree as he did in his first coming, nor to intercede any more for sins, but to work vengeance upon sinners.[30]

There is no sacrifice for sin in the second coming but only vengeance upon sinners. Note the substitutionary nature of the

---

29. Haimo of Auxerre, *In Epistolam Hebraeos PL* 117.888. *Ac si diceret: Primum quidem ille apparuit per hostiam suam, hoc est per corpus mortale, quod fuit hostia pro peccato, secundo autem apparebit sine hostia pro peccato, quia jam non erit hostia pro peccato, sicut prius fuit. Non enim poterit deinceps mori. Sicut enim unusquisque nostrum post mortem recipit justa opera sua: ita Christus devicta morte, et adepto regno,* secundo apparebit exspectantibus se in salutem, *ut juste vindicet suos, qui juste passus est ab alienis.*

30. Haimo of Auxerre, *In Epistolam Hebraeos PL* 117.888. Videbit eum omnis oculus, et qui eum pupugerunt. *Hoc est ergo secundo apparere sine peccato jam non videri in similitudinem carnis peccati, sed nec aliorum peccata portantem in corpore suo super lignum, sicut in primo adventu fecit, nec intervenire amplius pro peccatis, sed vindictam exercere in peccantes.*

atonement described in the first coming: bearing the sins of others upon the cross in his body.

HAIMO'S COMMENTARY ON HEBREWS 10

The first half of the tenth chapter of Hebrews continues the discussion of why Christ's sacrifice once for all is superior to the sacrifices of the old covenant. The author begins by explaining how the old covenant's sacrifices are shadows of "future goods," which may be interpreted as referring either to the new covenant realities like Christ's crucifixion, baptism, and the Eucharist or to the joys of heaven at the end of the age. Haimo then goes on to explain how, as the argument of Hebrews 10 notes, these sacrifices were not sufficient for the forgiveness of sins but were a reminder of sin. He comments:

> Hence the accusation of sinners was what was achieved, not their forgiveness; the accusation of weakness, not the demonstration of virtue. For in the fact that they were always making the offering lay the reproof of sinners, but in the fact that the offering was always necessary lay the reproof of the weakness of that same sacrifice. Because of this, he says, it was always offered on account of weakness since it was not able to completely cleanse, and so that it might be made a memory and reproof of sins.[31]

The sacrifices of the law of Moses were not meant to cleanse sins but to condemn them and remind the sinner of his sin.

---

31. Haimo of Auxerre, *In Epistolam Hebraeos PL* 117.889. *Proinde accusatio peccatorum fuit quod fiebat, non solutio: accusatio infirmitatis, non virtutis ostensio. In eo enim quod semper offerebantur, redargutio peccatorum erat: in eo autem quod semper necessaria, redargutio infirmitatis eiusdem sacrificii. Propter hoc, inquit, impetravit semper offerri propter infirmitatem, quia non poterat perfecte mundare, et ut memoria et redargutio peccatorum fieret.*

Haimo goes on to make a connection between the offerings of the old covenant and the Eucharist, which is likewise an "offering" made frequently. Is the Eucharist, he asks, useless for the cleansing of sin? By no means; for it differs fundamentally from the sacrifices of the old covenant.[32] Christ's presence resides in the bread and wine offered everywhere and every day by Christians since Christ is everywhere and fills all things; but the Eucharist is a remembrance of his one sacrifice, and it is the power of this sacrifice that cleanses Christians from sin.

The argument of Hebrews then proceeds to why God was not pleased with the sacrifices of the old covenant. Haimo explains that the sacrifices of the law of Moses did not please God in and of themselves but rather were efficacious only insofar as the desire of the one offering them was righteous. Haimo goes on to argue that they were instituted by God for two reasons: first, as a concession to the formerly pagan Jews who were used to sacrificing to their false gods, as marriage is a concession to those who cannot live a celibate life; and second, as a foreshadowing and enacted prophecy of Christ's true sacrifice.[33]

---

32. Haimo of Auxerre, *In Epistolam Hebraeos PL* 117.889. "For our sacrifice that is repeated in the same way differs in this way from that old sacrifice often repeated, since the former is the truth, the latter an image; the former makes a human being perfect, the latter not at all; and the former is not repeated by reason of its weakness: since it is not able to confer perfect salvation but is performed in remembrance of Christ's passion, just as he himself said: *Do this in remembrance of me*: and this is a single sacrifice, not many as the latter were." *In hoc enim differt ab illo veteri sacrificio saepius repetito istud nostrum quod similiter repetitur, quia istud est veritas, illud figura, illud perfectum reddit hominem, illud minime, et istud non causa infirmitatis suae repetitur: quod non possit perfectam conferre salutem, sed in commemorationem passionis Christi, sicut ipse dixit: Hoc facite, inquiens, in meam commemorationem: et una est haec hostia non multae sicut illae erant.*

33. Haimo of Auxerre, *In Epistolam Hebraeos PL* 117.889–90. "For this reason coming into the world he says: *Sacrifice and offering I did not desire, but you fitted my body for me. Burnt offerings for sin did not please you, then I said: Behold, I come. At the start of the book it was written about me that I should do your will O God.* The earlier sacrifices were shown by these words to be useless for a whole and complete cleansing and instead were images

Haimo then expounds the second part of the quoted passage of Hebrews in the comments explained above, connecting it to Christ's willing sacrifice. The former sacrifices were not sufficient for the forgiveness of sins, being, rather, concessions for the weak people of Israel and prophecies of Christ's sacrifice of himself to God. But what is the nature of Christ's sacrifice? He notes that the quotation in Hebrews 10:5–7 from Psalm 40:6–8 is assigned to Christ during his incarnation. These words explain Christ's mission on earth:

> Why does he say to God the Father: "*You did not desire a sacrifice and an offering, but you fitted or completed a body for me?* So that I might offer to you an acceptable sacrifice. *Burnt offerings for sin did not please you, then I said: Behold I come* through the mystery of the incarnation, so that I might redeem by my sacrifice the human race." Now a sacrifice was called a "burnt offering" [*holocaustus*]

---

not acceptable to God since from the start they did not please him. It must not be thought that God Almighty should have ever been delighted by the smell of flesh and the burning up of animals, even though it is read that he smelled the sweet aroma, but rather by the desire of the one offering, and so also through Jeremiah he says: *Your burnt offerings are not accepted* by me, *and your sacrifices do not please me*, and through Isaiah: *Do not offer any more sacrifices* to me, *the incense is an abomination to me; he who slaughters* a bull *is as one who stuns a dog*." Ideo ingrediens mundum dicit: Hostiam et oblationem noluisti, corpus autem aptasti mihi. Holocaustomata pro peccato non tibi placuerunt, tunc dixi: Ecce venio. In capite libri scriptum est de me, ut faciam, Deus, voluntatem tuam. *Anteriores hostiae ostenduntur his verbis inutiles esse ad integram perfectamque mundationem, et forma magis fuisse, nec esse acceptabiles Deo, quoniam ab initio non placuerunt ei. Non est putandum quod omnipotens Deus nidore carnium et concrematione animalium unquam delectatus fuerit, licet legatur odoratus esse odorem suavitatis, sed fide et desiderio offerentis, unde et per Hieremiam dicit:* Holocaustomata vestra non sunt mihi accepta, et victimae vestrae non placuerunt mihi, *et per Isaiam:* Ne offeratis (*inquit*) ultra sacrificium *mihi,* incensum abominatio est mihi; qui mactat *bovem,* quasi qui excerebret canem.

because the whole thing was burnt up on the altar as if it were all incense. For *holon* means all, and *caustus*, incense.[34]

Here Christ's mission is clear: come to earth in an incarnate body to offer to God the Father a sacrifice for sin that would be effective, unlike the sacrifices of the old covenant. This sacrifice was his body, associated previously by Haimo with the term *hostia*, sacrifice. Haimo then notes that prior to Christ's coming, sins were purged in part by repentance and faith, as David was forgiven for his sin with Bathsheba, but that at Christ's coming, there was a complete cleansing.

There then follows an explanation of the phrase "at the start of the book it was written about me that I should do your will, O God." Haimo discusses varying views of which book is meant, concluding that rather than the first chapters of Genesis or the Psalms, as some think, it refers instead to the first chapter of Leviticus, which opens with instructions about burnt offerings. Haimo argues that this makes better sense since it speaks about Christ's sacrificial death, unlike the other two possibilities. He writes:

> If anyone from you offers to the Lord from his flocks, he
> should offer a spotless male, that is, a bull-calf from the
> cattle, or from the drove. That calf taken from among
> the cows and offered as a sacrifice is Christ arisen from
> the race of the patriarchs and sacrificed for the salvation

---

34. Haimo of Auxerre, *In Epistolam Hebraeos PL* 117.890–91. *Et quid dicit Deo Patri: Hostiam, inquit, et oblationem noluisti, corpus autem aptasti sive perfecisti mihi: illud tibi offeram sacrificium acceptum. Holocaustomata pro peccato non tibi placuerunt, tunc dixi: Ecce venio per incarnationis mysterium, ut meo sacrificio redimam genus humanum. Holocaustum autem dicebatur sacrificium, quod totum concremabatur in altari, quasi totum incensum.* [Text modified from MS Paris BnF lat. 1762, f. 305v; digital version of MS from gallica.bnf.fr.]

of the human race. Therefore, Christ says to the Father,
"Since the sacrifices of irrational animals do not please
you, because they are not able to cleanse a person completely, behold, I come into the world through the mystery of the incarnation."[35]

Christ came into the world to be the sacrifice that all the burnt
offerings of Leviticus foreshadowed since they were unable to
cleanse humanity from sin and so please the Father. The sacrifice in question is one of expiation but has a propitiatory effect.

This sacrifice on the cross was done at the will of the Father,
who wished to save humanity from sin:

> For *at the head* of Leviticus *it was written about me that
> I should do your will*, that is, that I should die for the sal-
> vation of the human race. For the will of God the Father
> was that the Son should redeem the human race by his
> passion. And so the Son himself, nearing his passion,
> said: *But that the world might know that I love the Father:
> and just as the Father gave the command to me, so I do. Rise,
> let us go from here* to the passion.[36]

The Son goes to the cross to make a sacrifice of expiation not
apart from the will of the Father but in accordance with it. Thus,

---

35. Haimo of Auxerre, *In Epistolam Hebraeos PL* 117.891. Si quis ex vobis hostiam offert
Domino de pecoribus, masculum immaculatum offerat, *hoc est, vitulum de bobus, sive de
armento. Vitulus iste de bobus assumptus, atque in sacrificium oblatus, Christus est de genere
patriarcharum ortus, ac pro salute generis humani immolatus. Dicit ergo Christus ad Patrem:
Quia sacrificia irrationabilium animalium tibi non placent, eo quod perfecte hominem mundare
non possunt, ecce venio in mundum per incarnationis mysterium.*

36. Haimo of Auxerre, *In Epistolam Hebraeos PL* 117.891. In capite etenim libri *Levitici*
scriptum est de me, ut faciam voluntatem tuam, *hoc est, ut moriar pro salute generis humani.
Voluntas enim Dei Patris fuit, ut Filius sua passione genus humanum redimeret. Unde ipse Filius
approprinquans suae passioni dixit: Sed ut cognoscat mundus quia diligo Patrem: et sicut
mandatum dedit mihi Pater, sic facio. Surgite, eamus hinc ad passionem.*

the sacrifice is made by God in two ways: by Christ, who is himself God, and by God the Father, by whose will the Son performs the sacrifice. Haimo goes on to say that the passion, accomplished by the will of the Father, cleanses us from sin through baptism performed on someone who has faith.

Hebrews 10:11–18, the final section of Haimo's commentary that we will examine, explains how the new covenant removes the need for the sacrifices of the old. The sacrifices of the Mosaic law could not take away severe sins (*criminalia et capitalia*), but Christ through his passion could and did. Christ, after offering himself as a sacrifice that cleanses those who believe in him from sin, now sits at the right hand of the Father awaiting the time when all his enemies are placed under his feet. Enemies are to be understood as both the reprobate, that is, the Jews, heretics, and false Christians who are subjected to him for punishment, and the elect, that is, those who were once his enemies and now have voluntarily subjected themselves to his rule. These latter are recipients of the benefits of his passion: *"For by a single offering he perfected the sanctified forever*, that is, offering himself once, he made them sanctified forever."[37]

The argument of Hebrews 10:15–18 uses the citation of Jeremiah 31:33–34 to show how the sacrifices of the old covenant were brought to an end by Christ's single offering. Haimo comments:

> For *afterward* the omnipotent God through the prophet Jeremiah *said: But this is the covenant that I will invoke for*

---

37. Haimo of Auxerre, *In Epistolam Hebraeos PL* 117.892. Una enim oblatione consummavit in sempiternum sanctificatos, *id est semel se offerens perfectos fecit sanctificatos in sempiternum.*

them after those days, says the Lord: I will give my laws in
their hearts, and upon their minds I will write them, and he
immediately adds beneath: *And their sins I will remember*
no longer, showing that now the figurative sacrifices made
continually were not necessary, which also the Apostle
demonstrates when he adds beneath: *But where there is*
forgiveness of these sins there is now no required offering for
sin. For after this covenant was fulfilled, as God promised through the prophet, immediately those sacrifices
received their end since with the coming of the truth the
shadow went away. But it ought to be noted that where
there is no remembrance of sins that have been forgiven
in baptism through the faith of the Lord's passion, there
is now no required offering of the Law for sin.[38]

Once again, Haimo makes clear that Christ's death on the cross
was a sacrifice of expiation that is put into effect by the baptism of a faith-filled sinner. The sacrifices of the old covenant,
of the law of Moses, now pass away because they are fulfilled
by Christ's one-time sacrificial death.

Haimo's commentary on Hebrews 9:1–10:18 demonstrates
that he sees these crucial passages as teaching that Christ's
death on the cross was a sacrifice for sin. Our redemption is

---

38. Haimo of Auxerre, *In Epistolam Hebraeos PL* 117.892. Postquam enim dixit *omnip-*
otens Deus per prophetam Jeremiam: Hoc autem testamentum quod testabor ad illos post
dies illos, dicit Dominus: dabo leges meas in cordibus eorum et in mentibus eorum super-
scribam eas, *statim subintulit:* Et peccatorum eorum non memorabor amplius, *ostendens jam*
non fore deinceps necessarias hostias figurativas, quod etiam Apostolus manifestat, dum subdit:
Ubi autem horum peccatorum remissio jam non est *necessaria* oblatio pro peccato. *Nam*
postquam hoc testamentum adimpletum est quod Deus per prophetam promittebat, statim illae
hostiae finem acceperunt, quia veniente veritate umbra discessit. Notandum autem, quia ubi
recordatio peccatorum non est, quae in baptismate per fidem Dominicae passionis dimittuntur,
jam non est necessaria oblatio legis pro peccato.

achieved by his passion. Far from being a means of tricking the devil into losing his rights over his captives, the crucifixion is a sin offering, the true fulfillment of the useless sin offerings of the Old Testament, made by God to God. It is a sacrifice made by God in two ways: by the Son, who is himself the sin offering, and by the Father, by whose will the sacrifice is made. It is the fulfillment of the sin offering made on the Day of Atonement by the high priest, a sacrifice of both propitiation and expiation. Christ's death on the cross expiates our sin by its cleansing blood washing us clean in a faith-filled baptism. It propitiates God by two means: by making believers holy, thereby removing his wrath due to our sin, and by allowing Christ as the representative of the human race to enter into the heavenly Holy of Holies and there intercede with God on our behalf. It is thoroughly theocentric.

CHAPTER 7

HAIMO OF AUXERRE, PART II

Sacrifice and Satisfaction in
Christ's Crucifixion

W ith Haimo's understanding of the atonement now having been laid out, two contemporary commentators on these same passages, Claudius of Turin and Hrabanus Maurus, will be analyzed to see how Haimo's thoughts fit in with his contemporaries. We will then examine what another retiring scholar, Jean Rivière, contributed to our knowledge of Carolingian atonement doctrine and of the predecessors of Anselm of Canterbury. We will also look at how Rivière described the import of Anselm's own work on the atonement in the broader context of his predecessors.

Propitiation and Expiation
in Claudius of Turin

As we have seen, Haimo in his commentaries on Romans and
Hebrews conceives of the atonement mainly as a sacrifice of
propitiation and expiation made by God to God. What did his
contemporaries think of these passages? Is his view a unique
one? Two commentators on the Pauline epistles who wrote
roughly at the same time as Haimo, Claudius of Turin and
Hrabanus Maurus, provide useful comparative material. What
each has to say about the meaning of Romans 3:25–26 and
Hebrews 10:5–10 will be examined, and how they line up with
Haimo's interpretation will be outlined.

Claudius of Turin (d. 828) was born in Spain and came to
Gaul around 800. Trained in the Scriptures at Lyon, he became
bishop of Turin in 816 by the order of Louis the Pious, son
of Charlemagne, in whose court he was influential. He was a
fierce iconoclast; that is, he opposed the use of images (even
crucifixes) in worship. While this was official orthodoxy in
the Frankish court at the start of his episcopate, by 825, feel-
ing had turned against it, and so Claudius was condemned for
his heterodoxy, keeping his episcopate only by royal favor until
his death in 828.

Throughout his episcopate, he wrote commentaries on
Scripture, eventually completing twenty of them. These tended
to be quite derivative, mere compendiums of the works of the
fathers rather than original exegesis. Still, how he shaped his
borrowings from the fathers and what he added to them is of
considerable interest and provides a glimpse into his theological emphases and opinions. He has not, however, been extensively studied, in part because most of his commentaries lack a

printed edition and are found only in manuscripts. Moreover, his Latin is colloquial and inelegant, untouched by the reforms of Alcuin. Yet his exegesis was influential, on Haimo of Auxerre especially. Although due to the cloud of unorthodoxy that hung over Claudius, he is only ever mentioned by name to be criticized, Haimo in fact incorporated large portions of Claudius' commentary on the letters of Paul into his own work. It is therefore useful to compare Claudius with Haimo on the atonement.

In his commentary on Romans 3:25–26, Claudius first gives a very basic overview of the effects of a sacrifice of propitiation— the forgiveness of sins—and states that it fulfills the sin offerings of the old covenant. Then, he goes on to characterize the atonement as both the devil's overstepping his lawful bounds and a sacrifice of expiation and propitiation. Claudius writes:

Whom God put forward as a propitiation through faith in his blood. Therefore, inasmuch as he is a sacrifice, he is made a propitiation through the shedding of his own blood, insofar as he was proven to have been made a propitiation by the forgiveness of former faults. Indeed, when the forgiveness of sins is given, it is certain that a propitiation through the pouring out of holy blood has been carried out. For without the shedding of blood, as the apostle says, there is no forgiveness of sins, since the propitiation and forgiveness of sins have been conferred through the blood of Christ. As a type of him as well, the blood of victims was offered in the old covenant.[1]

---

1. Claudius of Turin, *Expositio in Epistolam Romanos*, MS Paris BnF lat. 2392 f. 14v, online at gallica.bnf.fr. Quem proposuit deus propitiationem per fidem in sanguine ipsius.

Claudius argues that since Christ's death on the cross is the means by which sins are forgiven, it must have been a propitiatory offering of blood. There is no clearer explanation of what exactly propitiation does, however.

He goes on to argue that God demonstrates his own justice through justly defeating the devil:

> For the demonstration of his own justice for the sake of the forgiveness of former sins. In this, he says that he demonstrated justice since he held to an unwearying patience in order to await our cleansing. Thus, the compassion of forgiveness is achieved for us when he suffers those things who did no sin. Since God does all things justly, justly did the devil lose the debtor since unjustly he slew an innocent man.[2]

Claudius of Turin emphasizes the defeat of the devil through Christ's death on the cross. We are cleansed from sin by Christ's blood, yes, but more to the point, the innocence of the sufferer condemns the devil. In this instance, at least, Claudius has more in common with the view of the atonement offered in the Eusebius Gallicanus sermons explored in the previous chapter than he does with Haimo.

Secundum hoc ergo quod hostia est per effusione sanguinis sui propitiatio efficitur, in eo quod ad remissionem praecedentium delictorum propitiationem probaretur effecta. Cum vero peccatorum remissio tribuatur certum est propitiationem per effusionem sacri sanguinis adimpletam; absque sanguinis enim effusionem sicut dicit apostolus, non fit remissio peccatorum, quia propitiatio et remissio peccatorum per sanguinem est christi conlata. In cuius typo etiam in veteri testamento pro peccatis populi victimarum sanguis offerebatur.

2. Claudius of Turin, *Expositio in Epistolam Romanos* f. 14v. Ad ostensionem iustitiae suae propter remissionem praecedentium delictorum. *In hoc dicit ostendisse iustitiam quod indefessam tenuit pro emundationis nostrae expectatione patientiam. Ita nobis misericordia fit remissionis, dum illa patitur qui nihil peccavit. Quia omnia deus iuste facit, iuste ergo diabolus perdidit debitorum quia iniuste occidit innocentem.*

Claudius of Turin's commentary on Hebrews 10:5–10 was used extensively by Haimo in his commentary on the passage, demonstrating the latter's dependence (even if he would not admit it) upon the former. Claudius covers the same exegetical bases as Haimo, including affirming the expiatory nature of Christ's death on the cross. So he writes:

> To sacrifice is not the will of God, and when these sacrifices did not please him, he came at once just as it was written: *Then I said, "Behold, I come."* This was said of no one other than Christ ... Indeed, for this reason, he ordered the aforesaid sacrifices to be offered: as an image of the true sacrifice that released the whole world from sin. And so he gives a rebuke since the true sacrifice was approaching and says to the prophet, "Behold I come, at the beginning of the book it was written about me." This book is Leviticus, the book that commands and talks about sacrifices. "But since I am the main and only sufficient sacrifice," therefore "at the beginning," that is in the beginning of the book of sacrifices, "it was written about me," as in the beginning God made heaven and earth. What does it mean, "That I should do your will?" "To hand myself over—this is the will of God." By that will we have been made holy.[3]

---

3. Claudius of Turin, *Expositio in Epistolam ad Hebraeos*, MS Paris BnF lat. 12290 f. 114v, online at gallica.bnf.fr. *Proinde sacrificare non est voluntas dei et dum illi illa non placuerunt, statim advenit sicut scriptum est:* Tunc dixi ecco venio. *Quod de nullo alio nisi de christo dictum est ... Ideo quippe hostias iamdictas offerre iussit, quia in figura erant ad hostiam veram quae totum mundum de peccato solveret, et propterea reprobat quia iam vera hostia adpropinquabat, et dicit prophetam,* Ecce venio, *in capite libri scriptum est de me. Idem levitici qui liber hostias imperat et narrat. Dum autem sum principalis et sola sufficiens hostia, ideo in capite id est in principio libri hostiarum de me scriptum est, ut in principio fecit deus caelum et terram. Quid*

Here at least the elements of Christ's sacrifice are the same as in Haimo: the crucifixion is a sacrifice that is the fulfillment of the sacrifices of the old covenant, and by the will of God, this final sacrifice is made to make us holy and cleanse us from sin.

Propitiation and Expiation in Hrabanus Maurus

What of the commentaries of Hrabanus Maurus, a far more dynamic character and elegant exegete than Claudius? This man, who lived from approximately 780 to 856, studied under Alcuin and then became a teacher in the abbey at Fulda, over which he was later appointed abbot. There he wrote an impressive number of works comprising such genres as biblical commentaries (the majority), editions of classical works, letters, sermons, and poems. In 847, he was appointed bishop of Mainz, where he served until his death.

His *Commentary on the Pauline Epistles* was written only slightly before Haimo's commentary, and Haimo may have used it as a source. What he says about the atonement in the two passages we have singled out is therefore of interest. For Romans 3:25–26, Hrabanus comments:

> *Whom God put forth as a propitiator of faith.* He says that God "put forth" in Christ, that is, he arranged that he would be made favorable to the human race if it believed. *In his blood.* "In his blood" for this reason: since we are freed by his death, so that he might show forth that same death and by his suffering condemn death. *For the*

---

est, ut faciam voluntatem tuam? *Memetipsum tradere, hoc est dei voluntas, in qua voluntate sanctificati sumus.*

demonstration of his justice, that is, so that he might make his promise publicly, by which he freed us from sins, just as he promised previously, since at the time when he fulfilled it, he showed that he was just. *On account of the declaration of preceding faults in the patience of God.* God, knowing that he "declared" his favor by which he decided to aid sinners—those who are dwelling above as much as those who are held in hell—vacating the sentence by which all justly are seen to be condemned to demon-strate to us that at that time he had decided to free the human race through Christ, just as he promised through Jeremiah the prophet, saying, *I will be propitiated with regard to their iniquities, and I will no longer remember their faults.*[4]

Hrabanus is drawing here from the commentary on Romans by Ambrosiaster, the anonymous fourth-century exegete, and thus his biblical text is slightly different. The verb *propono* is put in place of *remissio* or *propitio* on two occasions, and you can see the commentary struggling to make sense of it, given its context. At any rate, the meaning of the whole is clear enough: God put in process the redemption to make his own self favorable to

---

4. Hrabanus Maurus, *Expositio in Epistolam Romanos PL* 111.1343. Quem proposuit Deus propitiatorem fidei. *Hoc dicit quia in Christo proposuit Deus, id est, disposuit propitium se futurum humano genri, si credat.* In sanguine ipsius. *Ideo in sanguine ipsius, quia morte eius liberati sumus, ut manifestaret illum mortuum, et mortem passione eius damnaret.* Ad ostensionem justitiae suae, *hoc est ut promissum suum palam faceret, quo nos a peccatis lib-eraret, sicut ante promiserat; quod tum cum implevit, justum se ostendit.* Propter propositum praecedentium delictorum in patientia Dei. *Sciens Deus propositum benignitatis suae quo censuit peccatoribus subvenire, tam his qui sunt apud superos, quam qui in inferno tenebantur, utrosque diutissime exspectavit, evacuans sententiam, qua justum videtur omnes damnari: ut ostenderet nobis, quod olim decreverat liberare genus humanum per Christum, sicut promisit per Jeremiam prophetam dicens:* Propitius ero iniquitatibus illorum, et delictorum illorum non memorabor.

sinful humanity. Christ's death on the cross defeated sin and death even as it enabled God's change in attitude.

Hrabanus's commentary on Hebrews 10:5–10 focuses on Christ's sacrifice as one that expiates sin:

> The signs of the things promised were taken away because the promised reality showed itself. For this reason he says, *Burnt offerings and sacrifices you did not desire, but you have prepared a body for me.* That is, the sacrifices of the law were not able to expiate the sin of the human race, but a body you have prepared for me. This is said from the perspective of him who received the body of our mortality in order to possess what he offered up for our sake. *Then he said, Behold I come.* Then the time came for the sins to be taken away and the promised reality to come. *Then I said, Behold I come,* having taken away these things, offered those things, fulfilled these other things. Where are the sacrifices of the Jews? They passed away and are not in the church of Christ, since he himself came, who was the image of those sacrifices … *In whose will we are sanctified through the one-time offering of the body of Jesus Christ.* This offering was offered up one time but is always able to wash clean all those who believe and all those desiring to be cleansed in it.[5]

---

5. Hrabanus Maurus, *Expositio in Epistolam ad Hebraeos PL* 112.783–84. *Ablata sunt signa promittentia, quia exhibita veritas promissa. Ideo ait:* Holocaustomata et sacrificia noluisti, corpus autem aptasti mihi. *Hoc est, peccatum humani generis legalia sacrificia non potuerunt expiare, corpus autem aptasti mihi. Hoc ex persona dicitur eius, qui corpus suscepit nostrae mortalitatis, ut pro nobis haberet quid offerret. Tunc dixi, Ecce venio. Tum tempus fuit, ut ablata essent signa et veritas promissa veniret. Tunc dixi, ecce venio, ablata haec, illa oblata, haec impleta. Ubi sunt sacrificia Judaeorum? Transierunt et non sunt in Ecclesia Christi, quia venit ille, qui figurabatur illis sacrificiis … In qua voluntate sanctificati sumus per oblationem*

The crucifixion is a sacrifice, fulfilling the sacrifices of the old covenant, that cleanses those who partake of its benefits from sin. In other words, it is a sacrifice of expiation. The body that Christ takes up at the incarnation is taken up to be offered up as this sacrifice.

Both Claudius of Turin and Hrabanus Maurus composed their commentaries largely by extracting passages from the fathers and then combining them into a compendium of authoritative interpretations. We can see from their similarities with Haimo that the monk of Auxerre did something similar. However, unlike his contemporaries, Haimo weaves his sources into a more coherent whole. He also focuses more than they do on the sacrificial aspects of Christ's death. Yet all three center the understanding of the atonement on Christ's sacrificial death on the cross, a sacrifice made by God to God. The atonement is thoroughly theocentric; the devil is mostly put to the side. Our problem is sin and the coming judgment of God due to that sin, a problem that is solved by the shedding of Christ's blood.

SUMMING UP

What are we to make of all this? How did the most popular exegete of Paul's letters in the Middle Ages, the author of what was practically the standard textbook for monasteries, conceive of the atonement? There are two points I would like to make. First, Haimo's view of the atonement was thoroughly theocentric; second, at its center was the altar of the cross upon which a sacrifice of expiation and propitiation was made by God to God.

---

corporis Jesu Christi semel. *Haec oblatio semel oblata est, sed semper potens est abluere omnes credentes et omnes optantes in ea mundari.*

The atonement for Haimo of Auxerre is theocentric, not demonocentric. In other words, the cross solves a problem that revolves around God, not the devil, and solves it by a means that focuses on God, not the devil. In his commentary on Romans 3, Haimo insists that mankind's predicament is caused by sinning against God: "*For all have sinned and lack the glory of God,* that is, all lack forgiveness and pardon for sins, Jews as much as gentiles." Insofar as mankind's predicament is a captivity to the devil, it is a captivity caused by rebellion against God and could be remedied by turning back to God: "He subjected himself to the devil by transgressing the law of God and when he began to serve vices and idols. But this captivity was dissolved when the spirit returned to God and understood that it was sick, but God was a physician." The cross saves us from our predicament by changing God's attitude toward us: "God the Father put forward his Son, that is, he decreed and foreordained him as a propitiator and reconciler, so that he might make God the Father propitious toward us and easily appeased through the faith of his passion." There are, of course, two parts to God's attitude: on the one hand, he has wrath against us due to sin and needs to be appeased; on the other, he loves us and was the prime mover of the plan of salvation. Thus, Haimo also insists, "If he [the Father] had not wanted to make us righteous, he would not have handed his Son, who did no sin, over to death for our sake."

The theocentric character of the atonement continues in the commentary on Hebrews. Our predicament is caused by our sin, which could not easily be forgiven: "So great was our sin that there was no other way we were able to be redeemed and saved unless the only-begotten Son of God should have died for us." The remedy for this sin includes the presence of a mediator before God, a mediator who could only gain access to the Father's presence by means of blood: "With the blood of his passion, he opened heaven and entered into the hidden places of the heavenly homeland, where now he stands before the face of God the Father praying for us." Christ had to be free from sin so that he could please the Father, and he was enabled to be free from sin by the power of the Spirit: "The Holy Spirit, who filled that man in the virgin's womb, guarded him so that no sin from this world should pass into him and that he might be a sacrifice without stain in a pleasing aroma to God the Father." The purpose of the incarnation was to provide a sacrifice that would please the Father: "Therefore Christ says to the Father, 'Since the sacrifices of irrational animals do not please you, because they are not able to cleanse a person completely, behold, I come into the world through the mystery of the incarnation.'" It was not just a sacrifice made to the Father, however, but also one made by the Father: "The will of God the Father was that the Son should redeem the human race by his passion." And it was a sacrifice made by the Son of God to the Father: "For the bull that was usually the sacrifice of the priest indicates Christ, who, standing forth as the true priest, offered the bull, that is himself, to God the Father on the altar of the cross."

Haimo's atonement doctrine also centers around the cross as the altar upon which Christ died as a sacrifice of propitiation and expiation. It was a sacrifice of expiation because it cleansed believers from sin. In his commentary on Romans 3, Haimo has little enough to say about this aspect, but it is still there, although joined indissolubly to baptism: "Our own redemption, by which we are redeemed, and through which we are made righteous, is the passion of Christ; when it has been joined with baptism, it makes a man righteous through faith, and afterward, through repentance." In Hebrews, the crucifixion comes out as a sacrifice of expiation much more clearly, and Haimo's commentary reflects this; in comparison with the blood shed by the sacrifices of the old covenant, "how much more was the blood of Christ able to cleanse our own soul and to fully make it righteous!" It is an expiation because it destroys sin: "Once, he says, at the end of the ages he appeared for this reason, to destroy sin through his own sacrifice."

It is also a sacrifice of propitiation because it averts God's wrath. How it does this is complicated and needs some untangling. First, it averts God's wrath because it pays the debt we owed due to sin—in other words, our punishment: "He himself was made a mediator for us by his death, so that through his unowed death he might take away what we owed." Christ is also described as "bearing the sins of others in his body upon the tree" in his first coming to die on the cross. Second, it averts God's wrath because it allows mankind's representative, Christ, access to heaven and to God's throne, before which he can intercede on his people's behalf and change God's mind (in a certain sense). Christ is the great high priest, "who with the blood of his passion opened heaven and entered into the hidden places of the heavenly homeland, where now he stands before the face of God the Father praying for us." So too, "He appears before the face of God for our sake ... so that he might show forth his own self to the power of the Father and make him propitious towards us. And so John says, *We have an advocate with the Father, the righteous Jesus, and he is the propitiation for our sins."*

Third, propitiation involves pleasing God through a sacrifice that makes the recipients of its benefits holy: "Christ says to the Father, 'Since the sacrifices of irrational animals do not please you because they are not able to cleanse a person completely, behold, I come into the world through the mystery of the incarnation.'" Christ's sacrifice changes God's mind because it changes those who were once objects of his wrath due to their sin into righteous servants. So God put Christ forward so that "he might make God the Father propitious toward us and easily appeased through the faith of his passion." In other words, remembering that "faith of his passion" refers to the individual believer's faith in Christ's passion, God is propitiated not by the sacrifice itself but by the righteousness through faith that the sacrifice enables.

Haimo of Auxerre, the great teacher of Europe in the Middle Ages, thus held that the death of Christ on the cross was a sacrifice of propitiation and expiation made by God to God. Above all, I hope to have shown that the doctrine of the atonement in the ninth century, as exposited by its most influential exegete, was fundamentally theocentric. The fact that similar commentaries like those of Claudius of Turin or Hrabanus Maurus drew more on the older *Christus Victor* or "mousetrap" images of the atonement—although their theocentricity is also quite clear—illustrates Haimo's unique contribution. And it is Haimo's commentary, not that of Claudius or Hrabanus, that was instantly adopted by Christians across Europe. The number of surviving manuscripts tells the tale: three copies of Hrabanus Maurus's Hebrews commentary, seven copies of Claudius of Turin's—and a hundred twenty-four (and counting) of the commentary by Haimo of Auxerre.[6] What Haimo taught about the atonement, Europe from the ninth century onward clearly liked and affirmed.

Jean Rivière and the
Carolingian Commentators

The study of the theologians of the Carolingian era was not well advanced in the time of Jean Rivière, so it is not surprising that he did not give it much attention. However, he did not overlook it entirely, and it played a small but important part in his response to Joseph Turmel's critique of Anselm of Canterbury's *Cur Deus homo*. Haimo of Auxerre, who played such a large role in developing the Carolingian theological corpus, only appears a few times in Rivière's works, always through the inaccurate medium of the *Patrologia Latina*, which misidentified him as Haimo of Halberstadt. Still, what Rivière says about his writings is of interest to us, and what is of still greater interest is how the great historian of the atonement located Haimo and his contemporaries in the broad sweep of the history of the doctrine. What Rivière insists upon is that the work of Anselm, far from being a radical break with a dominant *Christus Victor* model of the atonement, was in essential continuity with the teaching of the fathers and the best of the Carolingians and their immediate successors. For all of them, the central feature of the atonement is Christ's sacrifice for sin made by God to God, reconciling mankind to God and God to mankind.

---

6. Data taken from the *Mirabile* online database, mirabileweb.it.

Rivière's last series of articles written against Turmel, *Le dogme de la rédemption au début du Moyen-Age*, "The doctrine of the redemption at the beginning of the Middle Ages," contains his treatment of the Carolingians and his assessment of their continuity with Anselm. His thesis about the doctrine of the atonement in the fathers and their immediate successors is clear: "Nowhere systematized, the doctrine of the redemption is then consistently summed up in the framework of a sacrifice of expiation at the same time as this theocentric aspect of the accomplished work of Christ is set alongside the enacting of a certain 'justice' with regard to Satan."[7] Is this affirmed by the Carolingian theologians? Or is their version of the atonement a skewed version of this that places the defeat of the devil at the center of the redemption? We have seen that the atonement in Haimo of Auxerre can scarcely be characterized by the latter; Rivière, despite his limited acquaintance with Haimo, agrees and extends this judgment to most of the Carolingians.

While a great deal of work has been done on Carolingian theology since Rivière's day, even now, his opinion of this era is all too commonly held: "Even taking account of the shadowy 'Carolingian Renaissance,' the period that lies between the eighth and eleventh centuries remains undoubtedly one of the poorest in the history of the church, in terms of both men and works."[8] This is mistaken, although he adds in a footnote that

7. Jean Rivière, "Le dogme de la Rédemption au début du Moyen-Age," *RevScRel* 11, no. 3 (1931): 23. *Nulle part systématisée, la doctrine de la Rédemption est alors assez uniformément résumée dans le cadre du sacrifice expiatoire, en même temps qu'à cet aspect théocentrique de l'oeuvre accomplie par le Christ se juxtapose l'accomplissement d'une certaine «justice» à l'égard de Satan.*

8. Rivière, "Rédemption au début du Moyen-Age," 357. *Même en tenant compte de l'éphémère renaissance carolingienne, la période qui s'étend depuis le VIIIe jusqu'au Xie siècle*

this view is perhaps too harsh and is reflective of the judgment of contemporary scholars that the Carolingians were unoriginal compilers of the fathers: "For this reason, this period is wholly neglected in the most learned histories of the doctrine of the redemption. This fact releases us from any bibliography, yet this may well come from an excessive disdain. Perhaps we will discover one day that these obscure intermediaries are not unworthy of all interest."[9] Indeed, as I hope to have shown in this chapter, one at least of these intermediaries is very interesting.

Yet this hesitant dismissal of the Carolingians does not prevent Rivière from affirming their essential continuity with the fathers. The theocentric atonement of the patristic era remained:

> To the one who knows how to receive texts and facts as they actually are [a dig at Turmel], it quickly appears that if the old teaching of the devil's "rights" survived to the threshold of the Middle Ages, it is by way of an accidental and optional element, following the caveats noted by the fathers, in an economy of redemption whose essential element does not stop for even a moment being understood as centering on God.[10]

---

reste, à n'en pas douter, l'une des plus pauvres qui soient dans l'histoire de l'Église sous le double rapport des hommes and des oeuvres.

9. Rivière, "Rédemption au début du Moyen-Age," 357n1. *Pour ce motif, cette période est entièrement négligée dans les histoires le plus érudites du dogme de la Rédemption. Fait qui nous dispense de toute bibliographie, mais qui pourrait bien procéder d'un dédain excessif. Peut-être s'apercevra-t-on un jour que ces obscurs intermédiaires ne sont pas indignes de tout intérêt.*

10. Rivière, "Rédemption au début du Moyen-Age," 358. *A qui sait prendre textes et faits tels qu'ils sont, il apparaît vite que, si l'ancienne doctrine des «droits» du démon survit jusqu'au seuil du Moyen-Age, c'est à titre d'élément accidentel et facultatif, suivant la nuance relevée chez les Pères, dans une économie rédemptrice dont l'essentiel ne cesse pas un moment d'être conçu en fonction de Dieu.*

There are two elements of the *Christus Victor* atonement (and the devil's place in it) that are qualified by the fathers and their Carolingian successors: the devil's rights over captive humanity and God's justice in rescuing us from his grasp. Rivière insists that both are essentially images that do not detract from the theocentric nature of the atonement. In other words, for the Carolingians as much as for the fathers, the death of Christ was a sacrifice made by God to God.

THE RIGHTS OF THE DEVIL IN PRE-ANSELMIAN THEOLOGY

With regard to the notion that the devil had rights over the human race, and so God had to act justly toward him, Rivière argues that this is essentially an image of a deeper reality: "Reduced to its concrete forms, the rule of the devil is nothing but a means of expressing the state of degradation that original sin places us in and that brings about our condemnation to the punishments of hell for eternity."[11] The devil's rights, properly understood, merely refer to the consequences of our sin. God does not have to pay the devil a ransom to rescue captive humanity, in other words. As we have seen, this is essentially the position of Haimo of Auxerre (and Caesarius of Arles as well). Rivière also notes that Haimo is in support of this interpretation.

Haimo in several of his sermons uses terminology that seems to agree with the idea of the devil having actual rights over humanity: "Although we used to be *in sorte Dei* ["in the

---

11. Rivière, "Rédemption au début du Moyen-Age," 299–300. *Ramené à ses formes concrètes, le règne du démon n'est qu'une manière de traduire l'état de déchéance où nous met le péché d'origine et qui entraîne notre condamnation aux supplices de l'enfer pour l'éternité.*

portion of God"], we became, for Haimo of Halberstadt [sic], *de sorte diaboli* ["in the portion of the devil"]. Indeed, according to the same author, Satan has made us his captives."[12] However, this captivity is not legitimate, and God is not obliged to honor the devil's lordship: "Haimo ... presents the devil as a *violentissimus praedo* ["extremely violent robber"] and, to restrict his power, makes use of this formula voluntarily pejorative: *Per mortem hominis in mundo principatum praesumpserat* ["Through the death of man he presumed himself to be the ruler in the world"]."[13] The first quote is from one of Haimo's sermons, the second from his commentary on Hebrews 2. Haimo's position is that of his contemporaries as well, and after citing a wide variety of Carolingian sources, Rivière insists, "Everything comes together, as a result, to exclude the idea that our authors, when they speak of the 'justice' observed toward our enemy, are thinking of a strict law that God would be obliged to respect."[14] A legal right, that God *must* respect, obeying a law outside of himself? No.

On the other hand, the devil's *moral* right over humanity gets more credit. As I noted in Chapter 2, this moral right is affirmed in a certain sense by Caesarius in that God cannot treat the devil differently than sinful humanity. However, in other authors (the Eusebius Gallicanus preachers, for example),

---

12. Rivière, "Rédemption au début du Moyen-Age," 359. *Alors que nous étions* in sorte Dei, *nous sommes devenus, pour Haymon d'Halberstadt,* de sorte diaboli. *En effet, d'après le même auteur, Satan a fait de nous ses captifs.*

13. Rivière, "Rédemption au début du Moyen-Age," 364. *Haymon d'Halberstadt présente le démon comme un* violentissimus praedo *et, pour qualifier son empire, se sert de cette formule volontairement péjorative:* Per mortem hominis in mundo principatum praesumpserat.

14. Rivière, "Rédemption au début du Moyen-Age," 370. *Tout concourt, par conséquent, à exclure l'idée que nos auteurs, quand ils parlent de la «justice» observée envers notre ennemi, pensent à unde loi stricte que Dieu serait tenu de respecter.*

this moral right becomes something more like a legal right in that the devil seems to have a just title to the human race. Rivière argues that this latter understanding is present in at least two later texts, a commentary on Hebrews by Bruno of Cologne (1030–1101) and an anonymous treatise entitled *De redemptione humana* ascribed to the Venerable Bede. Both use language describing God as being obliged to deal with the devil's rightful claim over humanity in a just manner. They represent a viewpoint that grew naturally from the language of their predecessors:

> Because it was not required, the observance of "justice" with regard to the devil was therefore nonetheless sovereignly appropriate to God's wisdom. Up to what point must this sense of "fittingness" be pushed? After the problem of the metaphysical right, henceforth settled in the negative, it is now, one might say, that the problem of the moral right opens up.[15]

Of course, God acting justly toward the devil is properly construed in the fathers and most of their successors as being fitting (*convenire*) as opposed to necessary. As Rivière notes, "The claim of 'justice' toward Satan never takes the form of a strict law and is reduced, in sum, to the affirmation of this sovereign wisdom that, being one of the essential attributes of God, ought to be discovered in each one of his actions."[16]

---

15. Rivière, "Rédemption au début du Moyen-Age," 370. *Pour n'être pas exigée, l'observation de la «justice» à l'égard du démon n'en était donc pas moins souverainement convenable à la sagesse de Dieu. Jusqu'où faut-il pousser le sens de cette convenance? Après le problème du droit métaphysique, désormais tranché par la négative, c'est, peut-on dire, celui du droit moral qui s'ouvre.*

16. Rivière, "Rédemption au début du Moyen-Age," 377. *La revendication de la «justice» envers Satan ne prend jamais la forme d'une loi rigoureuse et se ramène, au total, à l'affirmation*

But to what extent did this fittingness lend itself to maintaining that the devil still had some kind of right that bound God? A little, but not much; Rivière, after noting the presence of this tendency in Bruno and the treatise of Pseudo-Bede, states, "In the eyes of the historian, their exuberance has the main advantage of making stand out all the better, by contrast, the sobriety of the rest."[17] In other words, most theologians and exegetes did not make this mistake of emphasizing the devil's moral right so much that it became a travesty of justice if God did not trick him into giving up his power.

At the same time, this notion of the devil's moral right was sufficiently popular in mainstream Christian writing (sermons, poetry, etc.) that it aroused the opposition of Anselm in the eleventh century. To describe the redemption mostly in terms of the just removal of the devil's rights over humanity was the *manière courante*, the "common way," of expressing the matter by the eleventh century, even if most theologians were more balanced. So in a famous passage of his *Cur Deus homo*, Anselm launches an assault against this common view:

> But also as for that which we are accustomed to say—
> namely, that God had first to proceed against the devil
> through justice to free humanity rather than through
> strength, so that when the devil slew him in whom no
> reason for death was found, and who was God, justly
> did he lose that power which he used to hold over sin-
> ners; for otherwise God would have done unjust violence

---

de cette souveraine sagesse qui, étant und es attributs essentiels de Dieu, doit se retrouver en chacune de ses actions.

17. Rivière, "Rédemption au début du Moyen-Age," 377.

upon him, since justly he possessed humanity, which he had not violently taken to himself but rather the same humanity had given himself over freely to him—as for that, I do not see how it has any force.[18]

We can see in this outline of Anselm a clear echo of the Eusebius Gallicanus sermons as well as some of the import of Caesarius's rhetoric. Rivière notes, "Saint Anselm clearly has before his eyes a theology in which, whether by the manner of presenting the facts or by the principles called upon as justification, the law of 'justice' governs all the redemptive providence of God."[19] It is worth observing that Anselm calls out a view of the redemption whose provenance he only vaguely mentions: *illud quod dicere solemus*, "that which we are accustomed to say." The target he is aiming at is a distortion of the teaching of the church, not any sort of official dogma.

Our investigation of Haimo of Auxerre has demonstrated the theocentricity of the official understanding of the atonement at least two hundred years before Anselm put pen to parchment. So what the bishop of Canterbury addresses is in no small part a contemporary popular misconception brought about by irresponsible rhetoric, alongside an increasing tendency of

---

18. Anselm of Canterbury, *Cur Deus homo* 1.7, PL 158.367. *Sed et illud quod dicere solemus, Deum scilicet, debuisse prius per justitiam contra diabolum agere, ut liberaret hominem, quam per fortitudinem; ut, cum diabolus eum, in quo nulla mortis erat causa, et qui Deus erat, occideret, juste potestatem, quam super peccatores habebat, amitteret; alioquin injustam violentiam fecisset illi, quoniam juste possidebat hominem, quem non ipse violenter attraxerat, sed idem homo se sponte ad illum contulerat, non video quam vim habebat.*

19. Rivière, "Rédemption au début du Moyen-Age," 378. *Saint Anselme a manifestement devant les yeux une théologie dans laquelle, soit par la manière de présenter les faits, soit par les principes invoqués à titre justificatif, la loi de «justice» commande toute la Providence rédemptrice de Dieu.*

the clergy themselves to endorse this misconception. Rivière describes this regrettable situation as follows:

> Without bypassing the order of "fittingness," the "justice" with regard to the devil tended to take a more and more central place in the rational justification of the economy of redemption, until it became the principal—even the only—element of the small-scale *Cur Deus homo*s that medieval homiletic and theology was beginning to put together.[20]

THE ECONOMY OF REDEMPTION IN PRE-ANSELMIAN THEOLOGY

If the rights of the devil were more ephemeral than is commonly supposed, what of the notion that Christ's death on the cross was principally a victory over the devil? Was Anselm's insistence upon the centrality of the sacrificial, theocentric aspect of the crucifixion an innovation? If what we have seen from Caesarius of Arles and Haimo of Auxerre is any indication, the answer is no. Rivière makes the argument that while the devil's defeat was an important part of the redemption for the fathers and the medieval theologians pre-Anselm, it was matched in prominence, and even subordinate to, the notion of a sacrifice to God:

> For the fathers, this preoccupation that must be called "demonocentric" is far from being the only one, as

---

20. Rivière, "Rédemption au début du Moyen-Age," 381. *Sans dépasser l'ordre de la convenance, la «justice» envers le démon tendait à prendre une place de plus en plus centrale dans la justification rationnelle de l'économie rédemptrice, jusqu'à devenir l'élément principal, sinon unique, des humbles Cur Deus homo que l'homilétique et la théologie médiévales commençaient à ébaucher.*

developed as it may be. The Middle Ages, despite the shapeless character of its theology of redemption, was not lacking either in awareness at the same time of the aspects wherein the redemption orders itself directly toward God.[21]

He cites a wide variety of texts, including Haimo of Auxerre's commentary on Hebrews, to provide evidence that "the Middle Ages did not let perish the doctrinal tradition that resolved itself, in the fathers, in the Pauline idea of the mystery of the reconciling expiation brought about by the Savior's cross."[22]

A sacrifice of expiation and propitiation made by God to God for the purpose of dealing with humanity's sin and reconciling God and the human race after they had been estranged: this was at the core of the atonement for theologians of the early Middle Ages. There are three areas Rivière addresses that demonstrate this focus. First, the exegesis of the book of Hebrews during the early Middle Ages dwells on the heavy weight of human sin, unable to be expiated save by Christ's death on the cross: "The Letter to the Hebrews above all lent itself to the development of the philosophy of the divine plan, at the end of which we see appear, in a sense still poorly defined,

---

21. Rivière, "Le dogme de la de Rédemption au début du Moyen-Age (suite)," *RevScRel* 11, no. 4 (1931): 578. *Autant que chez les Pères, pour développée qu'elle puisse être, cette préoccupation qu'il faut bien appeler démonocentrique est loin d'être la seule. Le Moyen-Age non plus, malgré le caractère amorphe de sa théologie rédemptrice, n'a pas manqué d'apercevoir en même tems les aspects par où elle s'ordonne directement en vue de Dieu.*

22. Rivière, "Rédemption au début du Moyen-Age (suite)," *RevScRel* 11, no. 4 (1931): 579–80. *Le Moyen-Age n'a pas laissé périr la tradition doctrinale qui se résumait, chez les Pères, dans la notion paulinienne du mystère d'expiation réconciliatrice réalisé par la croix du Sauveur.* He cites such authors as Bede, Walafrid Strabo, Hrabanus Maurus, Lanfranc, and Bruno of Cahors in addition to Haimo.

the necessity of the Incarnation."[23] He then goes on to show how two commentators on Hebrews, Atto of Vercelli (885–961) and Bruno of Cologne, make the case from the text that Christ's death was a sacrifice that did what all the preceding sacrifices of the old covenant could not do: result in the forgiveness of sin. Rivière makes a brief note of Haimo of Auxerre's concurrence with this view in his own commentary, noting that it makes use of Walafrid Strabo's (808–849) exegesis of Hebrews 9 to likewise affirm the necessity of Christ's sacrificial death due to the gravity of sin.[24]

A sermon of Peter Damian (1007–1072) is also brought forward to supplement the evidence; here, the great theologian affirms the inefficacity of the sacrifices of the old covenant to forgive humanity's sin and the necessity of Christ as high priest and sacrificial victim to achieve what the old sacrifices could not.[25] More than this, however, Peter Damian makes use of a pregnant term in another one of his sermons to describe the import of Christ's sacrifice: *satisfecit,* "he made satisfaction." Rivière notes Peter Damian's exegetical conclusions:

> The only way to get out of the impasse [of the gravity of sin and the uselessness of the sacrifices of the old covenant] was the mystery of the incarnation, thanks to which the Son of God becomes our priest and our sacrificial victim. And if we add to it that in a nearby sermon,

---

23. Rivière, "Rédemption au début du Moyen-Age (suite)," *RevScRel* 11, no. 4 (1931): 580. *L'Épître aux Hébreux surtout prêtait à développer cette philosophie du plan divin, au terme de laquelle on voit apparaître, dans un sens encore mal défini, la nécessité de l'Incarnation.*

24. Rivière, "Rédemption au début du Moyen-Age (suite)," *RevScRel* 11, no. 4 (1931): 580n2.

25. Rivière cites Peter Damian, Sermon 45, *PL* 144.744–45.

to mark the value of Christ's death, the author uses the word *satisfecit*, we see that here again we are on the road leading straight to the *Cur Deus homo*.[26]

Was Anselm therefore making a wholesale innovation when he wrote his great work? No: "Saint Bruno sketched the doctrine of Saint Anselm; Saint Peter Damian even heralds its terminology. These two facts show the state of maturity to which the development of medieval soteriology had already attained."[27] Anselm was clarifying and developing a doctrine of redemption based on a solid substratum of theology that was preserved in the exegesis of the early medieval theologians, Haimo among them.

Second, Rivière makes the point that the concept of Christ's *mors indebita*, his "unowed death," was interpreted in terms of a ransom paid to satisfy not the devil, nor even death, but the justice of God. Human beings owed a death because of our sin, but to whom was this debt paid? The recipient is unnamed in most texts from this period; Rivière uses Haimo as an example of this discretion. But what the early medieval exegetes in fact do is frequently interpret the *mors indebita* of Christ in a substitutionary sense:

---

26. Rivière, "Rédemption au début du Moyen-Age (suite)," *RevScRel* 11, no. 4 (1931): 582–83. *Le seul moyen de sortir de l'impasse était le mystère de l'Incarnation, grâce auquel le Fils de Dieu devient notre prêtre et notre victime. Et si l'on ajoute que, dans un sermon voisin, pour marquer la valeur de sa mort, l'auteur emploie le verbe* satisfecit, *on voit qu'ici encore nous sommes sur le chemin direct qui mène au* Cur Deus homo. [The sermon cited is Peter Damian, Sermon 48, *PL* 144.766.]

27. Rivière, "Rédemption au début du Moyen-Age (suite)," *RevScRel* 11, no. 4 (1931): 583. *Saint Bruno esquissait la doctrine de saint Anselme; saint Pierre Damian annonce même sa terminologie. Ce double fait montre à quel état de maturité le développement de la sotériologie médiévale était déjà parvenu.*

This idea of the *mors indebita* becomes also at times the kernel of small theological systematizations in which the redemption resolves itself into a mystery of penal substitution. For many writers, this theme adds itself to that of sacrifice without being able to easily see if they are synonymous or complimentary concepts. But it is affirmed as well in autonomous developments that have all the appearance of being self-sufficient.[28]

He goes on to cite as examples several texts from Bruno of Cologne and Jonas of Orléans (780–843). Rivière then concludes, "The least that we are able to say is that in the Middle Ages, as in the fathers, the concern to satisfy the 'rights'—very relative in any case—that the devil had acquired over us never prevented the perception of the properly theocentric side of the redemption."[29] Anselm was therefore not doing a new thing by insisting that Christ's death be thought of in terms of what it did for God rather than what it did for the devil.

Third, the defeat of the devil by the payment of a ransom is subordinated in every way to Christ's sacrifice to God. As we saw in Caesarius of Arles, the defeat of the devil is only possible once our sin has been atoned for; it is a side effect of the main object of the crucifixion, the forgiveness of our sin and

---

28. Rivière, "Rédemption au début du Moyen-Age (suite)," *RevScRel* 11, no. 4 (1931): 585. *Cette idée de mors indebita devient elle aussi parfois le noyau de petites sytématisations théologiques où la Rédemption se résout en un mystère de subsitution pénale. Chez plusieurs écrivains, ce thème s'ajoute à celui de sacrifice, sans qu'on puisse bien voir s'il s'agit là de concepts synonymes ou complémentaires. Mais il s'affirme aussi en développements autonomes et qui on tout l'air de se suffire.*

29. Rivière, "Rédemption au début du Moyen-Age (suite)," *RevScRel* 11, no. 4 (1931): 586. *Le moins qu'on puisse dire, c'est donc qu'au Moyen-Age comme chez les Pères le souci de satisfaire aux «droits»—très relatifs du reste—que le démon s'était acquis sur nous n'a jamais empêché d'apercevoir le côté proprement théocentrique de la Rédemption.*

our reconciliation with God. The concept of ransom is even absorbed into the concept of the sacrifice for sin. Rivière cites Bede, Atto of Vercelli, Fulbert of Chartres (952–1028), Bruno of Cologne, Peter Damian, and Manegold of Lautenbach (1030–1103) as exegetes who insist upon the priority of the sacrifice to God over the defeat of the devil and who make ransom synonymous with sacrifice. One example, that of Peter Damian, will suffice for our purposes. Rivière writes:

> The sermon already cited [Sermon 45] of Saint Peter Damian on the philosophy of sacrifice supports this conclusion, of which the synthetic intention is no more debatable than the meaning: *Quia … in rebus inveniri non poterat pretium nostrae Redemptionis, Redemptor noster semetipsum obtulit Patri pro nobis hostiam in odorem suavitatis. Sic ipse factus est sacerdos et sacrificium, ipse redemptor et pretium.* [Since … there was not able to be found in material things the price of our redemption, our Redeemer offered himself to the Father in a sweet aroma. Thus he himself was made priest and sacrifice, redeemer and price.][30]

The price of our redemption, our ransom, is here, as elsewhere, a sacrifice of propitiation (*in odorem suavitatis*) made to God the Father by Christ his Son. Rivière concludes, "Instead therefore of the sacrifice coming to be absorbed in the ransom, it is

---

30. Rivière, "Rédemption au début du Moyen-Age (suite)," *RevScRel* 11, no. 4 (1931): 587. *Le sermon déjà cité de saint Pierre Damien sur la philosophie du sacrifice about it à cette conclusion, don't l'intention synthétique n'est pas plus contestable que le sens:* Quia … in rebus inveniri non poterat pretium nostrae Redemptionis, Redemptor noster semetipsum obtulit Patri pro nobis hostiam in odorem suavitatis. Sic ipse factus est sacerdos et sacrificium, ipse redemptor et pretium. [Citing Peter Damian, Sermon 45, *PL* 144.745.]

ultimately, for Manegold as for many of his contemporaries, the ransom that is absorbed in the sacrifice."[31]

Rivière thus makes the case that for the exegetes of the early Middle Ages, prior to Anselm's *Cur Deus homo*, the doctrine of the redemption was firmly, if somewhat vaguely, based on a theocentric view of the atonement. This does not mean there were no problems; as noted before, the imagery of the devil's conquest tended to overgrow its proper boundaries, prompting Anselm's sharp retort. Rivière thus closes his description of the prelude to Anselm in this way:

> The humble medieval commentators did not, any more than the fathers, lose contact with the evangelical and Pauline doctrine that connects the salvation of the human race to the sacrifice offered to his Father by the Son of God; the citations given previously, and which no doubt would not be impossible to multiply, bear witness to the continuity of a theological effort seeking to explain this dogma, an effort that both preserves and, on occasion, even enriches the patristic heritage on this matter. Yet these first sketches of a theology of redemption are still lacking in two ways: the theme of sacrifice that forms their base remains as carelessly drawn as it is feebly deepened, and the old overloading with import of the devil and his rights did not stop working against their development.[32]

---

31. Rivière, "Rédemption au début du Moyen-Age (suite)," *RevScRel* 11, no. 4 (1931): 588. *Au lieu donc que le sacrifice arrive à s'absorber dans le rachat, c'est, en définitive, pour Manegold comme pour beaucoup de ses contemporains, le rachat qui s'absorbe dans le sacrifice.*

32. Rivière, "Rédemption au début du Moyen-Age (suite)," *RevScRel* 11, no. 4 (1931): 579–80. *Les humbles glossateurs médiévaux n'ont pas plus que les Pères perdu le contact avec*

Such was the situation at the start of the second millennium
of the Christian era. But a stiff gale was about to blow through
the theological world of Latin Christendom, a wind that would
scour the rust of overwrought imagery from the pure theocentric metal of the doctrine of the redemption.

The Achievement of
Anselm of Canterbury

The largest part of Jean Rivière's *Le dogme de la Rédemption au
début du Moyen-Age* is taken up with responding to Turmel's
critique of Anselm. The two parts of his defense of Anselm that
are of interest to us are his insistence upon the essential continuity of the archbishop of Canterbury's teaching on atonement
with the tradition of the fathers and his careful explanation of
the import of the term "honor" when applied to the doctrine
of satisfaction. At root, Anselm's satisfaction theory (a term
Rivière dislikes) is a clear expression of the biblical and traditional view of Christ's crucifixion as a sacrifice of expiation and
propitiation made by God to God.

Rivière recognizes that it is a commonplace (at least among
tous les historiens superficiels, "all superficial historians") to hold
that Anselm was making a clean break with the atonement
doctrines of the past, but he has no time for this commonplace:

---

*le doctrine évangélique et paulinienne qui rattache le salut du genre humain au sacrifice offert à
son Père par le Fils de Dieu, les citations qui précédent et qu'il ne serait sans doute pas impossible
de multiplier attestent la continuité d'un effort théologique en vue d'expliquer ce dogme, où l'on
voit se conserver et, à l'occasion, s'enrichir l'héritage patristique sur ce point. Mais ces premières
ébauches de théologie rédemptrice sont encore doublement déficitaires, parce que le thème du
sacrifice qui en forme la base y reste aussi mollement dessiné que faiblement approfondi et que
l'antique surcharge du démon et de ses «droits» ne cesse pas d'en contrarier le développement.*

Usually, the weightiest objections made to the work of
Anselm come from history. The relative novelty of the
concept of satisfaction that forms its axis has always
served as a pretext to see there a complete break with
the patristic tradition ... We have no need to return to
this question again, having sufficiently demonstrated that
the death of Christ never stopped, in the Church, from
being conceived as a sacrifice offered to God for our sins.
This closely corresponded to the satisfaction that the
archbishop of Canterbury would make the cornerstone
of his treatise.[33]

Anselm was not departing from traditional doctrine but instead
expressing it in different and more developed ways.

Key to this argument is a proper understanding of what
God's honor is for Anselm. It is an image that corresponds to
a deeper reality, and it is necessary not to confuse the image
with the reality. It is important, Rivière writes, not to "dwell at
length ... on the deficient part of the image to the detriment
of the idea that it transmits."[34] What honor means with regard
to God for Anselm is not a divine attribute, since God's honor
cannot be taken away by anything, but an external reality:

---

33. Rivière, "Le dogme de la Rédemption au début du Moyen-Age: Deuxième partie,
voies nouvelles," *RevScRel* 12, no. 2 (1932): 169–70. *D'habitude, les plus graves objections faites
à l'oeuvre anselmienne lui viennent de l'histoire. La nouveauté relative du concept de satisfaction
qui en forme l'axe a toujours servi de prétexte pour y voir une complète solution de continuité avec
la tradition patristique ... Nous n'avons pas à y revenir davantage, ayant suffisamment montré
que la mort du Christ n'a jamais cessé, dans l'Église, d'être conçue comme un sacrifice offert à
Dieu pour nos péchés. Ce qui, au terme près, correspondait à la satisfaction dont l'archevêque de
Cantorbéry allait faire la clef de voûte de son traité.*

34. Rivière, "Rédemption au début du Moyen-Age: Deuxième," 179. ... *à s'appesantir
... sur la part déficiente de l'image au détriment de l'idée qu'elle traduit.*

Therefore Saint Anselm never conceived, as H. Gallerand [i.e., Turmel] imputes to him, that sin stripped God personally of that which belonged to him, but only that it took away from him the external glory that the willing homage of rational creatures ought to make shine forth in the universe. Here is the reason why the sanctions of the divine justice have some sense when this honor due to God has not been given to him.[35]

Rebellion against God is what sin in its essence is. This rebellion results in humanity not worshiping God, which he, because of who he is, cannot tolerate: "Do not worship any other god, for the LORD, whose name is Jealous, is a jealous God" (Exod 34:14). This is by no means out of step with the teaching of the fathers and the earlier medieval authors, as, for example, in the Eusebius Gallicanus preachers' use of the term *maiestas*, "treason," to describe Adam's sin.

Against the argument of Turmel and the general perception he represented—that Anselm broke with the demonocentric atonement of the fathers and the early Middle Ages—Rivière argues that both were based on the same essential substrate:

The fathers did not limit themselves to defending the "rights" of the devil, nor were the first scholastics limited to fighting them. Between the former and the latter there was common ground, both knowing the continual affirmation of the expiating death of Christ and its value with

---

35. Rivière, "Rédemption au début du Moyen-Age: Deuxième," 181. *Jamais donc saint Anselme n'a conçu, comme le lui impute H. Gallerand, que le péché dérobe personnellement à Dieu quoi que ce soit de son bien, mais seulement qu'il le prive de la gloire extérieure que l'hommage volontaire des créatures rasissonnables doit faire rayonner dans l'univers. Voilà pourquoi les sanctions de la justice divine ont un sens quand cet honneur dù à Dieu ne lui a pas été rendu.*

regard to the forgiveness of our sins. [This was] a fundamental point of the Christian revelation that the fathers
all maintained, until the time when medieval theology
undertook a more rigorous investigation of it.[36]

This more rigorous investigation was occasioned by the problem we saw Rivière identify earlier, that the imagery of the devil's defeat tended to overwhelm the core theology of sacrifice.
Rivière goes on to note:

> This continuity of background is, however, not incompat-
> ible with some surface differences. The most prominent,
> in the sight of the one who sees only the external, is in the
> very unequal preoccupation with Satan and his "rights,"
> which held for the fathers an important place among the
> "fittingnesses" [convenances] of the economy of redemp-
> tion and which the early scholastics resolutely banished.[37]

The work of Anselm was, for Rivière, an important development not because it marked a significant departure from the
foundational understanding of the atonement that came before,
but because it countered a mistaken overemphasis on the devil's
role in the redemption.

---

36. Rivière, "Le dogme de la Rédemption au début du Moyen-Age (suite)," *RevScRel*
13, no. 2 (1933): 213. *Ni les Pères ne se sont contentés de défendre les «droits» du démon, ni les
premiers scolastiques de les combattre. Entre les uns and les autres il y a un trait d'union, savoir
l'affirmation constante de la mort expiatoire du Christ et de sa valeur pour la rémission de nos
péchés. Point fondamental de la révélation chrétienne que les Pères ont tous maintenu, en atten-
dant que la théologie médiévale en entrepît une plus rigoureuse investigation.*

37. Rivière, "Rédemption au début du Moyen-Age (suite)," *RevScRel* 13, no. 2 (1933):
213. *Cette continuité de fond n'est pourtant pas incompatible avec des divergences de surface. La
plus saillante, au regard de qui ne voit que les dehors, est dans la préoccupation très inégale de
Satan et de ses «droits», qui tenait, chez les Pères, une place importante parmi les convenances
de l'économie rédemptrice et que les initiateurs de la scolastique en ont résolument bannie.*

Another surface difference was in the systematic development of a theology of satisfaction and merit, whose flowering
resulted in the later medieval doctrine of redemption. Rivière,
faithful Roman Catholic that he was, of course approved of
this development; Protestants might point out that it led to its
own set of unnatural growths that obscured the reality of the
foundation. But in any event, the thread linking both earlier
and later doctrines was the same: a sacrifice of expiation and
propitiation made by God to God. Rivière argues that a study
of the development of the doctrine of the redemption makes
this clear: "When it does not content itself with a collection
of isolated pieces, it does not fail to grasp ... the lasting con-
firmation of an objective efficacy of the death of Christ with
regard to our reconciliation with God."[38] Whatever developments Anselm contributed to in the doctrine of the redemption,
they were not a break with the truth that had never ceased to
be handed down.

Rivière concludes his refutation of Turmel by reiterating
his position on the nature of the devil's rights during the
patristic and early medieval era.[39] According to Rivière, the

---

38. Rivière, "Rédemption au début du Moyen-Age (suite)," 214. *Quand elle ne se borne
pas à une collection de singularités, ne manque pas de saisir ... l'attestation permanente d'une
efficacité objective de la mort du Christ en vue de notre réconciliation avec Dieu.*

39. Rivière, "Rédemption au début du Moyen-Age (suite)," 217. "For him who wishes
to see and knows how to see things as they are, it is clear that, taken for itself, the
consideration of Satan and of his 'rights,' whatever place it may occupy in the patristic
or medieval literature, is only one of those secondary motifs—a good part of whose
nature is metaphoric when it comes down to it—that the Christian imagination has
often embroidered around the truths of the faith, but which never had anything but an
incidental connection with them. ... It is nonetheless certain in any case that far from
being the only or even the dominant one, this theory as it exists only represented, in the
thought of the fathers ... one part of the economy of redemption, of which the doctrine
of the expiating and reconciling sacrifice served as the other part to express ... the aspect
pertaining to God." *Pour qui veut et sait voir les choses comme elles sont, il est clair que, prise*

patristic concept of the conquest of the devil by Christ on the cross is an image that expresses an element of the atonement that is, at the same time, not its center. So what was Anselm's achievement?

> That being so, the role of the great originators of scholasticism was to cut down the ancillary concept to the benefit of the main concept, to prune the foliage of a particularly bushy tree to extricate—and by that means even to strengthen—the branches and the trunk. Such is the work accomplished by Saint Anselm.[40]

Conclusion

It is fitting to conclude our three vignettes of the medieval teaching on the atonement with a look at the great medieval exegete Haimo of Auxerre because it is a reminder that medieval Christians read the same Bible we do. If they read the same Bible, it would be odd if they missed the clear centrality of the sacrificial aspects of Christ's crucifixion. Jean Rivière puts it well:

---

en elle-même, la considération de Satan et de ses «droits», quelle que puisse être la place qu'elle occupe dans la littérature patristique ou médiévale, n'est qu'un de ces motifs secondaries—de caractère pour une bonne part métaphorique, au demeurant—que l'imagination chrétienne a souvent brodés autour des vérités de la foi, mais qui n'est jamais avec elles qu'un lien accidentel ... Il n'est pas moins sûr d'ailleurs que, loin d'être unique ou seulement prépondérante, cette théorie telle quelle ... ne représentait, dans la pensée des Pères ... qu'une partie de l'économie rédemptrice, don't la doctrine du sacrifice expiatoire et réconciliateur leur servait d'autre part à exprimer ... l'aspect relatif à Dieu.

40. Rivière, "Rédemption au début du Moyen-Age (suite)," 217. *Cela étant, le rôle des grands initiateurs de la scolastique fut de faire tomber l'accessoire au profit du principal, d'émonder la frondaison d'un arbre particulièrement touffu, pour dégager—et par là même fortifier d'autant—les branches et le tronc. Tel est le sens général d l'oeuvre accomplie par saint Anselme.*

How can we imagine that these preachers and exegetes, bound so to speak to the text of Scripture—and most especially to that of Saint Paul, on whom they loved to comment—perceived none of those innumerable texts that speak of reconciliation and of sacrifice when speaking of the cross of Christ?[41]

How can we imagine, indeed? And yet far too many do so imagine, and so assert, and so dismiss. But as we have seen, Haimo of Auxerre grasped the theocentric import of the atonement quite easily in his commentaries on Romans and Hebrews. Not only did he grasp it, but his exposition of the nature of Christ's sacrifice is both subtle and wide ranging. For Haimo, as for his contemporaries Claudius of Turin and Hrabanus Maurus, the centerpiece of the atonement is Christ's sacrificial death on the cross: a sacrifice of expiation and propitiation made by God to God to reconcile mankind to God and God to mankind.

This understanding is, I would suggest along with Rivière, the center of the atonement in the Middle Ages. Thus, the reason why Anselm only appears at the end of this book, and only indirectly: he was building on that solid foundation of sacrifice made clear by Haimo of Auxerre. Our final vignette encompasses the first two, which are variations on this central theme of sacrifice. The cross was an altar upon which our redemption was purchased, our sin washed away, our punishment averted. So one of the greatest medieval hymns on the

---

41. Rivière, "Rédemption au début du Moyen-Age (suite)," *RevScRel* 11, no. 4 (1931): 579. *Comment imaginer que ces prédicateurs et ces exégètes, rivés pour ainsi dire au texte de l'Écriture et tout spécialement de saint Paul qu'ils se plaisent à commenter, n'aient rien aperçu des textes innombrables qui parlent de réconciliation et de sacrifice à propos de la mort du Christ?*

cross, the *Vexilla regis prodeunt*, written in the sixth century by the poet Venantius Fortunatus, concludes:

> *Salve ara, salve victima*
> *De passionis gloria*
> *Qua vita mortem pertulit*
> *Et morte vitam reddidit*

> *Hail, O altar*
> *Hail, O Victim*
> *From the glory of your Passion*
> *In which Life endured death*
> *And in death restored life*

CHAPTER 8

CONCLUSION

T
hus ends the experiment. Three vignettes of the medieval doctrine of the atonement, the first from the end, the second from the beginning, and the third from the middle of the Middle Ages, have been explored. I hope to have given readers a glimpse of the immensity and subtlety of the medieval tradition of the atonement and to have shown that at its core lay the mystery of Christ's sacrifice on the cross, a sacrifice of expiation and propitiation made by God to God. Contrary to the usual narrative, medieval teaching on the atonement prior to Anselm was thoroughly theocentric, not demonocentric, however popular the imagery of *Christus Victor* was. This book is, of course, not a comprehensive treatment of the subject—for an early effort to that end I have pointed to Jean Rivière—but a blueprint for an approach that will serve two ends: to introduce evangelical Protestants to a broader

historical world and to give believers confidence that orthodoxy is not a novelty in Christian history.

The section on Dante serves these two purposes by laying out the variety of engagements with the doctrine of the atonement of a major figure of late medieval Italy and demonstrating how his approach integrated penal substitution into a conception of atonement as satisfaction. In his *Monarchia*, we see penal substitution leveraged as an argument for the authority of the Roman Empire as ordained by the mysterious providence of God; in the *Divina Commedia*, we see it stand side by side with a doctrine of satisfaction and the two doctrines together contribute to Dante's spiritual growth and delight in God. At root, however, we have seen how Dante's conception of the atonement is a sacrifice of propitiation and expiation made by God to God. It displays God's attributes in their full glorious panoply, summed up by the phrase the *divina bontà*, "the divine goodness."

The section on Caesarius of Arles shows how the atonement was preached in the beginning of the Middle Ages in post-Roman Gaul by an innovative and powerful bishop. While remaining deeply attached to the striking imagery of the conquest of death and the devil by Christ on the cross, Caesarius made it clear that this conquest was dependent upon humanity's forgiveness through Christ's sacrifice of propitiation and expiation offered to God. Moreover, the devil was not our rightful conqueror but our fellow criminal. And for Caesarius—as for his contemporaries—this sacrifice and the economy of redemption at whose center it stood displayed God's justice and mercy in a way that brought forth their praise and resolve to pursue holiness.

The section on Haimo of Auxerre brings forward a critically important commentary on the letters of Paul and shows how it taught an atonement focused on the sacrifice of Christ. This was a commentary not by a famous theologian but by a humble monastic teacher seeking to instruct his ninth-century pupils in the grandeur of Scripture. His doctrine of the atonement reflects this and hews closely to the teaching of Scripture on the subject: it was a sacrifice made by God and to God, a sacrifice of propitiation and expiation. Haimo's teaching on the atonement also demonstrates that Anselm's project was not one of invention but one of clarification. For Haimo, as for his contemporaries, we see the love of God displayed for his beloved creation in the atonement: why the God-man? To provide a spotless lamb for a sacrifice for sins and the redemption of the human race.

All three were thoroughly mainstream thinkers in their time and place; this is important to emphasize. And throughout these three vignettes, and summed up by the final one, we see the common thread of sacrifice. The cross is a sacrifice of propitiation, by which God is made favorable toward those on whom his wrath previously lay, and a sacrifice of expiation, by which sins are cleansed and forgiven. A sacrifice made by God himself both because it was the will of the Father for the Son to die and because the Son is God himself who chose to die. A sacrifice made to the Father by the Son and by God to his own self. A sacrifice for sin since without the shedding of blood there can be no forgiveness. A sacrifice that demonstrates the obedience of the representative Man, the Second Adam, to God and therefore satisfies his wrath. A sacrifice that sheds the blood that enables the Mediator of all mankind to enter into the divine presence and intercede before God for those who believe. A sacrifice that imposes the punishment deserved by

all sinners upon the Second Adam. A sacrifice that cleanses
those who believe from sin. A sacrifice that purges believers
from sin by shedding the blood of a spotless lamb. A sacrifice
that lies at the heart of our redemption.

JEAN RIVIÈRE AND THE ATONEMENT

The insight that sacrifice lay at the center of the medieval conception of the atonement was the foundation of Jean Rivière's
work. This is why I have placed it alongside the three medieval figures treated in this book. Not only is it precisely the sort
of treatment that should be held up as an exemplar of superb
scholarship on the doctrine of the atonement, but also, the
dispute in which he engaged has uncanny similarities with the
discussions raging today. Against Joseph Turmel, a modernist
historical theologian insisting upon the primacy of *Christus
Victor*, Rivière deployed all his skill and knowledge of the history of the atonement with devastating effect.

His three books on the atonement that we have already mentioned (comprising the articles we used in the body of the text)
were further supplemented in 1931 by an expanded third edition of his classic *Le dogme de la Rédemption: Étude théologique.*
Of these works against Turmel, his friend Ferdinand Cavallera,
professor of patristics at the University of Toulouse, wrote:

> Certainly, these seventeen hundred pages of discussion
> and investigation shot through with primary texts are not
> always easy reading, but it is very obvious that nowhere will
> we find information as abundant and as certain and that all
> people of good faith have to recognize that between him
> and his adversary, M. Turmel (whom he follows footstep

by footstep and lets no error escape, especially no error of
interpretation), the superiority, with regard to the criticism
as much as to the erudition, is not on the side of the one
decked out in a mask in order to attack at his pleasure the
fundamental doctrine of salvation.[1]

Rivière's work is indeed intimidating, which perhaps explains
the lack of engagement with him. His French is idiomatic and
complex, while he disdains to translate his numerous Latin
citations. Yet the hard work it takes to read and comprehend
him pays tremendous dividends.

The only work of Rivière's that has passed into general use
in the English-speaking world is his first, published in 1905:
The Doctrine of the Atonement: A Historical Essay, translated
into English by Luigi Cappadelta in 1909. With stubborn con-
sistency, this is the work that crops up again and again in the
study of the history of the atonement. So Gustav Aulén breezily
dismisses Rivière with two brief mentions of this early work,
neither of which show any sign of engagement with the French
historian.[2] More recently, take, for example, William Lane

---

1. Ferdinand Cavallera, "Les travaux récents de M. *Rivière sur la Rédemption*," *BLE*
36, nos. 3, 4 (1935): 87. *Certes, ce n'est pas une lecture toujours facile que celle de ces dix-sept
cents pages de discussions et d'examen serré des textes, mais il saute aux yeux que, nulle part,
on ne trouvera d'aussi abondants renseignements et aussi sûrs et que tout homme de bonne foi
devra reconnaître qu'entre lui et son adversaire, M. Turmel, qu'il suit pied à pied et auquel il ne
pardonne aucune défaillance, à plus forte raison aucune erreur d'interprétation, la supériorité,
pour la critique comme pour l'érudition, n'est pas du côté de celui qui s'est affublé d'un masque,
pour attaquer plus à son aise le dogme fondamental du salut.*

2. Aulén, *Christus Victor*, 21, 52. In fact, Aulén shows no sign of even having read
Rivière's works; his critique on p. 52 is drawn from Hastings Rashdall's book *The Idea of
the Atonement in Christian Theology*, published in 1919. He does not, in short, cite Rivière's
book directly even when criticizing it. It seems from this that Aulén had certainly heard of
Rivière, but rather than do the hard work of actually reading him, he lets Rashdall do his
work for him. One trembles to imagine what Rivière's response to this insouciance would
have been. Actually, we can get a taste from one of his takes on Turmel: "M. Turmel shares
in the pretention of incarnating purely and simply in his own person the results of the

Craig's book *Atonement and the Death of Christ*, which treats Rivière more respectfully but still relies exclusively upon the English translation of his first book.[3] Turmel adhered to this habit when responding to Rivière's criticisms, choosing to attack a small part of this early work rather than the more recent articles attacking him.[4] He also refused to refer to Rivière by name, only briefly mentioning anonymous attacks in the *Revue des sciences religieuses*—although perhaps we might forgive him for that, given that Rivière was one of the drivers of his excommunication. In response, Rivière remarked that it seemed Turmel was trying to discredit his later articles by finding fault with the scholarship of his youth done some twenty-five years earlier:

> It is easy to grasp the key to this maneuver. Since it is the same person, in noting what he believes to be the mistakes of his earlier works, M. Turmel hopes to devalue those of today. A method that cannot exceed the value of an *ad hominem* argument.[5]

---

analysis. This permits him up to this point to remain faithful to this Olympian method where nothing counts except the conviction of the author, without any regard for the vulgar necessities of discussion." M. *Turmel partageait la prétention d'incarner purement et simplement en sa personne les résultats de la critique. Ce qui lui permettait jusqu'ici de rester fidèle à cette méthode olympienne où rien ne compte que la conviction de l'auteur, sans aucun égard aux nécessités vulgaires de la discussion.* Jean Rivière, "Le dogme de la Rédemption devant l'histoire," *RevScRel* 15, no. 4 (1935): 493.

3. William Lane Craig, *Atonement and the Death of Christ: An Exegetical, Historical, and Philosophical Exploration* (Waco: Baylor University Press, 2020). See especially the notes for Chapter 6, pp. 91–112, where the English translation of Rivière's work is cited not only for his insights but also as a source for some of the translations of the primary texts that Craig uses (to Craig's credit, however, he does not buy into the typical narrative laid out in the introduction of the history of the doctrine of the atonement; 110–11). This habit of citing Rivière's first work as a source for primary texts or even for English translations of these texts appears all too frequently, as, for example, in David Brondos, *Paul on the Cross: Reconstructing the Apostle's Story of Redemption* (Minneapolis: Fortress, 2006), 214n25.

4. Joseph Turmel, *Histoire des dogmes* vol. 4 (Paris: Rieder, 1935), 477–85.

5. Rivière, "Rédemption devant l'histoire," 497. *Il est facile de saisir le secret de la manoeuvre. Comme il s'agit d'un même personnage, en relevant ce qu'il croit être les défaillances de ses*

Rather than engage with Rivière's actual critique, then, Turmel chose to go after the earlier, more popular work. But as Rivière wryly notes, "He has no doubt dismissed the idea that the author, during the quarter of a century since then, has learned to master any more of his subject."[6] To rely, as Turmel and most others do, solely on Rivière's first venture into the subject area of the history of the doctrine of the atonement is to overlook the great mass of his mature work.

Rivière's passionate and learned defense of orthodox doctrine (Catholic orthodoxy, to be sure, but he was a generous reader of Protestant authors as well) is instructive for us in two ways. First, he was confident that a thorough and skilled account of the historical record supported the essential doctrinal continuity of the Christian faith throughout its existence—a confidence that we would do well to emulate. Second, he engaged directly in defending a key doctrine of the faith, the redemption, whose size and complexity in the historical record might deter less determined scholars; we too should not fear to tackle big subjects and burrow down into the marrow of history to expound them in their fullness.

The assault by Turmel against the work of Rivière, his sneers about the "apologists," and his rude attempts at *damnatio memoriae* were taken by his foe not as personal assaults but as part of a broader attack on the core of the Christian faith, to be answered accordingly. Rivière writes:

---

travaux d'autrefois M. Turmel espère démonétiser ceux de maintenant.

6. Rivière, "Rédemption devant l'histoire," 497–98. *Car il n'est sans doute pas exclu que l'auteur, pendant ce quart de siècle, ait appris à maîtriser davantage son sujet.*

Let us first not mistake the nature of the case. It is plainly not a wretched personal conflict, but also not one of those ongoing debates that engage the interest of none save a few specialists. What the point of contention is here, whether we want it to be or not, is a dogmatic question of the first rank, considering the importance of the Catholic tradition to the matter of the redemption and, as a result, given the specifics of this particular case, its qualifications for the role it claims in the transmission of the deposit of faith. M. Turmel boasts of catching it in a blatant inconsistency, where his opponent defends its continuity: we need to know on whose side the impartial verdict of history lies.[7]

Rivière is concerned, as a faithful Roman Catholic, to defend the continuity of the tradition of the church. Yet he does so not by dogmatic assertion but through a careful, nuanced assessment of all the facts at hand. Yes, the doctrines taught by Scripture have undergone development, but that development is based on clarifying and going deeper into fundamental truths that have always been affirmed by the church in every era, so long as it was faithful to Scripture. For Rivière, the fundamental truth in the case of the atonement was a theocentric sacrifice. History, he was confident, would back that up against the attacks of the church's enemies.

---

7. Rivière, "Rédemption devant l'histoire," 525. *Et d'abord qu'on ne se méprenne point sur la nature du cas. Il ne s'agit évidemment pas d'un misérable conflit personnel, mais pas davantage d'un de ces débats toujours pendants qui n'intéressent que la curiosité de rares techniciens. Ce qui est en cause ici, qu'on le veuille ou non, c'est une question dogmatique au premier chef, savoir la valeur de la tradition catholique en matière de Rédemption et par conséquent, sous les espèces de ce cas particulier, ses titres au rôle qu'elle de la saisir en flagrant délit d'inconsistance, au lieu que son contradicteur en défend la continuité: il s'agit de savoir à qui l'histoire impartiale donne raison.*

LESSONS FROM HISTORY

What I would suggest is that evangelical Protestants should take this confidence in history to heart. Although it was (and is) a special problem for Roman Catholics, for whom the sacred tradition of the church has special importance, for evangelicals as well, a blatant inconsistency in the content of orthodoxy among various historical periods can prove problematic. Yet there is a tendency for evangelicals either to dismiss the Middle Ages entirely as Catholic or to seek out proto-Protestants who stood against the bleak tide of superstition and unbelief. Both takes are to be avoided. The medieval church was neither Roman Catholic nor Protestant but a *tertium quid*. It was not monolithic but varied between times and places. It had its unorthodox doctrinal encrustations that were periodically cleared away, with the solutions (as is all too often the case even today) causing new encrustations. But above all, it was a Christian church, a church whose devout adherents were as likely to grasp the true gospel as we are. We can learn from them, allowing their insights and struggles to inform our theology and practice. We can be confident as well that the fundamental doctrines of the faith, in all their thickness and grandeur, have remained present at the core of church teaching. Finally, we can rejoice in discovering this common faith. They read and believed the same Bible we do and held allegiance to the same Lord Jesus Christ.

What does this mean for how we, as evangelical Protestants, approach the atonement? We should begin with having confidence that what we see taught in Scripture was seen as well by those who read it before us. I would also suggest that like the medieval authors studied in this book, we should begin from the base of Christ's death on the cross as a sacrifice of propitiation and expiation. We need to regain the full panoply of meanings behind these two terms, including a proper regard for the mystery inherent in how such a sacrifice operates. Above all, and as ever, we need to return to Scripture's presentation of the atonement. The Protestant tradition rightly emphasizes the priority of Scripture over tradition, and the medieval authors we have studied were eager and obedient readers of the Bible. Thus, they make good conversation partners as we engage with the inspired text's teaching on the atonement and can help correct our blind spots, just as we can see and correct theirs. Moreover, reading them helps us to delve down to the foundation of the atonement because the very real differences that we have with them in language and imagery, as well as the doctrinal differences, should provoke us to seek out the common ground we have in Scripture. And that is the most valuable thing of all, for, as Dante wrote:

> You mortals do not proceed along one same path in philosophizing, so much does the love of show and the thought of it carry you away; and even this is borne with less anger up here than when the Divine Scripture is set aside or when it is perverted. They think not there how much blood it costs to sow it in the world, nor how much he pleases who humbly keeps close to it.[8]

---

8. Dante Alighieri, *Paradiso*, trans. Charles Singleton. *Voi non andate giù per un sentiero/ filosofando: tanto vi trasporta/ l'amor de l'apparenza e 'l suo pensiero!/ E ancor questo qua sù si comporta/ con men disdegno che quando è posposta/ la divina Scrittura o quando è torta./ Non vi si pensa quanto sangue costa/ seminarla nel mondo e quanto piace/ chi umilmente con essa s'accosta.*

ACKNOWLEDGMENTS

This book would not have been possible without the support of family and friends. Its origins lie in a conversation in a Toronto restaurant with Michael Haykin, who urged me to expand my idea of a few online articles on the history of the medieval atonement into a book. His encouragement and advice while I was crafting my book proposal were both invaluable, and I am extremely grateful to Dr. Haykin for his support for the book as a whole. Jon Neufeld and Howard McPhee read parts of the first draft of this book, and I am thankful for their suggestions and encouragement. Todd Hains and the staff at Lexham Press deserve a great deal of thanks as well, not only for taking on the publication of this book, but for allowing me such a free hand in crafting it as I wished. Dr. Hains's enthusiasm for this book and extraordinary patience as I continually missed deadlines were both blessings.

Part of the reason for the missed deadlines was the fact that most of this book was written during the COVID-19 pandemic. In addition to closed libraries, this meant for me a sustained period of unemployment. Without the financial and moral support of my family, therefore, this book would have been utterly impossible. My thanks go to my grandparents, Barbara and Chester Wheaton, and to my parents, Byron and Jackie Wheaton, for their financial aid and encouragement. My father also read substantial portions of the first draft, and his suggestions improved the text greatly.

Most of all, I am indebted to the generosity of my sister, Laura Wheaton. In the midst of the tremendous stresses placed upon the medical profession (of which she is an honored member) by COVID-19, she provided me with financial support and a place to live. It is in the pleasant confines of her home that I have written this book, and it is through her library account at Queen's University in Kingston that I have obtained many of the texts necessary for its completion. Authors need patrons, and I could not have asked for a kinder one than my sister. To her this book is dedicated.

I believe that what I have written contributes to our knowledge of the truth. But as the sixth-century churchman Venantius Fortunatus reminded me: *Unde in homine mendace causa veritatis sit, nisi ipsa veritas se ministret, hoc est, nisi in hominem ipsam bonam voluntatem Deus veritatis inspiret qui et velle tribuit et posse conplevit?* Therefore I conclude, in gratitude: *Soli Deo gloria*—to God alone be the glory.

BIBLIOGRAPHY

Andrieu, Michel. "In Memoriam: Mgr. Victor Martin et M. Jean Rivière."
    Revue des sciences religieuses 21, no. 3–4 (1947): 5–16.

Bailey, Lisa Kaaren. *Christianity's Quiet Success: The Eusebius Gallicanus
    Sermon Collection and the Power of the Church in Late Antique
    Gaul.* Notre Dame, IN: Notre Dame University Press, 2010.

Baudreu, Hervé. "«Une Vie d'Hircocerf»: Joseph Turmel (1859–1943)."
    Annales de Bretagne et des Pays de l'Ouest 114, no. 1 (2007): 185–98.

Boucaud, Pierre. "Claude de Turin († ca. 828) et Haymon d'Auxerre (*fl.*
    850): deux commentateurs d'*I Corinthiens.*" In *Études d'Exégèse
    Carolingien: Autour d'Haymon d'Auxerre,* edited by Sumi
    Shimahara, 187–236. Turnhout: Brepols, 2007.

Brondos, David. *Paul on the Cross: Reconstructing the Apostle's Story of
    Redemption.* Minneapolis: Fortress, 2006.

Caesarius of Arles. *Sermones.* Edited by G. Morin. CCSL 103. Turnhout:
    Brepols, 1953.

Cassell, Anthony. *The Monarchia Controversy.* Washington, DC:
    Catholic University of America Press, 2004.

Cavallera, Ferdinand. "Les travaux récents de M. *Rivière* sur la
    Rédemption." *Bulletin de littérature ecclésiastique* 36, nos. 3, 4
    (1935): 83–87.

Chazelle, Celia and Burton van Name Edwards. "Introduction: The Study of the Bible and Carolingian Culture." In *The Study of the Bible in the Carolingian Era*, 1–16. Turnhout: Brepols, 2003.

Craig, William Lane. *Atonement and the death of Christ: An Exegetical, Historical, and Philosophical Exploration*. Waco, TX: Baylor University Press, 2020.

Delaplace, Christine. "La Provence sous la domination ostrogothique (508–536)." *Annales du Midi* 115, no. 244 (2003): 479–99.

De Maeyer, Nicolas and Gert Partoens. "Preaching in Sixth-Century Arles: The Sermons of Bishop Caesarius." In *Preaching in the Patristic Era*, edited by Anthony Dupont, Shari Boodts, Gert Partoens, and Johan Leemans, 198–231. Leiden: Brill, 2018.

Evenson, George O. "A Critique of Aulén's *Christus Victor*." *Concordia Theological Monthly* 28 (1957): 738–49.

Eusebius 'Gallicanus': Collectio homiliarum. Edited by F. Glorie. CCSL 101. Turnhout: Brepols, 1970.

Fairweather, Eugene R. "Incarnation and Atonement: An Anselmian Response to Aulén's *Christus Victor*." *Canadian Journal of Theology* 7, no. 3 (1961): 167–75.

Ferguson, Sinclair, David F. Wright, and J. I. Packer, eds. *New Dictionary of Theology*. Downers Grove, IL: InterVarsity Press, 1988.

Fiorentini, Luca. "Archaeology of the *Tre Corone*: Dante, Petrarca, and Boccaccio in Benvenuto da Imola's Commentary on the *Divine Comedy*." *Dante Studies* 136 (2018): 1–21.

Flood, Derek. "Substitutionary Atonement and the Church Fathers: A Reply to the Authors of *Pierced for Our Transgressions*." *Evangelical Quarterly* 82, no. 2 (2010): 142–59.

Gunzbert, Lynn M. *Strangers at Home: Jews in the Italian Literary Imagination*. Berkeley: University of California Press, 1992.

Heil, Johannes. *Kompilation oder Konstruktion? Die Juden in den Pauluskommentaren des 9. Jahrhunderts*. Hannover: Hahnsche Buchhandlung, 1998.

———. "Haimo's Commentary on Paul: Sources, Methods and Theology." In *Études d'Exégèse Carolingien: Autour d'Haymon d'Auxerre*, edited by Sumi Shimahara, 103–22. Turnhout: Brepols, 2007.

Heydemann, Gerda. "The People of God and the Law: Biblical Models in Carolingian Legislation." *Speculum* 95, no. 1 (2020): 89–131.

Hollander, Robert. "Dante and His Commentators." In *The Cambridge Companion to Dante*, edited by Rachel Jacoff, 270–80. Cambridge: Cambridge University Press, 1993.

———. *Dante: A Life in Works*. New Haven: Yale, 2001.

Iogna-Pratt, Dominique. "L'oeuvre d'Haymon d'Auxerre." In *L'école carolingienne d'Auxerre: De Muretach à Remi 830–908*, edited by Dominque Iogna-Pratt, Colette Jeudy, and Guy Lobrichon, 157–80. Paris: Éditions Beauchesne, 1991.

Jeffery, Steve, Michael Ovey, and Andrew Sach. *Pierced for Our Transgressions: Rediscovering the Glory of Penal Substitution*. Wheaton: Crossway, 2007.

Kay, Richard. *Dante's Monarchia*. Toronto: PIMS, 1998.

Klingshirn, William. *Caesarius of Arles: The Making of a Christian Community in Late Antique Gaul*. Cambridge: Cambridge University Press, 1994.

Leonardi, Claudio. "Une école au carrefour de la culture carolingienne." In *L'école carolingienne d'Auxerre: De Muretach à Remi 830–908*, edited by Dominque Iogna-Pratt, Colette Jeudy, and Guy Lobrichon, 445–53. Paris: Éditions Beauchesne, 1991.

Levy, Ian Christopher. "Trinity and Christology in Haimo of Auxerre's Pauline Commentaries." In *The Multiple Meanings of Scripture: The Role of Exegesis in Early-Christian and Medieval Culture*, edited by Ineke Van 't Spijker, 101–24. Leiden: Brill, 2009.

Matteini, Nevio. *Il piu' antico oppositore politico di Dante: Guido Vernani da Rimini*. Padua: Casa editrice dott. Antonio, 1958.

Mazzoni, Francesco. "Alighieri, Pietro." In *Enciclopedia Dantesca*, edited by Umberto Bosco, vol. 1. Rome: Istituto dell'Enciclopedia Italiana, 1970.

———. "Benvenuto da Imola." In *Enciclopedia Dantesca*, edited by Umberto Bosco, vol. 1. Rome: Istituto dell'Enciclopedia Italiana, 1970.

———. "Lana, Iacopo della." In *Enciclopedia Dantesca*, edited by Umberto Bosco, vol. 3. Rome: Istituto dell'Enciclopedia Italiana, 1971.

———. "Lancia, Andrea." In *Enciclopedia Dantesca*, edited by Umberto Bosco, vol. 3. Rome: Istituto dell'Enciclopedia Italiana, 1971.

———. "Ottimo commento, L'." In *Enciclopedia Dantesca*, edited by Umberto Bosco, vol. 4. Rome: Istituto dell'Enciclopedia Italiana, 1973.

McKitterick, Rosamond. "The Carolingian Renaissance of Culture and Learning." In *Charlemagne: Empire and Society*, edited by Joanna Story, 151–66. Manchester: Manchester University Press, 2005.

McNall, Joshua M. *The Mosaic of Atonement*. Grand Rapids: Zondervan, 2019.

Munier, Charles. "La patristique à la Faculté de Théologie Catholique de l'Université de Strasbourg." *Revue des sciences religieuses* 66, no. 3–4 (1992): 319–32.

Nardi, Bruno. "Discussioni dantesche: Di un'aspra critica di Fra Guido Vernani a Dante." *L'Alighieri* 6, no. 1 (1965): 43–47.

Parker, Deborah. *Commentary and Ideology: Dante in the Renaissance*. Durham, NC: Duke University Press, 1993.

Rivière, Jean. "Dante et le «châtiment» du Christ." *Revue des Sciences Religieuses* 1, no. 4 (1921): 401–6.

———. "Le dogme de la rédemption chez saint Augustin." *Revue des Sciences Religieuses* 7, no. 3 (1927): 429–51.

———. "Le dogme de la rédemption chez saint Augustin (suite et fin)." *Revue des Sciences Religieuses* 8, no. 1 (1928): 24–49.

———. "Le dogme de la rédemption après saint Augustin: deuxième partie: au temps de saint Grégoire." *Revue des Sciences Religieuses*, 9, no. 3 (1929): 305–42.

———. "Le dogme de la rédemption après saint Augustin: deuxième partie: au temps de saint Grégoire." *Revue des Sciences Religieuses* 9, no. 4 (1929): 477–512.

———. "Le dogme de la Rédemption au début du moyen âge." *Revue des Sciences Religieuses* 11, no. 3 (1931): 353–81.

———. "Le dogme de la Rédemption au début du moyen âge (suite)." *Revue des Sciences Religieuses* 11, no. 4 (1931): 566–89.

———. "Le dogme de la Rédemption au début du Moyen-Âge." *Revue des Sciences Religieuses* 12, no. 2, (1932): 161–93.

———. "Le dogme de la Rédemption au début du Moyen-Âge (suite)." *Revue des Sciences Religieuses* 12, no. 3 (1932): 355–88.

———. "Le dogme de la Rédemption au début du Moyen-Âge (suite)." *Revue des Sciences Religieuses* 12, no. 4 (1932): 533–71.

———. "Le dogme de la Rédemption au début du Moyen-Âge (suite)." *Revue des Sciences Religieuses* 13, no. 1 (1933): 1–24.

———. "Le dogme de la Rédemption au début du Moyen-Âge (suite)." *Revue des Sciences Religieuses* 13, no. 2 (1933): 186–218.

———. "Le dogme de la Rédemption devant l'histoire." *Revue des sciences religieuses* 15, no. 4 (1935): 493–531.

———. "La doctrine de la Rédemption chez saint Césaire d'Arles." *Bulletin du Littérature Ecclésiastique* 44 (1943): 3–20.

Shimahara, Sumi. *Haymon d'Auxerre, Exégète Carolingien.* Turnhout: Brepols, 2013.

Shimahara, Sumi. "Introduction." In *Études d'Exégèse Carolingien: Autour d'Haymon d'Auxerre,* 9–20. Turnhout: Brepols, 2007.

Singleton, Charles. *The Divine Comedy: Paradiso 2: Commentary.* Princeton: Princeton University Press, 1975.

Stott, John. *The Cross of Christ.* Twentieth anniversary ed. Leicester: Inter-Varsity Press, 2006.

Talar, Charles J. T. "Une passion partagée pour la vérité: Joseph Turmel et Alfred Loisy." *Revue de théologie et de philosophie* 142 (2010): 161–73.

Toynbee, Paget. *Dantis Alagherii Epistolae.* Oxford: Clarendon, 1966.

Turmel, Joseph. *Histoire des dogmes,* vol. 4. Paris: Rieder, 1935.

Vlach, Michael. "Penal Substitution in Church History." *The Master's Theological Journal* 20, no. 2 (2009): 199–214.

Waltke, Bruce K. *An Old Testament Theology*. Grand Rapids:
    Zondervan, 2007.
Wenham, Gordan J. *The Book of Leviticus*. The New International
    Commentary on the Old Testament, vol. 3. Grand Rapids:
    Eerdmans, 1979.
Williams, Garry J. "Penal Substitutionary Atonement in the Church
    Fathers." *Evangelical Quarterly* 83, no. 3 (2011): 195–216.

SUBJECT INDEX

SCRIPTURE INDEX